Key to front cover

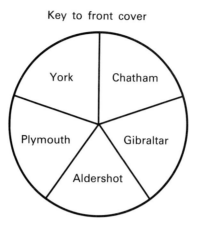

GARRISON

Ten British Military Towns

Other Brassey's titles of related interest

Sword and Mace
Twentieth Century Civil-Military Relations in Britain
JOHN SWEETMAN

Very Special Relationship
Field-Marshal Sir John Dill and the Anglo-American Alliance 1941-44
ALEX DANCHEV

Brassey's Battles
3,500 Years of Conflict, Campaigns and Wars from A-Z
JOHN LAFFIN

A Nation in Retreat?
Britain's Defence Commitment
CHRISTOPHER COKER

GARRISON

Ten British Military Towns

Edited by

PETER DIETZ

BRASSEY'S DEFENCE PUBLISHERS
(a member of the Pergamon Group)

LONDON · OXFORD · WASHINGTON · NEW YORK
BEIJING · FRANKFURT · SÃO PAULO · SYDNEY · TOKYO · TORONTO

U.K. (Editorial)	Brassey's Defence Publishers, 24 Gray's Inn Road, London WC1X 8HR
(Orders)	Brassey's Defence Publishers, Headington Hill Hall, Oxford OX3 0BW, England
U.S.A. (Editorial)	Pergamon-Brassey's International Defense Publishers, 1340 Old Chain Bridge Road, McLean, Virginia 22101, U.S.A.
(Orders)	Pergamon Press, Maxwell House, Fairview Park, Elmsford, New York 10523, U.S.A.
PEOPLE'S REPUBLIC OF CHINA	Pergamon Press, Qianmen Hotel, Beijing, People's Republic of China
FEDERAL REPUBLIC OF GERMANY	Pergamon Press, Hammerweg 6, D-6242 Kronberg, Federal Republic of Germany
BRAZIL	Pergamon Editora, Rua Eça de Queiros, 346, CEP 04011, São Paulo, Brazil
AUSTRALIA	Pergamon-Brassey's Defence Publishers, P.O. Box 544, Potts Point, N.S.W. 2011, Australia
JAPAN	Pergamon Press, 8th Floor, Matsuoka Central Building, 1-7-1 Nishishinjuku, Shinjuku-ku, Tokyo 160, Japan
CANADA	Pergamon Press Canada, Suite 104, 150 Consumers Road, Willowdale, Ontario M2J 1P9, Canada

First edition 1986

Library of Congress Cataloging in Publication Data
Dietz, Peter.
Garrison: ten British military towns.
Bibliography: p.
1. Military towns — Great Britain. 2. Gibraltar — History, Military. 3. Rheindahlen (Mönchengladbach, Germany) — History, Military.
I. Title.
UA649.3.D54 1986   355.1'2   86-17560

British Library Cataloguing in Publication Data
Dietz, Peter.
Garrison.
1. Cities and towns — Great Britain — History. 2. Great Britain — History, Military.
I. Title.
355'.00941   DA50

ISBN 0-08-31192-X

Printed in Great Britain by A. Wheaton & Co. Ltd., Exeter

FOR VIVIEN, FOR HER RESEARCHES,
HER MANY HELPFUL SUGGESTIONS
AND CONSTANT SUPPORT

Acknowledgements

The editor and publishers thank the following individuals and institutions for their help and for permission to reproduce copyright material in this book:

The British Library for the *Articles of Surrender, York*. The Imperial War Museum for photographs. *Soldier* Magazine. The Scottish United Services Museum for the Castle Garrison Lists. Scottish Portrait Gallery for the John Kay print. Plymouth Art Gallery for the map of Plymouth. The Royal United Services Institute for Defence Studies Library and The Prince Consort's Library, Aldershot for help with referencing. The Royal Engineers Corps Library, Chatham. The York City Library. Mrs M. Huart and the Staff of the Gibraltar Garrison Library. The Edinburgh Military Tattoo. The Woodlands Local History Library, London Borough of Greenwich.

The Gibraltar Museum. The Royal Armoured Corps Museum, Bovington. The Aldershot Military Museum. The Gibraltar Tourist Office. Wesley Harry the Archivist, and The Royal Arsenal, Woolwich.

Laurie Lee for the extract from *Cider With Rosie*. Major Colin Innes (Retd) for extracts from *The History of Craigiehall*. Peter Dix, Leamington Spa for extracts from *The Great and Close Siege of York 1644*. The Woolwich District Antiquarian Society and Dix-Instance Publishers (4th Edn) for permission to quote from *The Woolwich Story* by E. F. E. Jefferson. Century Hutchinson Ltd. for extracts from John Walters, *Aldershot Review*. George E. Lanning for his essay, *From Rifle Range to Garrison, An Essay on Bovington Camp (1899-1925)*. Essex County Library for *Colchester as a Military Centre*. Colchester Borough Council for quotations from their many publications.

The Commander and Royal Army Educational Corps Staff at HQ, North East District, York for *Some Military Associations of the City of York*. Major Peter Aston (Retd) for assistance at Craigiehall and introductions in Edinburgh. Major Nigel Legge (Retd) for assistance at HQ South East District, Aldershot. John Murray Ltd. for permission to quote from *A Subaltern's Love Song* by Sir John Betjeman. Stanley Goodman and C. W. Woodward for help with the chapter on Plymouth. Dr D. J. P. Waldie, Lieutenant Commander Henry Nash and Sydney Bradford for information and help with Bovington. Vivien Dietz for research in York, Edinburgh and Gibraltar. Cecil Gomez for very valuable assistance in Gibraltar. Simon G. Anholt for research in Moenchengladbach, Federal Republic of Germany.

Brigadier Stuart Lee MBE and the RAEC and civilian staff at HQ BAOR and 34 Army Education Centre, for assistance at Rheindahlen. The Royal Tank Regiment for permission to quote from the *RTR 50th Anniversary Souvenir Book* (1967), and from early copies of the *Tank Corps Journal*. The Royal Engineers Institution for permission to quote from *The Royal Engineers Journal*. Jonathan Cape Ltd. for permission to quote from *Tinned Soldiers* by Alec Dixon. David Higham Associates Ltd. for permission to quote from *The Tanks* by Basil Liddell-Hart.

Cover photographs reproduced courtesy of the *Aldershot News*, the *Illustrated London News*, Peter Dietz and the Topham Picture Library.

Contents

List of Illustrations

Aldershot

Bovington

Rheindahlen

Gibraltar

Endpapers: Front   Edinburgh *(Print: John Kay, National Galleries of Scotland)*
                Back   Gibraltar *(Photo: Gibraltar Tourist Office)*

Cover photographs

Front
Monk Bar, York: *Peter Dietz*
Rochester bridge being 'blown', Chatham: *Illustrated London News*
Elliot's statue Alameida Gardens, Gibraltar: *Peter Dietz*
Brunel's Bridge, Plymouth: *Peter Dietz*
Army parade, Aldershot: *Aldershot News*

Back
Cadets with bicycles outside 'The Shop', Woolwich: *Topham Picture Library*
View from the Castle, Edinburgh: *Peter Dietz*
Colchester Castle: *James Stone*
Tank Museum, Bovington: *Peter Dietz*
J.H.Q. Rheindahlen: *Peter Dietz*

Introduction

In putting together this account of ten British military towns the editor and his fellow authors are naturally conscious of the element of selection in their choice of locations. However, despite appearances, certain principles have been applied to the task. Limited in scope to ten towns only we have tried to cover a cross section of cities and towns and have included at least one overgrown village which will together represent those very many areas where soldiers, sailors and airmen are living 'in garrison' in Britain today. By way of contrast, or perhaps to point the lesson, we have included two other peculiarly British military settlements on the continent of Europe. Everyone has a favourite town and the serviceman no less than his civilian fellows. Whether it becomes a favourite because of its history, its surroundings, its amenities or even on the grounds put forward by a young officer with a new sports car who said in praise of Bovington Camp, it's easy to get away from, will depend upon individual taste. Nevertheless we are aware that our highly partial selection must disappoint some readers who will look in vain for the town where, they believe, they spent the happiest years of their lives.

We have tried to present a truly representative sample of towns with a service connection and we have tried to describe them in ways which suit us best as individuals. In every case we have felt it necessary to give some kind of historical background to the development of our garrison towns but these will differ in length and intensity and after this common introduction we each go our own way. Some accounts will be frankly historical, others will tend towards social if not sociological matters. Local politics cannot be avoided in one story whilst in another the writer's approach is almost romantic. In yet another contribution an autobiographical style is used consciously as against the half-conscious use of experiences and impressions gained from living, as we all have, in the communities which we describe. Taken together, these different approaches will we hope provide some approximation of the way in which garrison towns emerge and evolve, and what it was and still is like to live in them as a serviceman, member of a service family or as a civilian.

Our ten towns can be seen as falling into four sections. Some towns, like York and Colchester, can provide evidence of a military presence which stretches back into pre-history but still they have sufficient reasons, geographical and political, to justify the maintenance of a modern garrison and a military area headquarters. Sometimes, of course, the military are still in or around the old towns from sheer inertia, or from the now astronomical cost of moving barracks and offices. Sometimes the military are still there because they are very pleasant places to be, and why not? But often, in the case of our older towns, what were good reasons for the Romans to be based there held at least until the Second World War. Route centres, national and provincial capitals, strategic facilities and distinctive tribal concentrations, which latter are still important to some sections of the military, have traditionally provided the focal points for military settlements. In York and Colchester and even more in Edinburgh the historic and political role of the cities has justified their inclusion and will provide the main framework for their examination as 'military towns'.

An interesting feature of these three towns is their historical interrelatedness. This emerges to an extent in the individual studies but overall one cannot help but notice for example, the all-pervasive nature of the Roman connection. Six of the eight United Kingdom towns we deal with have some Roman remains of interest and in the case of the three towns in this section York is of national significance, closely followed by Colchester; and even Edinburgh, on the frontier of the Roman Empire had the port of Cramond. Fitzroy Maclean, in his *Concise History of Scotland*, writes of the old Emperor Severus, who held court and died in York, as 'pushing northwards as far as the Moray Firth' from his naval base at Cramond. Our two overseas garrisons, Gibraltar and Rheindahlen were both known to the Romans and it is likely that most of the towns garrisoned by British troops in Europe today were lived in by Roman legionaries and compared, discussed and rated much as they are today. It is not surprising that the Tudors, Henry VIII and Elizabeth, left their mark on so many military strongholds but what is surprising perhaps is how easily we forget the widespread and serious fighting in our Civil War. Plymouth, Colchester, York and Edinburgh were all besieged and even Aldershot, long before the establishment of the camp, was the scene of several engagements between the Cavaliers holding Basing House and the Roundheads of the London-trained bands who were holding Farnham.

The importance of sea power to an island nation is another theme which runs through most of the book. Although our second group of towns includes only Chatham, Woolwich and Plymouth, two of our other garrisons, Colchester and York were important as ports in their day. It has been said that the Romans never really understood the importance of sea power, and despite old Severus and his naval base at Cramond it was probably the withdrawal of the Roman fleet from the North Sea which signalled the beginning of the dark ages in Britain. The Firth of Forth has always been an important anchorage and from medieval times has contributed through Leith, Musselburgh and more recently Rosyth to the prosperity and security of Edinburgh. Gibraltar, it need hardly be said, was seized and held by the British in furtherance of a policy based on the maintenance of British sea power in the Mediterranean.

Our second group of towns then, whilst they have long and obvious associations with the armed forces, are included because they represent that period in British history when the sea acted as the cradle from which our power and greatness as a nation first emerged. The sea became an almost impregnable defence and at the same time the one element on which we could, through our world trade and maritime supremacy, rank as a world power. Plymouth was the base from which British sailors and soldiers first seized a share of the New World, established Britain as a world trading nation and played a prominent part in the defeat of the Spanish, the first real world power. Chatham, like Plymouth with its great dockyard and Woolwich with its vitally important arsenal, also had their *raison d'être* in the sea. The growth of commerce and Empire, the development of a thriving European *entrepôt* system and the increasing need to import food and raw materials made these naval and military bases more and more important. The defence of these sea and dockside towns, whilst they were primarily naval bases and in Chatham and Plymouth housed Royal Marines, was for all immediate purposes the task of a military garrison which would always include a high proportion of army gunners.

Woolwich, whilst a great arsenal and navy yard in its own right, is now predominantly the home of the Royal Artillery, but it was also the site of the first Royal Military Academy. At times the Arsenal, the Gunners and the Academy were under the same roof in the aptly named 'Warren', but each of the three developed separately although together they provided a nucleus around which the town grew. The Military Academy was set up to train the young men destined to be officers in the 'Scientific Corps', the gunners and sappers. The Royal Engineers have counted nearby Chatham as their home from the late eighteenth century and although the complex of forts, camps, townships and yards of which it is the centre has been an important naval base and repair yard, and been a base for the Royal Marines its naval importance has now declined. It is the sappers with their engineering schools, depots and barracks who are now the senior partners amongst the forces in the Medway area.

All three towns in this section reflect, through their location, in their architecture and in their spirit, the Golden Age of British military and naval power. Looking out towards the oceans, docks, depots and yards bustled with life and energy. In addition they represented the engineering and scientific achievements of the Victorian age, not only in structures like Brunel's futuristic bridge above the naval base at Saltash but in the shipyards, arsenals, munitions factories and training and experimental institutions themselves which were so much a feature of these particular towns.

A third type of military town or settlement is exemplified first by Aldershot. It was selected, planned and developed during and immediately after the Crimean War as the main base and training area for the Army in Britain. As we shall see it came into existence partly through a lucky combination of circumstances and partly through the driving force of a few highly placed individuals, and apart perhaps from Bovington is unique amongst British garrison towns for that reason. Bovington in Dorset is the second example from this section. Bovington would probably not exist even now if the Army had not required a large new training area for the tank forces which came into being during the First World War. Aldershot had appeared on maps showing the 'Hundred of Crondal' in the County of Hampshire at least since the Middle Ages and in Parish Records from 1248. But its sudden growth into a town dates from the arrival of the Army in the mid-nineteenth century and its emergence as 'The Home of the British Army', as it now proudly calls itself, took rather less than a hundred years. It is unlikely that Bovington appeared on maps at all before the twentieth century and even now there is no civilian town as a centre of the training establishments of the Royal Armoured Corps. Despite this, the training schools and workshops, military and civilian, the barracks, messes and clubs together with the civilian housing estate and the officers' and soldiers' quarters and the shopping and recreational facilities which go with them, do together make up a small town. In both cases the military requirement has dictated the growth of the urban settlement, and even in Aldershot which now has a population of over 32,000, the military presence dominates the area. In Bovington it is almost possible to say that it is the military machines, tanks, transporters, recovery vehicles and all the other paraphernalia of mechanised warfare, with its inevitable noise, dust and stench which provide the constant reminder of the military presence.

Finally, Rheindahlen and Gibraltar. These two military towns at almost the opposite ends of continental Europe are included because they are both examples of how the British serviceman takes his country abroad with him and how, when his settlement has any degree of permanence overseas it becomes almost indistinguishable in essentials from its United Kingdom model. Thus Rheindahlen in West Germany, a military town built around a Headquarters complex is not unlike Aldershot, Bovington or Catterick. There was no original civilian town in the British camp at Rheindahlen but it is laid out like its English counterparts. It is self-sufficient, neat and tidy, almost surburban, open to the world and unmistakably what it is. There are many other British camps and garrisons in West Germany but they are all part of a larger German community and they are always known by the name of the German town of which they are sometimes more and sometimes less a part. Rheindahlen, although called by the British by the name of a small German town three miles away, is clearly a town in its own right. The Germans themselves call the whole camp area JHQ (Joint Headquarters). The Churches, cinemas, stadia, clubs, gymnasia, restaurants, sports grounds, schools, swimming pool, golf links, theatres, houses, flats, barracks, offices and workshops do make up a community which can cater for all interests and activities. Sadly this is so much the case that some individuals and even families have no desire to explore outside the camp and for a whole overseas tour Germany remains a closed book for them.

Gibraltar too, whilst the climate and location modify to some extent the architecture and way of life of its inhabitants, can only be British. The Britain it reflects, rather like Woolwich or Chatham, is a Britain of the eighteenth or nineteenth century. The barracks and family quarters were, until recently, in many cases over two hundred years old. Service facilities and accommodation existed there cheek by jowl with a lively, noisy and cheerful civil population. An existence reminiscent perhaps of an earlier, more innocent age. Even today, despite modernisation and the arrival, on a permanent basis, of the Royal Air Force in 1939, the geography of the Rock so limits expansion that there is still a dimension of proximity which characterises life there. The 'British style' policemen and pubs, the oddly British shops, the Library and even the beaches, despite a Mediterranean climate, speak more of Britain than the Costa Brava. The profusion of Union Jacks and the loudly voiced pro-British sentiment also speak of a loyalty and affection enhanced by shared hardships. The history of Gibraltar is a history of outside pressures and often of real sieges. The last of a long series of sieges started in 1962 and only ended in 1985. Gibraltar is unique but it has been a British military town since 1704 and has an honoured place in this collection.

What then, if any, are the common characteristics of these ten towns? Clearly the presence, and in some of the towns the overriding presence of the military has tended to produce a uniformity of outlook. Even within the military, variety and difference of background and outlook has been reduced in our selected towns. One need not read far in this book to come across the outstanding role played by the Royal Engineers, and before them their predecessors the 'Sappers and Miners' in the story of so many of the towns we describe and nor is it surprising that with them in the forts, and on the walls of the medieval towns we everywhere find the gunners. The Royal Artillery and the Royal Engineers are by no means the only soldiers to serve in garrison towns and indeed many famous regiments are associated with the towns in our book. But, especially in the past, the Engineers have built and maintained the fortifications and the Gunners have manned the batteries which have defended them and they have tended to be more permanent in their occupation. The 'Scientific Corps' have made a mark on our military towns which is peculiarly theirs.

The garrison town looks inwards; its inhabitants are more supportive, less radical and more conservative, more patriotic and more self-sufficient than their supposedly more unfortunate neighbours. These are the most sweeping of generalisations but they are true to a degree of all garrison towns. Historic memories and physical reminders in walls, gatehouses, butts, batteries, barbicans, citadels and exercise grounds serve to reinforce these attitudes in some towns. In others ties of marriage between servicemen and civilian families strengthen the pro-service feeling. In yet other towns, especially the more recent military settlements, commercial interests inevitably promote a regard for the services and the social and political values they seem to represent. In all the towns which have a military presence the frequent parades, martial music and everyday evidence of the nation's power and purpose in its disciplined and well-armed forces encourage the will and lift the spirit. It is this *joie de vivre* and sense of common purpose, confidence and steadfastness which is characteristic of the true military town.

The Historic Garrisons

1

Colchester

JAMES STONE

THE VISITOR to Colchester who is seeing it for the first time will quickly register the fact, as he wanders through its streets, that it is a market and manufacturing town with a long history. Its history is visible everywhere — in the Roman walls and remains which fringe the old town centre, in the Norman castle with its imposing keep and in its buildings and churches which range, in period, from the medieval, through the Georgian and Victorian, to the present day. Colchester's history is also registered in its street names — for example, Cumulodunum Way, Claudius Road, Boadicea Way, Saxon Close, Fairfax Road. Other street names such as Military Road, Barrack Street, Artillery Road, Ypres Road, Tobruk Road, serve to remind the visitor that Colchester is also a garrison town and has been so, in one form or another, for a very long time. Colchester is, in fact, Britain's oldest recorded town still functioning as a borough and for almost 2,000 years it has also served as a military garrison town. Over the years it has quartered Roman legionaries, warriors of the Danish 'Great Army', the Norman troops of William the Conqueror, and soldiers who fought at Blenheim, Waterloo, Mons and Alamein.

The present garrison is located largely in the area south of the town centre and this is where one finds the barracks, military headquarters and training areas. On the eastern outskirts of the town is the Hythe, Colchester's port ('hyth' being Old English for haven or harbour). Colchester has been a port throughout its history thanks to its position on the Colne. The River Colne has been one of the routes to inland Essex for thousands of years and has played a crucial part in Colchester's development. It is commonly supposed that the town takes its name from the river (from the Saxon word 'Colne-ceaster' meaning 'the fortress on the Colne') although it has also been suggested that the 'Col' in Colchester comes from the Roman word 'Colonia', referring to the colony of veteran soldiers set up on the site by the Emperor Claudius after its capture by the Roman Army. Be that as it may, the River Colne besides providing a vital form of communication for the settlement which developed in pre-Roman times also afforded it protection from the north and east. The site was admirably suited for settlement since it enjoyed a pure water supply, was situated on a ridge and was free of the dense forest which surrounded it and which provided added protection. It was also only eight miles from the mouth of the Colne at its highest navigable point so that from the Iron Age period the settlement became a centre of trade — trade which extended to the Continent.

Archaeological finds in the area around Colchester show that the area was inhabited during the Bronze Age as early as 3000 BC and by the end of the Bronze Age (about the fifth century BC) a clearly identifiable settlement had emerged at Colchester. It was developed by the Trinovantes, an Iron Age people who were displaced by the Belgae, a civilised aggressive people from the Continent who, having occupied Kent and Hertfordshire, proceeded to bid for the kingdom of the Trinovantes which approximated roughly in area with the present county of Essex. By the beginning of the first century AD the kingdom of the Trinovantes had become part of the domain of Cunobelin, a Belgic king whose dominion extended over Kent and Hertfordshire as well as Essex. Cunobelin (known, through Shakespeare, as Cymbeline) made his capital at Colchester which at this time was called Camulodunum, meaning the Fortress of Camulos after the Celtic God of War. Camulodunum thus became the capital of south-eastern Britain. A great system of defensive earth works was built to the west of the area extending three miles south to cut the Roman river which flows eastwards into the Colne. Long stretches of these ramparts still remain as visible evidence of the importance of this pre-Roman capital. Other evidence of the wealth and achievements of Belgic society is to be found today in Colchester's Castle Museum which contains examples of their coinage, pottery, bronze and silver work of an impressive standard. The name of Camulodunum appears on gold coins struck about 10 BC.

Julius Caesar in his second expedition to Britain in 54 BC had intervened in the struggle between the Belgae and the Trinovantes in favour of the latter but his stay was short and had no lasting influence. Nearly a hundred years passed before Britain saw another Roman Army and meanwhile a considerable trade grew up between Britain and the Continent in which Camulodunum shared and prospered. This added to its wealth and importance. Politically and strategically Camulodunum and the kingdom of which it was capital was an attractive prize and after the death of Cunobelin (AD 40), who had held south-eastern Britain in comparative peace and prosperity for many years, there was a struggle for power. In the continuing unrest, some of the chieftains who were faring badly appealed to Rome to intervene. Julius Caesar, a century before, had demonstrated how easily Britain might be invaded and subdued, and Rome had long considered the desirability of annexing Britain to round off and settle the north-west frontier of the Empire. The disorder in Britain prompted the Emperor Claudius to act in AD 43. The Roman Army which crossed the Channel under Aulus Plautius quickly overran Kent despite resistance led by Cunobelin's sons, Togodumnus and Caratacus (Togodumnus was killed but Caratacus survived to continue resistance for some years until his capture by the Romans). So easy was the invasion that the unwarlike Emperor Claudius travelled from Gaul to see his forces cross the Thames and occupy Camulodunum. The Emperor personally led his army, with elephants, into the capital where he received the submission of a number of chieftains before returning to Rome.

The Romans built a permanent fortress in what is now the south-west part of the town and stationed a legion in the area but otherwise in the early years of occupation the local community was left to itself. However in AD 49 the Roman troops stationed there were moved to Gloucester and it was decreed that the town should become a colony — or colonia — for retired Roman soldiers, the first of its kind to be founded in Britain. In honour of the Emperor it was called Colonia Claudia Victriensis. The development of the new town along Roman lines quickly followed on the ridge along which today's High Street now runs. Dominant in the new building was a great temple dedicated to the Emperor Claudius.

As the Roman occupation was consolidated in Britain oppression and exploitation of the subject people increased. The Iceni, a tribe which dwelt in what is now East Anglia, suffered particularly. After the death of their King, who had been vassal to the Roman Emperor, the Iceni endured wholesale plunder and confiscation and when the widowed Queen Boudicca (or Boadicea as she is more popularly known) protested she and her daughters suffered personal outrage (the Queen was flogged and her daughters raped). This last cruel act stimulated the revolt of the Iceni under Boudicca in AD 60. The Iceni were quickly joined by the Trinovantes and other tribes in eastern Britain who had similar grievances against their Roman rulers. The rebels cut the Ninth Legion to pieces, destroyed by fire the Colonia and its temple and slaughtered its inhabitants. London and Verulamium (St. Albans) suffered a similar fate. In all, many thousands of men and women (as many as 70,000 it is claimed) were savagely put to death before the revolt was quelled, with frightful severity, by the Roman Army. Boudicca took poison when she saw the struggle was lost (AD 61).

Once Roman order was fully restored the rebuilding of the town began although it never regained its former importance as a Roman centre; it was outstripped by London which from then on was the undisputed capital of Roman Britain. However, Colchester[1]* flourished again as a prosperous market and manufacturing town reflecting Roman ways and Roman culture. Archaeologists have identified temples, theatres and a Roman cemetery, and there is good evidence that the houses, at least of the wealthy, were substantial with warm-air heating and mosaic floors. The town walls, which are still impressively in evidence today, were built by Roman military engineers probably in the early part of the second century AD. What is equally remarkable is the fact that the main streets laid down by the Roman engineers have become, substantially, the main streets of modern Colchester.

What else did the Romans bequeath to Colchester? Possibly their greatest contribution was their road building. The Roman road which was built from London to Colchester ensured good communications with the capital and other important centres which, combined with the town's advantageous position on the River Colne, ensured Colchester's future development. The point has been made that the Roman roads, generally, greatly increased the speed of the Saxon, Danish and Norman conquests with, again, important consequences for Colchester. Colchester has been famous for its oysters (the 'Colchester Natives') throughout its history and it was the Romans who developed the oyster fishery. Not only did they prize British pearls but the oysters themselves were exported to Rome as a special luxury. The Romans also developed the harbour, moving its site downstream. To the Romans can also be attributed the start of Colchester's long history as a garrison town. Fortunately, later garrisons have managed to avoid the fate which the Roman garrison suffered at the hands of the Iceni although the lives of the various garrisons remained insecure, for one reason or another, until the mid-nineteenth century.

The Roman Empire, rent by political intrigue and under pressure from the Germanic tribes which attacked it increasingly from the third century onwards, finally withdrew the Roman legions from Britain in 410 to fight on the Continent. This left the country open to attack and seizure from the invading Anglo-Saxons. The territory north-east

* Superscript numbers refer to Notes at the end of the book.

of the Thames to the Stour was seized by the East Saxons from whom Essex derives its name. There was an early Saxon settlement at Colchester which might have been a mixed settlement on the evidence of pottery found in the town which combined Roman-British and Saxon features. The Saxons were not town dwellers and tended to destroy the Roman cities and dwellings. Colchester survived and was used by the Saxons because of its strategic importance, its accessibility by river and road and its value as a trading centre. There is one example left in the town of Saxon building and that is the Saxon tower of Holy Trinity Church now used as a museum, but this was built in the year 1,000 when Saxon rule was nearing its end. Before this, Saxon control of Colchester was interrupted with the next wave of invaders from the Continent, namely the Danes. The Vikings, as they were called, carried out their first raids on Britain towards the end of the eighth century and gradually co-ordinated their attacks in the form of a confederacy which called itself the 'Great Army'. Part of the Danish 'Great Army' conquered East Anglia in 870, and soon after this Colchester was occupied by the Danes who were now thinking of permanent occupation of Britain. The Saxons never accepted Danish hegemony and there was a prolonged struggle between the two contenders for supremacy in Britain which culminated finally in victory for the Saxon kings. The Saxon reconquest of East Anglia began in the early part of the tenth century and in 917 the Danish garrison in Colchester was driven out. It appears that from this time Colchester was no further troubled although the conflict between Saxons and Danes was not resolved for many years.

By the time of the Norman Conquest Colchester was a considerable centre of trade and administration — 'a town known to all men' as it was described in 931. It had its own court and mint and was regarded, because of its geographical position and its defensive works, as an important fortress. It featured — as 'Colecestra' — in the Domesday Survey of 1086 and from the information given there it has been deduced that the total population was something around 2,000 and that the wealth of the leading citizens rested on trade. The Normans, immediately after their arrival in England, built a great number of mound castles (high mounds crowned by timber forts). It is a sign of the importance that King William attached to Colchester that the castle that was started in 1076 was of stone and was considerably larger than the White Tower in London which William also commissioned. The keep, in fact, was the largest of its kind ever built in Europe. The castle, which like those in London and Norwich was a royal fortress, was built on the foundations of the Roman temple dedicated to the Emperor Claudius. It was built as a strong point to strengthen the East Anglian coast against a threatened invasion by the Danes under Cnut but it also served to deter outbreaks of rebellion which were always likely to occur among the English who were far from reconciled to Norman rule. The Danish invasion never occurred and although the castle may have contributed to the peace and stability of the area during the unsettled period of Norman rule it gradually became redundant. King John stayed there five times before he was obliged to put it to siege in 1216 while it was in the hands of a rebellious garrison representing the barons against the king. By the end of the thirteenth century the castle had become a county gaol and continued to be used as a prison until it fell into disuse and ruin. It was saved from total disintegration through the efforts of Charles Gray, an eighteenth-century lawyer. Today all that remains of the castle is the keep, much reduced from its original size, and the Roman vaults beneath. The castle now houses the Archaeological Museum with its impressive collection of Roman and other antiquities.

The story of Colchester during the medieval and Tudor periods is one of commercial and ecclesiastical development with little reference to military matters. Richard I granted the town its first Borough Charter in 1189 and by the beginning of the thirteenth century cloth-making was an established trade. The cloth trade grew in importance and the growing prosperity of the town was reflected in the increasing number of parish churches which were built, most of them favoured by endowments from the more wealthy of the town's burgesses. Colchester successfully survived the ravages of the Black Death in the fourteenth century and while the disappearance of its monasteries during the sixteenth century made little difference to the town it was seriously affected by the slump in the cloth trade around the 1550s. Enlightened self-interest saved the cloth trade when Colchester admitted Flemish cloth-makers fleeing from religious persecution in the Netherlands. The special skills which the Flemish brought to cloth-making gave rise to the 'New Draperies' — the cloths known as bays and says — which made Colchester internationally famous.

When the Civil War broke out in 1642 Colchester sided with the Parliamentarians. London and East Anglia were solid in support of Parliament and there was no fighting of any consequence in the region until 1648. By this time the King (Charles I) was a prisoner on the Isle of Wight and most of the Royalist strongholds had fallen to the Parliamentary forces. However, Royalist feeling was still strong in various parts of the country and a plot was devised for a general rising of Royalists. Between April and June 1648 insurrections broke out in Wales, Kent, Essex, Cornwall and in the North. In early June a Royalist force was raised in Kent, led by Lord Goring. It was pursued and attacked by a large Parliamentary force under Lord Fairfax, causing Goring to move his troops across the Thames to a temporary camp at Bow and Stratford. On 9 June they proceeded to Brentwood in Essex to link up with another Royalist group led by Sir Charles Lucas. The total force, which now numbered between 4,000 and 6,000 men, moved to Colchester on 12 June. Lord Goring, the senior nobleman, was in general command but lacked military experience. Sir Charles Lucas, on the other hand, was an experienced military commander having been Commander-in-Chief in Suffolk and Essex and a Lieutenant General in the Royalist Army. Sir George Lisle who joined Lucas had also fought in the Civil War. Lucas had been captured at Stow-on-the-Wold and Lisle at Faringdon and both men had been released by their opponents on undertakings that they would not bear arms again. Lord Capel completed the Royalist leadership.

The people of Colchester, still loyal to Parliament, had closed the town gates and manned them against the Royalists but quickly decided that they would not be able to resist such a large force. It seems that the Royalist leaders originally intended that their stay at Colchester should be a short one and they entered the town on that understanding. However, Fairfax and the Parliamentary Army, which had been in hot pursuit, arrived at the outskirts of the town at Lexden Heath the following day (13 June) and demanded the immediate surrender of the Royalists. This was rejected and fierce fighting took place as Fairfax tried to force his way in. The attack was repulsed with hundreds of casualties on both sides and Fairfax thereupon put the town to siege.

The siege lasted until 27 August — almost eleven weeks. During this time Fairfax methodically encircled the town, systematically closing off access to sources of supply for the besieged and building forts from which the town could be bombarded. At first the Royalists were able to reach the Hythe where provisions were available and successful forays for food and other supplies were also made beyond the North Gate of the town but, gradually, access routes were closed by the Parliamentarians until by the beginning of July the Royalists were completely cut off. This meant that not only could they not get out but they were also denied the possibility of relief from outside. To make matters worse, Fairfax about this time received forty additional guns with which to increase his bombardment of the town.

The Royalists continued to take the battle to the enemy where they could; the East Street sortie of 5-6 July was an example of this where the Royalists attempted, with partial success, to dislodge the Parliamentarians from the mill at East Bridge. The attack was initially successful with the Royalists charging down the hill and across the footbridge. Under the impetus of the attack the Parliamentary forces gave ground but later rallied so that finally the Royalists had to retreat back to their positions. They did so in good order having taken prisoners and inflicted numerous causalties. It was a short but bitter action which was good for the Royalists' morale but made no real difference to their position. Without hope of relief it could be only a matter of time before they would be forced to surrender. Food became increasingly scarce and before the end of the siege horse flesh was the only meat available. It is said that people were also eating cats and dogs. Ammunition was scarce and the town suffered intensive bombardment. By early August the townspeople were gathering outside Lord Goring's quarters demanding surrender.

The Royalist leaders might have agreed to surrender earlier but were unhappy with the terms which Fairfax offered since officers were excluded from the honourable conditions he promised to soldiers. Fairfax made a number of offers all of which were rejected on the same grounds. In desperation the Royalists finally considered a last general assault to cut their way out to freedom but the troops, fearing that the officers were planning to desert them by getting away on the remaining horses, refused to move. With no hope left the Royalist leadership on 26 August sent emissaries to negotiate a treaty of surrender. The terms which Fairfax laid down were severe. All private soldiers and officers under the rank of captain would receive 'fair quarter' — that is while remaining prisoners they would be free of ill treatment; nor would they be allowed to retain anything but the clothes they wore. Officers would not be allowed to retain their horses and senior officers would be 'rendered to mercy' — that is their fate would be at the discretion of Parliament.

The surrender was signed on 28 August when over 3,500 men surrendered. The Royalist leaders had good cause to be apprehensive about the treatment they would receive. On the same day as the surrender Lucas, Lisle and Sir Bernard Gascoigne were brought before Fairfax's Council and told they would be shot forthwith. Lucas and Lisle were executed that evening; Gascoigne was reprieved when it was discovered that he was a Florentine. Lord Capel was imprisoned in the Tower and beheaded in 1649 after his escape and recapture. The common soldiers were imprisoned and many of them suffered transportation. The people of Colchester, who were largely innocent victims of the prolonged struggle between the Parliamentarians and the Royalists, were fined £14,000 of which £2,000 was later remitted. £10,000 of the fine was paid to the Parliamentary Army. Given that many innocent citizens were killed, that many had lost their homes through bombardment and fire and had suffered near starvation and many other privations during the siege, and that through it they had lost work and trade, this forced payment to the Army must have caused great bitterness. Certainly the siege and its outcome could have done nothing to endear the Army to the civil population, particularly as it took the town a long time to recover economically. Colchester today still shows some of the scars left by the siege; for example, in the ruins of St. Botolph's Priory which was destroyed during the siege, in the fallen section of the town walls, near to the Balkerne Gate, which was demolished after the siege and in the bullet holes left by Royalist shots in the timbers of the Siege House Inn.

Colchester was seriously affected by the outbreak of bubonic plague in 1665 which is reputed to have killed nearly 5,000 people.[2] This calamity, occurring relatively soon after the siege, further delayed the town's return to prosperity and recovery was not properly achieved until towards the end of the century. The accession of William III in 1689 probably helped in this direction because the King frequently passed through Colchester on his way from London to Harwich where he crossed to the Hook of Holland. This meant that the road from London to Colchester was better maintained than it might otherwise have been and improved communications helped the flow of trade and people into Colchester. By the turn of the century, the town was visibly restored so that visitors could comment on 'the fair and beautiful streets' and on 'the abundance of good and well-built houses'.

During the second half of the seventeenth century and for a substantial part of the eighteenth century Britain was involved in Continental wars and British troops saw a lot of action in the Netherlands during this period. Harwich is only one hundred and six miles from the Hook of Holland and one hundred and thirty-five miles from Antwerp and consequently the port was increasingly used for the transport of troops and supplies. Colchester, being just nineteen miles from Harwich and on a good road, was ideally situated to serve as a staging post for troops *en route* to and from the Continent. There were no permanent barracks and the practice, sanctioned by law, was to billet troops in the local inns and alehouses, using their stables for the horses. This was not popular with the innkeepers and publicans concerned because it meant that often their establishments were overcrowded with troops for which they were poorly recompensed compared with what they might otherwise have obtained from the more lucrative civilian trade. There was some relief after 1741 when it was decided to establish a military camp at Lexden Heath on the western outskirts of the town. Britain had pledged support to the Empress Maria Theresa of Austria whose accession to the Austrian throne was opposed by the Elector of Bavaria in coalition with France, Spain and Prussia. All available British troops were to be sent to Germany to join Hanoverian forces who were in British pay and the camp at Lexden Heath was needed to accommodate the large body of men who assembled there in preparation for the move to the Continent. In fact, owing to a change of plan, the departure of these troops to Germany was considerably delayed which resulted in cases of desertion, drunkenness and fighting among those soldiers who remained in Colchester. When, finally, they joined their Hanoverian allies in Germany they took part in the Battle of Dettingen (1743) under the command of King George II — the last occasion that a King of England was under fire in battle.

Lexden Heath camp was used as an encampment for the remainder of the eighteenth century although it was not in continuous use. The camp, lacking permanent barracks, was unsuitable for quartering troops over a long period and so if a regiment was stationed in the Colchester area it would be dispersed for billeting in local inns and

The Siege House. This late fifteenth century house stands in East Street. It came under Royalist fire during the siege of Colchester in 1648 and holes from musket shots are still discernible in the timbers.

alehouses and brought togther periodically for exercises and official inspections. These inspections, or 'reviews' as they were called, attracted much interest among the local people who seem to have treated them as a form of public entertainment, according to contemporary accounts. For example, when Major General George Preston and his staff arrived at Lexden Heath on 2 May 1775, to inspect the 4th Regiment of Dragoons the local population crowded round the saluting base and joined in the cheers. The march past must have been a pretty sight with the squadrons arrayed in scarlet and green preceded by two farriers with axes and two negro trumpeters with turbans and scimitars and since it was concluded with the squadrons performing thirty-six movements the onlookers must have gone home well satisfied.

With the frequent arrival and departure of regiments and the pomp, ceremony, excitement and entertainment provided by the military in the setting-up of camps and in the many parades, exercises and manoeuvres which ensued, it is not surprising that Colchester was a popular recruiting centre. It was used by recruiting parties of many regiments and a variety of emblandishments were employed to attract volunteers. Those of us who have served may appreciate the refined approach of Captain Fenner of the 22nd (Cheshire) Regiment who, in March 1766, was inviting 'gentlemen volunteers . . . to try so genteel and commendable a life' (a bounty of a guinea and a half was also promised perhaps with more effect). The Prince of Wales's Dragoon Guards in their recruiting advertisement (1770) tried a more hearty approach assuring volunteers that 'by enlisting in this Corps', a young man would 'find a release from his cares and enter a life of Ease and Jollity'. Not all soldiers have found military life so attractive and certainly some of the volunteers of that time did not. Desertions were not uncommon and the local paper from time to time advertised rewards of a guinea for the apprehension of a deserter. Soldiers could be shot for desertion so it was not an act to be lightly undertaken; at the least they could expect the lash if apprehended which itself was a fearsome punishment.

Although Colchester lacked a permanent garrison until the nineteenth century it became habituated to the constant presence of troops well before this. At peak times large bodies of troops were assembled either to meet the threat of invasion or to make ready for Continental campaigns. It has been estimated, for example, that in 1741 at the beginning of the War of the Austrian Succession there were nearly 10,000 men stationed on Lexden Heath in addition to a vast number of horses. The feeding and supplying of such a host must have been a prodigious task, adding to the great increase in traffic which the movement of troops engendered. Local shopkeepers and suppliers would benefit enormously but it was not all gain for the town. Inevitably, at a time when society was much less well ordered than it is today and social behaviour was less constrained, the presence of large numbers of troops in what was relatively still a small town (in 1801 the first National Census showed that the population of Colchester was just over 11,520) would often lead to an increase in violent behaviour which occasionally flared up into something larger when regimental loyalties or rivalries were involved. This must have been the case in 1741 when a fierce clash between the Royal Welch Fusiliers and another regiment led to the death of one man and a number of woundings.

On these occasions relations between the military and the civilian population were bound to become strained unless the country was at war or faced with some serious international crisis when the physical presence of the military was reassuring and misdemeanours could be condoned. At other times efforts were made to maintain a rapport between the two sides. Officers and leading citizens of the town would meet socially; civilian dignitaries would be invited to military ceremonies; and regiments would entertain invited ladies and gentlemen of the district at balls arranged by the officers' mess. Illustrative of this was the occasion when General Lord Amherst visited Colchester in September 1779 to review regiments including the Royal Dragoons and the Light Dragoons who were encamped on Lexden Heath. The troops held a field day at Boxted Heath which was observed by his lordship, the military staff and a 'prodigious concourse' of people; 'after which his lordship and the field officers dined together at the White Hart and, it being assembly night at the same inn, his lordship, 4 generals and officers were present and a great number of the ladies and gentlemen of the town and neighbourhood'.

With all the military activity which affected Colchester and the surrounding area during the eighteenth century, billeting became an increasing problem. As the *Ipswich Journal* put it in 1778, 'the burden of the soldiery in Essex is found insupportable, particularly in Colchester where the principal inns have 150 men each; a petition has been sent up to the war office praying relief'. War between Britain and Revolutionary France broke out in February 1793, and there was a rapid build-up of troops as 20,000 men were prepared for what turned out to be a disastrous campaign in the Netherlands under the command of the Duke of York. It promised to be a long war and this prompted the innkeepers and publicans of Colchester in 1793 to petition the government to build barracks in the town. The need was finally recognised by the government and barracks, of wooden construction, began to be erected. Infantry barracks were built in 1794 followed by barracks for the artillery; additional infantry barracks were begun in 1797 and cavalry barracks were erected in 1799. By July 1805, the Commissioners of Military Enquiry could report that Colchester Barracks could accommodate over 200 officers, more than 7,000 NCOs and men and 450 horses while the hospital there could cater for 414 patients. Thomas Neill, a local builder, was responsible for most of the building at a cost of £129,078; the total cost of the new barracks and hospital is estimated to have been in the region of £177,000. The barracks were built to the south-east of the town centre where the names of Barrack Street and Artillery Street still exist to remind us of where the barracks once stood.

Permanent barracks enabled regiments to stay longer. The 11th Regiment, for example (the North Devonshire Regiment which later became the Devon and Dorset Regiment), arrived in barracks in 1796 and remained there for over a year. The degree of permanency which the barracks gave to the garrison was good for the town because it helped to sustain trade by providing a steady demand for goods and services. During the eighteenth century Colchester's cloth trade had seriously declined and although there was still money to be made out of the industry there was much unemployment and poverty in the town. Help came, ironically, from the French Revolutionary and Napoleonic Wars which lasted virtually for twenty years during which time Colchester and the surrounding area prospered. Local markets, shops, service industries and smallholders benefited not only from the presence of large numbers of troops but also from the high incomes of farmers arising from the price of corn which shot up during the War. Greater affluence was reflected in the heightened social life of the town in which the officers of the garrison were conspicuous. There were public breakfasts and dinners and dances, racing at Lexden and Mile End Heaths which were well supported and the theatre became so popular that a new theatre, the Theatre Royal, was opened in 1812 with a capacity of 1,200.

It was not all beer and skittles. The prolonged war took its toll on the fighting troops as was evident from the regiments which marched into Colchester. Regiments like the 20th Foot (later known as the Lancashire Fusiliers) arrived in Colchester in 1799 from campaigning in Holland where they had suffered heavy losses. This regiment, like the 22nd Regiment which was also stationed for a time in Colchester, had previously served in the West Indies where yellow fever had decimated both regiments. Walcheren fever was, later, to strike down regiments like the 28th (North Gloucestershire) Regiment and the 43rd Regiment (which later became the 1st Battalion Royal Green Jackets) which took part in the Antwerp-Flushing expedition before returning to Colchester. The town also saw troops returning from Corunna where the hard fighting had greatly reduced the regiments which had fought in that campaign. Colchester itself provided a volunteer force in aid of the war, raising about 600 infantry and two small troops of cavalry.

The second phase of the War began in 1803 with Napoleon hoping to bring it to a swift conclusion by invading England. The threat of invasion was very real as the French troops concentrated in great numbers on the French coast and thousands of flat-bottomed boats were assembled at French ports for the crossing. In Colchester the barracks were enlarged and troops were constantly on the move. By August 1803 four brigades of infantry were at Lexden Heath and the garrison was geared to move at twenty minutes' notice. In October the Colchester commander, General Craig, called the leading citizens together, warned them of the serious danger the civilian inhabitants were in and strongly advised that as many women and children as possible should be evacuated from the town. Those people who were able to left the town hurriedly. The signal that the invasion had started was to be the lighting of beacons and there was great excitement when officers of the garrison attending a ball at a local inn were informed that a beacon had been seen burning towards the coast. It turned out to be a local man who despite the ban on outdoor fires was burning weeds.

In the end there was no invasion and the War was brought to a final, successful conclusion in 1815. Troops returned to Colchester from Waterloo but now that the War was over the decision was taken to disband the Colchester garrison. The last regiments moved out in 1816 and the barracks were demolished or put up for sale with their contents. The period immediately following Waterloo was one of bad harvests and high food prices and the departure of the garrison from Colchester added to the town's economic difficulties. Many local tradesmen had depended on the garrison for business and the employment of many labourers in various trades rested on work provided by the military. The cloth trade failed to recover and finally came to an end in the 1830s with the closure of the last cloth manufacturer. There was a small silk industry which had started towards the end of the eighteenth century but generally Colchester depended upon agriculture and remained a country town. Unemployment and poverty were rife among farm labourers and weavers and there was unrest and violence in the countryside. Just before the garrison closed troops from Colchester had to be used to restore order in Cambridgeshire, Halstead and Bury St. Edmunds.

With the closure of the barracks troops brought to Colchester for exercises or review again had to be billeted in local public houses and beer-shops. There were particular problems when the cavalry were involved because many of these establishments lacked stables. Only the larger inns kept stables and these were monopolised by the coaching trade which flourished in Colchester in the nineteenth century until it was killed off in the 1840s by the railways.[3] Publicans required to accommodate cavalry complained to the Local Bench but received short shrift. They were told that under the law publicans were obliged to billet troops and that if they had no stabling they should arrange it with neighbours. Fortunately troops only visited Colchester occasionally. When they did, however, public concern was voiced about how to provide entertainment for them in order that they might avoid disgracing themselves by getting involved in drunken brawls and the like.

Britain had not been involved in a European war for almost forty years since Waterloo and during this time the Army had been woefully neglected. Thus when war was declared on Russia in March 1854, the country was totally unprepared. Troops were hurriedly assembled and it became immediately obvious that the country needed more barrack accommodation. In Colchester a new military camp was made south of the city centre between the Mersea and Military Roads. It was later extended westwards over the Abbey Field. The new hutted barracks, which included a large timbered church and a hospital, were first occupied in January 1856 by the Depot of the 11th Foot. In April of the same year Prince Albert visited the town, inspected the camp and reviewed the 88th Connaught Rangers and four regiments of militia. The wooden huts which formed the barracks were to remain in use until the end of the century. Today, all that survives is the garrison church; the churchyard is the old military burial ground dating back to the Napoleonic War (1807).

Inside the church there is a memorial plaque to sixty-four marriages between Colchester girls and German soldiers which took place at the church all on the same day, 20 October 1856. These soldiers were members of German regiments which were recruited to serve with the British Army in the Crimea. After the war some of these German regiments were ordered to Colchester pending a decision about their future. In the end most of the soldiers elected to return to Germany but a number of them accepted an offer to go to Cape Colony as military settlers. This scheme was mainly for married men and so during October 1856, nearly a hundred and fifty marriages between German soldiers and Colchester girls were solemnised at the garrison church.

After the ending of the Crimean War the government, learning from the mistake of allowing the Army to run down which had caused so many problems during the campaign, decided that some permanent camps were necessary; among these the camp at Colchester was included. By 1864 the garrison had doubled in size through the completion of a new cavalry barracks on the Abbey Farm which the government had bought. Many of the buildings, which were of red brick, continue to exist and can be seen today, still bearing the name 'Cavalry Barracks', along Butt Road. An interesting feature in the development of a permanent garrison was the establishment of a temporary building for military offenders. This was to be the forerunner of the Military Corrective Training Centre which, today, is the only one of its kind in the British Army. Another significant step in the development of Colchester as a garrison town was the creation, in 1866, of Eastern District as part of the Army command structure. The new district originally included troops and military installations at Colchester, Harwich, Ipswich, Langguard Fort and Norwich with its headquarters at Colchester where it has remained ever since. Since then, however, the District has been greatly extended and now stretches over eleven counties from the Thames to Humberside.

The Garrison Church. Built of wood as a temporary chapel in January 1856, it is still used regularly by the garrison today.

The permanent garrison which from this time remained at Colchester brought important economic benefits to the town particularly after the mid-1870s when agricultural depression, which was to last on and off until 1914, seriously affected the area. Colchester's population between 1851 and 1881 increased by 9,000, most of which is attributable to the growth in the garrison, counting soldiers and their dependants. All sorts of trades benefited — such as coachmakers, saddlers, wheelwrights, blacksmiths, farriers, builders, shopkeepers of all kinds, domestic servants, innkeepers and brewers. By 1869 the Army, it has been estimated, was spending around £80,000 a year in the town. Social life was also rejuvenated and it was quite like old times to have the garrison officers appearing in all the splendour of their dress uniforms at gala nights at the theatre or at regimental balls to which the local gentry were invited. Regimental bands played at public functions and regimental teams participated in cricket matches and other sporting activities with local sides.

The new permanent garrison was not universally popular and there was criticism of it on a number of issues in the early years. The Army was blamed for the increase in drunkenness and prostitution in the town. Certainly, brewing was a growth industry in Colchester during the second half of the nineteenth century and the number of licensed premises grew accordingly, rising from 154 in 1866 to 186 by 1885. Drunkenness was not peculiar to the Army but when it led to brawling between troops as happened during the Christmas season of 1869-70 when fighting between the 18th (Royal Irish) Regiment and 33rd (Duke of Wellington's) Regiment extended over two days, it attracted public censure. Occasional brawls between soldiers and civilians did not help. In the summer of 1885, for example, fighting between civilians and soldiers was only stopped when a force of three officers and 100 soldiers with fixed bayonets from the Durham Militia arrived on the scene. Prostitution had also been growing in Colchester for some time but got worse with the establishment of the garrison, attracting girls from other districts to the town and encouraging some innkeepers to organise brothels. Matters got bad enough for clergymen of all denominations to petition in 1869 against the relicensing of inns that kept brothels. In 1870 the matter featured in a by-election at Colchester when rival contestants clashed over the Contagious Diseases Act which could be said to provide a licence for prostitution in the garrison towns. The official Liberal candidate, Sir Henry Stokes defended the Act on the grounds that prostitution was essential to the Army's health. Sir Henry lost the election to his opponent who wanted the Act abolished but the brothels continued in business for quite a long time after this.[4]

The friction which existed between the town and the garrison subsided as both sides learned to live with each other. In a country town suffering from the decline in agricultural trade a permanent garrison was a blessing which the townspeople came to recognise. The garrison continued to expand. Between 1898 and 1906 the War Office bought more land for the building of Goojerat Barracks, Reed Hall Camp, the Ordnance Depot and the Kirkee and McMunn Barracks. This expansion was of great importance to the local building trade. Earlier, in 1885 the War Office had leased the Old Barrack Field, the parade ground of the Napoleonic garrison, to the town which converted it to a recreation ground. The reconciliation between the town and the garrison is observable in Wright's *Guide to Colchester*, 1899, in which he talks in admiring terms of the garrison — 'not the least interesting of the town's possessions' and recognises in the new barracks that he enthusiastically describes that 'Colchester is an important garrison town'. He enthuses also about the social side of the garrison 'which other less blessed towns have not the privilege of enjoying' such as the imposing church parades, the regimental bands playing in the public bandstand and the military exercises and manoeuvres 'bringing within easy reach of the townspeople in the sham fights all the glory of war with none of the dangers'.

The continuing presence of the military in the life of the town tended to make the average Colcestrian more imperialistic and patriotic than most. When the Boer War broke out in 1899 and the first garrison troops for South Africa left Colchester by train they were seen off by a large and enthusiastic crowd and there were public demonstrations of concern and loyalty throughout the duration of the war. So it was that a reporter, writing in 1900, could observe that 'Colchester's celebration of Mafeking will never be forgotten in the borough'. Lord Roberts, who finally brought the war to a conclusion in 1902, was given a warm welcome from the municipal authority and the townspeople when he visited the garrison in 1903.

Colchester in 1914 showed clear signs that it had weathered the agricultural depression and had made a successful economic adjustment. Its population in the 1911 Census was over 45,000, having practically doubled since 1861 and the town now had engineering works and iron foundries, clothing factories and printing firms, nurseries (including Cant's who made Colchester famous for roses) as well as its oyster fisheries and, of course, the garrison. The railway played a vital part in the rapid growth of industry in the area and was also of great service to the garrison. The outbreak of the First World War demonstrated this. The bulk of the troops in the existing garrison were moved quickly so that for a time there was, as a contemporary noted, 'the sudden and total disappearance of soldiers from the streets of the town'. More troops arrived later in vast numbers so that very soon up to 40,000 men were training in the area. The effect on the town can be imagined. As the fighting increased on the Western Front the military hospital and the Essex County Hospital filled with wounded and it became necessary to requisition a newly completed school for hospital use. During the war the town suffered air attack from Zeppelins and, later, aircraft but the effect was negligible. Where the town did suffer, in common with most other towns and villages in Britain, was in the loss of its young manhood — 1,200 Colchester men were killed in the war.

After demobilisation the regular army settled back to a peacetime routine although time was needed to re-organise and re-equip regiments for their peacetime and overseas roles. Colchester saw many regiments who were posted there for this purpose. During the inter-war period the garrison also housed officers who were later to distinguish themselves in the Second World War. Among these were Field-Marshals Lord Gort and Lord Wavell. Field-Marshal Wavell, who was born in Colchester when his father was stationed there, was later made High Steward of Colchester by the town in honour of his achievements during the Second World War.

With the return of the men from the Services there was a sudden demand for housing and large new suburbs grew up in Colchester. There was also a steady increase in motor traffic to which the garrison undoubtedly contributed because of mechanisation which proceeded apace in the Army during the 1920s and 30s. The traffic congestion led to the opening of a by-pass on the north side of the town in 1933 which must have considerably eased driving problems for civilian and military drivers alike. As the garrison's horses began to disappear from Colchester's streets so equally soldiers in uniform became less evident as the rules were changed to allow soldiers to wear civilian clothes off duty. Sunday church parades remained, however, and continued to provide entertainment for the townspeople as the troops were marched to and from church led by their regimental bands. Meanwhile as a result of the Government's rearmament programme which started in the mid-thirties Colchester garrison continued to expand. Hutted accommodation was replaced by brick buildings at Kirkee and McMunn barracks and new camps — Roman Way and Cherry Tree — were constructed. The Command Workshops were greatly increased in size and facilities while the introduction of national conscription early in 1939 necessitated the building of emergency barrack accommodation on various sites in the garrison area.

The Second World War greatly accelerated the pace of technological change in the garrison. Gone were the pre-war cavalry, replaced by armoured units; mechanisation affected all units, including the infantry, and weapons and weapon systems became ever more advanced and sophisticated. Training became increasingly technical although this might not have been obvious to local civilians who would still see the troops out on route marches and conventional military training on the barrack square. Now that it was wartime soldiers were back in uniform all of the time and the town would be thronged with troops during their off-duty hours. Among these were Allied and Commonwealth troops, later to be joined by Americans after the United States had entered the War. The number of troops in the area built up rapidly as D-Day approached. Colchester also housed prisoners-of-war. The Italians were the first to arrive and in 1943 completed a Nissen-hutted camp which was later occupied by German prisoners-of-war. This camp which was at Berechurch Hall later became the Military Corrective Training Centre.[5] During the War Colchester was bombed a number of times and anti-aircraft batteries were established at Abbey Field. In total, 54 people died from air attack and factories, shops and houses were destroyed although Colchester did not suffer from the heavy bombing which was inflicted on other British towns and cities.

The barracks were greatly enlarged during the War and with the retention of National Service until 1960 the garrison was maintained as a large and important military centre. The town itself continued to grow — by 1951 its population was over 57,000 — so that major units including the Command Workshops found themselves very much town-based. This caused difficulties for both the town and the garrison. On the one hand, Army vehicles unavoidably added to the traffic congestion in and around the town centre and, on the other, attempts to restrict army traffic within the town hampered the garrison's movements and activities. To relieve the situation a plan was accepted in 1962 aimed at rationalising the garrison's location. Broadly the intention was to concentrate the garrison in the south of the city and otherwise to confine specific units to particular zones. Hyderabad and Meanee infantry barracks on the Mersea Road had recently been modernised at a cost of one-and-a-quarter million pounds and were re-opened in June 1960 so there was no question of their being moved to a new zone.[6]

However, the location of the newly rebuilt Roman Barracks, previously known as Roman Way Camp, which were opened in July 1962 and occupied by the 2nd Green Jackets, fitted into the plan and the rebuild of Goojerat Barracks, which was completed in 1974, was also part of the new scheme of things. Today although parts of the Victorian garrison are still functional — for example, the stables of Le Cateau

The war memorial was designed by H. C. Fehr and completed in 1923 in the open space especially created for it in front of the castle.

Barracks are used today by the present garrison Saddle Club and the garrison chapel, as mentioned previously, still has regular weekly services — most of the older buildings have been modernised or demolished. There is a Colchester garrison planning group, involving both town and military representatives, to control the future development of the garrison. As a former garrison commander (Brigadier Mervyn McCord) put it, 'One part of the aim is to preserve the status of the garrison as part of the town. Where possible we shall modernise rather than destroy. We want to retain the historic atmosphere of Britain's oldest garrison while bringing it up to date'.

The garrison today includes 19 Infantry Brigade which has been associated with Colchester since September 1950 when it was re-formed and moved into Le Cateau Barracks. Its headquarters is now at Goojerat Barracks. The Brigade was renamed 19 Airportable Brigade in September 1970, became 7 Field Force in April 1978, and reverted to its original title in January 1982. These changes reflect the changes in military thinking which have occurred during this period although for some time now the main task of the Brigade has remained constant, namely to train for its wartime role as part of 1st British Corps in NATO's Northern Army Group which is responsible for the defence of Northern Germany. In addition the Brigade may be deployed to any part of the world for operational duties and regular units from the Brigade have served in Northern Ireland, in the United Nations Force in Cyprus, in Belize and in the Falklands. So it is not uncommon to find articles in the Colchester press which feature the activities of units from the Brigade currently serving in some exotic overseas theatre. The town is also reminded of the garrison's wider role when the Sea Transit Centre at Cavalry Barracks takes part in NATO exercises. On such occasions Colchester is used as the forming-up and distribution point for troops reinforcing NATO forces in Europe and the town teems with troops and vehicles.

The senior military headquarters in Colchester is HQ Eastern District which is at Flagstaff House and is commanded by a Major General. The presence of the District Headquarters in Colchester adds importance to the garrison and shows that the historical and geographical factors which have made Colchester militarily so dominant in the region for so long are still significant today. There is a third headquarters in Colchester and this is HQ Colchester garrison which is the adminstrative centre for the garrison. The garrison is commanded by the Brigadier who also commands 19 Infantry Brigade. Apart from administering to the needs of the units based in Colchester, garrison headquarters is also responsible for the management of Ministry of Defence land which now extends to 5,000 acres in and to the south of Colchester. This is a sizeable domain although much of it — over 4,000 acres — is used for military training purposes. The Army is anxious that local people should not be denied access to this countryside so when training is not taking place those parts of the training area which are safe to use are open to the public. The Garrison also controls extensive sports facilities — football and cricket pitches, an indoor swimming pool, a gymnasium and a running track — and, again, these facilities are available to local civilian organisations, by arrangement.

Many local civilians in Colchester are dependent, either directly or indirectly, on the garrison for their livelihoods. Apart from the three headquarters and the operational units which make up 19 Infantry Brigade, the garrison contains a number of static units and establishments. Among these can be mentioned the Stores and Clothing Research and Development Establishment which works on the improvement of military stores and clothing for the Services, 36 Command Workshop which repairs Army weapons, vehicles and equipment for local units, and 48 Squadron RCT which provides transport of all types for military staff and units in the Colchester area. These establishments are staffed very largely by civilians. Altogether, the garrison employs something in the order of 1,200 civilians which makes it one of the leading employers in the town. Then there is the considerable demand for goods and services which is generated by the garrison and from which local shopkeepers and tradespeople benefit. The garrison's military population, including servicemen and women, and soldiers' wives and families, numbers about 9,000, which makes it an important element in the economic life of the town.

Although military garrisons develop close working relationships with the civilian communities in which they find themselves, they tend otherwise to lead separate lives. This is to be expected since they are separately accommodated (billeting appears to have gone forever), enjoy their own amenities and lead a varied and turbulent existence markedly different from that of the local community. This is possibly what Henry Benham, a distinguished Colcestrian, was referring to when he suggested some years ago that the garrison was a thing apart. However, this separation should not be exaggerated. Post-war changes are helping to link the garrison and town closer together. An obvious example is the Colchester Tattoo which is a biennial event run jointly by the town and the garrison. It is claimed to be the largest tattoo held in the United Kingdom and raises funds which are shared between civilian and Army charities. Individual members of the garrison are also in closer touch with townspeople. Service regulations have eased and soldiers are better paid. With more freedom and more money, they tend to be less unit-centred and to look, more frequently, beyond the barracks into the community for entertainment and company in their off-duty hours. Soldiers are also getting married at a younger age than previously. This means that there are more Army families than before so that more members of the garrison are involved in the daily life of the town. Army children go to local schools; some Army wives take local employment when they can get it; others join local societies and associations and help with local charities and voluntary services. Increasing numbers of married servicemen are buying their own houses and many who have been stationed in Colchester have bought houses in the area. Others, at the end of their service, who remember Colchester as a friendly and pleasant town elect to settle there as their Roman predecessors did so many years ago.

All of this helps to draw the town and the garrison closer together. Of course, from time to time, individual soldiers kick over the traces and cause friction with local inhabitants but this does not last long. Colcestrians have been used to soldiers living in their midst for a very long time and seem to value the connection. As C. J. M. Alport, the MP for Colchester when Colchester was celebrating the 1,900th anniversary of its official beginning, put it in an address to the House of Commons, 'We in Colchester like soldiers and we think we understand them. As a senior officer told me not long ago, in his experience there is no town where the atmosphere of friendliness and understanding between civilians and military is greater than in Colchester . . . Colchester is a self-contained town with a strong local life. The town has always been accustomed to having soldiers and so there is no fear or suspicion of soldiery'. These sentiments were expressed in 1950 but they have been re-echoed publicly on numerous occasions since. Perhaps the last word on Colchester as a garrison town should rest with Councillor James Jackson, the first Mayor of the newly enlarged Borough of Colchester, who in 1975 invited the Army to stage the biggest military parade that had been seen in Colchester for thirty years. Said the Mayor: 'Nowhere else in the country is the Army as much part of the community as in Colchester. We are a garrison town and proud of it. And this is what the Mayor's parade through Colchester is about — to show our appreciation of the soldiers who live on our doorstep and are part of our lives'.

Bibliography

Colchester as a Military Centre, Chloe Cockerill & Daphne Woodward, Essex County Library, February 1978

I have found this work most valuable, particularly in its use of contemporary sources, and I am very grateful to the authors and to Essex County Library for kindly permitting me to use quotations from the book.

I have also relied heavily on the following:

The Story of Colchester from Roman Times to the Present Day, Geoffrey Martin, Benham Newspapers Ltd., 1959

Colchester — Official Guide, G. H. Martin, Colchester Borough Council, 1984

'Colchester through the Ages', J. J. Maling, *East Anglian Magazine*, 1984

Colchester 1815-1914, A. F. J. Brown, Essex County Council, 1980

Roman Colchester, David T. D. Clarke, Colchester Borough Council, 1980

The Siege of Colchester 1648, David T. D. Clarke, Colchester Borough Council, 1980

Soldier Magazine, various articles

Material provided by Public Information, Headquarters Eastern District.

2

York

PETER DIETZ

York is by almost any definition a 'military town', but by virtue of its walls, which are uniquely preserved by British standards, it also meets James's criteria and more than justifies its place in this collection. From Roman times onwards the history of York is an old soldier's story of armies, of fortifications, of sieges and of the interaction of the civil population of the town with the military garrison. The streets of York have echoed to the sound of marching soldiers for nearly two thousand years, and whether the reaction from the town has been friendly or hostile the arrivals and departures of bodies of troops through its now marvellously restored gates, have been a fact of life for most of the town's existence. The origins of York are obscure, but as with Colchester there are good topographical and military reasons for its existence and development. Placed where the confluence of the rivers Ouse and Foss provided natural protection, and located at the head of tidal water where glacial mounds formed a bridge over the swampy valley, the position could hardly fail to be of considerable strategic importance.

When the Romans moved north from Colchester and then Lincoln to pacify the Brigantes, after having finally crushed the revolt of the Iceni under Queen Boadicea, they built a new fortress at Eburacum. The fortress was first garrisoned by the Ninth Legion only recently recovered from their mauling in the revolt of the Iceni. Boadicea and her allies rose against the Romans in AD 60, but it was not until AD 74 that Brigantia was finally overrun, and the Northern Territories were not finally incorporated into the Province of Britain until another six years had passed. Eburacum, which eventually became York, was built by Quintus Petillius Cerialis who had been sent by his friend the Emperor Vespasian expressly to subdue the Brigantes. His choice of the site for the future York was a highly professional decision, it was the key to the whole of Northern Britain and it has remained the most important military garrison in the north of England ever since.

One can still be aware of Cerialis's Roman fortress beneath the city plan of today and even though his hasty structure of wood and clay and sand with a turf covering was rebuilt by Agricola in AD 79 and replaced by stone in the reign of Trajan in AD 107 and 108, the basic outline remained the same. The fortress measured 1,590 feet from south-west to north-east and 1,370 feet from south-east to north-west and covered about 50 acres. This was the standard size for a camp housing one legion. Each of the four walls of the fortress had a gate. The main gate was on the river front, the south-west side and it was connected to the headquarters building by the via praetoria and to the north-east gate gate by the via decumana. The main gate, the porta praetoria, was situated where St. Helen's Square now stands and the via praetoria followed roughly the line of Stonegate to the headquarters which must now be below the Minster. The Roman road, becoming the via decumana, continued north-east along the line of Chapter House Street to the porta decumana which would have been on the line of Lord Mayor's Walk opposite the end of Grove's Lane. Crossing this main axis the Roman via principalis joined the north-west gate at Bootham Bar to the south-east gate now below King's Square, along the line of Petergate. The barrack blocks for the five or six thousand legionaries, built in the usual long low pattern, must have occupied most of the remaining space within the ramparts. The Roman Governor was no doubt glad to get away from the crush and noise of the military camp to his own house which seems to have been located across the Ouse on the right bank. The Centurions, as is ever the way however, were quartered within the walls close to the south-west ramparts. Eburacum, Roman York, served as a base and springboard for Agricola's conquest of what remained of independent Northern England and Lowland Scotland, and it continued to be developed and strengthened during the whole of the Roman occupation. After the stone rebuilding in AD 107-8 settlements sprang up outside the walls. By the beginning of the third century AD the tradesmen, hucksters and camp followers who served the military had established themselves between the walls and the River Foss on the south-east side of the fortress. The settlement included quays along the river bank. Across the Ouse another settlement came into being, partly made up from discharged veteran legionaries who, as elsewhere on the frontiers of the Roman Empire, were encouraged through land grants to settle in permanent and loyal colonies around the military stations. Before AD 237 it seems, this settlement had achieved the status of a 'colonia', the highest rank of chartered town. Not much is known of this town outside the walls but its buildings included a temple of Serapis and some large public baths.

Whilst the Legions were 'in station' the fortress towns like Eburacum were secure. But despite the inevitability of Roman return and vengeance every opportunity was taken by the half subjugated tribes to rise against the conqueror whenever the Legions had to be withdrawn, for whatever reason. In AD 196, Clodius Albinus, then Governor of Britain, led a revolt against Rome. He took all the veteran Roman soldiers in Britain to Gaul where he was defeated by the Emperor Septimius Severus. Meanwhile the Mercatae tribe had streamed south over the now deserted Hadrian's Wall and had overrun Northern Britain. Eburacum was destroyed and its walls rased to the ground. Although the legions returned it was not until the Emperor Severus himself crossed to Britain and took charge of the punitive campaigns against the Caledonii and the Mercatae that the situation was finally restored. Severus remained to die in Eburacum in AD 210, but whilst he lived there the walls were rebuilt on concrete foundations and the parapet raised to twenty feet. The presence of the Emperor, planning and conducting the campaigns against the northern tribes, brought new prestige to the town and, in addition to the official residence of the Governor of Britannia Inferior, a palace for the Imperial Court of Severus and his Empress Julia Domna was built.

At the end of the third century AD, in 296, a rebellion led by the British Chief Allectus drew the Roman Army into the south of England, and brought about a second invasion by the northern tribes. Eburacum was again looted and burnt to the ground. Rebuilding started immediately. The barrack blocks discovered near Davygate were reconstructed at this time and it is likely that the fourth century bath house under the Mail Coach Inn, in St. Sampson's Square was built at the same time. The whole of the fortress defences, except for a small section between the porta decumana on the north-east wall and the porta principalis sinistra, which was all that remained of Severus's walls and towers, were rebuilt. The walls were made wider, higher and stronger than the orginal fortifications. At the south and west angles of the fortress walls, projecting multi-angular towers, each with a ten sided front and of considerable size were constructed. The western tower can still be seen in the museum gardens where about nineteen feet of the original Roman work is capped by a medieval superstructure. With the gates and six majestic, projecting interval towers, three on either side of the main gate, the south-west front, built to dominate the River Ouse must have, in Professor Sheppard Frere's words 'excelled in magnificence the other known fortresses of the Empire'.[1]

From about the time of the second major rebuilding of Eburacum a second menace to Roman order and civilisation began to make itself felt. Not only was there danger from the unsubdued tribes in the far north but, from the end of third century the Saxons began to take to the sea where they carried out piratical raids, especially on the English Channel and North Sea coasts of Britain. By the year 364 the Province of Britain was being harassed by the raids of Angles, Saxons and Jutes. The Romans, in their increasingly weakened and distracted condition, foreshadowing their ultimate withdrawal, stood everywhere on the defensive. Typical of this situation was the need for them to build a chain of posts along the coast to provide the command at York, and the northern garrisons with early warning of seaborne attack.

The Yorkshire Museum provides much evidence of the comparatively peaceful and stable period of Roman occupation. In over three hundred years only two Legions were permanently associated with the town. The Ninth Legion was stationed there from AD 74 until they disappeared from the historical records around AD 138 probably after being disbanded following defeat in battle. It is thought that the Emperor Hadrian brought the Sixth Legion to Britain with him in AD 122 and there is evidence of its presence in Eburacum from about AD 130. In any event the Sixth remained based on the town until the withdrawal of the Legions for the defence of Rome against the barbarian invaders in AD 410. The Legions in York must have been 'trickle posted' and to some extent locally recruited and they must have developed a relationship rather like that of a 'County Regiment' to its county town. Another interesting parallel with more recent practices is the seeming importance of religious observances to the Roman soldiers and particularly their officers. All military units and the civic authorities were expected to join in the formal worship of Jupiter Optimus Maximus or in the ceremonies in honour of the Emperors and their families. The British were allowed complete freedom of religion as long as they were prepared to take part in the Imperial cult. Troops sent to Britian from other Provinces often continued to worship their own native deities. The cult of the Earth-Mother goddesses which was popular in the Rhineland, appears particularly in the military areas of Britain. The temple dedicated to the Egyptian God Serapis by a Legionary Commander, discovered in the Colonia, across the Ouse from Roman York reminds us that eastern cults often attracted officers, probably for their mystic and intellectual content. It is only necessary to

Rebuilt at the end of the third century, the western multi-angular tower stands today in the museum gardens.

think of 'Chinese Gordon', who furnished the inspiration for the 'Military Sunday' parades in York up to the Second World War, to realise that spiritual and religious interests are often of great importance to the officer. This is particularly so when he is serving overseas, regardless of the age in which he lives or the secular power he serves. Mithraism, originally a Persian religion, became especially popular with Roman officers because of its high moral principles, rivalling and impeding the growth of Christianity in its early days.

After the withdrawal of the Legions in AD 410 Britain fell prey to increasing raids from across the North Sea until by the sixth century the raids had become full scale invasions with the object of conquest and permanent settlement. Britons, Saxons and Danes fought for control of the island and each gained only a temporary ascendancy. York was repeatedly besieged, taken and retaken and in the process, through neglect and deliberate vandalism, lost most of its Roman magnificence. During the seventh century York was an Anglo-Saxon town with the name of Eorforwic. It was the Capital of the Kingdom of Northumbria and after AD 627 when King Edwin of Northumbria was baptised, the small wooden church in the courtyard of the old Roman praetorium became the first York Minster. In the middle of the ninth century, the Danes, also known in some areas as the Vikings, succeeded in establishing control over much of central and north-eastern England. Their Capital, on the site of Anglo-Saxon Eorforwic renamed Jorvik was the scene of what was meant to be a great final battle to regain control between the Saxon kings and the Danes. Both Saxon kings were killed and their armies cut to pieces by the Danes who remained masters of 'Viking York' until the middle of the tenth century. The pre-Viking Eorforwic is believed to have been located to the south-east of the medieval walls of York, within the natural protection of the confluence of the rivers Ouse and Foss. Recent excavations have confirmed the existence of the monastery and library for which York was famous in the eighth century and in which the important post-pagan scholar Alcuin worked. The newly opened Viking Museum in the Coppergate, on the site of Viking Jorvik, carries the visitor back through time to an incredible reconstruction of the Viking settlement on the banks of the Ouse. The reconstruction perforce, shows the Vikings in a peaceful, domestic, trading setting but we know this was far from typical of their temperament or their preferred way of life. Eric Bloodaxe, the last Viking King of Jorvik, from the same mould as his predecessors, is presented in what is probably a more realistic way in the famous *Egils Saga*:

> The war lord weaves
> His web of fear,
> Each man receives
> His fated share;
> A blood-red sun's
> The warriors shield,
> The Eagle scans
> The battlefield.
>
> As edges swing
> Blades cut men down.
> Eric the King,
> Earns his renown.[2]

The Northumbrian Danes were clearly an unruly, quarrelsome, fickle people. Eric was twice deposed as King, being finally driven out of Jorvik in the spring of 954. Before this the Danes had gradually been subdued, first by Alfred leading the Wessex Saxons and then by his son King Edward I, his grandson Aethalstan and finally by Aethalstan's half brother Edmund. The King of Jorvik had submitted to Edmund in 943 but Eadred, Edmund's brother, who succeeded him after he was murdered in 946, had to march into Northumbria on at least two separate occasions and threaten to lay waste the whole of the Province in order to persuade the Danes that Eric Bloodaxe was not a really acceptable vassal King for Jorvik. It is said that the Danes complied out of sheer dread of the Saxon Eadred who must have been an absolute monster if he frightened them more than Eric. Even after the final submission of the Danish Kingdom of Northumbria Jorvik was not left in peace. After a further century of disorder and turbulence the climax came in September 1066 when an invading Norse army supporting a deposed Earl of Northumbria, Tostig, defeated the allied armies of Northumbria and Mercia who had remained loyal to King Harold of England, marched on Jorvik and plundered it. Harold, meanwhile was marching north to support his vassals. Although he quickly learnt of the defeat of his allies he advanced on Jorvik and finding that the Norse Army was encamped near Helmsley immediately launched his army on the invaders. The battle of Stamford Bridge ended in the complete rout of the Norse army and Tostig, and Hardrada the Norwegian King, were both killed. Over three hundred ships had been required to bring the invaders to England but twenty-four were sufficient to remove the survivors. Harold at once set off south to tackle William of Normandy, whose army landed near Pevensey in Sussex on 28 September. This time Harold was not successful and was killed in the battle which, in 1066, led to the last military conquest of Britain.

It was not until 1068 that William 'The Conqueror', became master of York. In order to protect the city and maintain his domination of the north he built two castles to the south of the old town, on either side of the River Ouse. The first castle was built in 1068 on the site of the 'Old Baile', an ancient castle on the west or right bank of the river whilst the second castle was built in 1069 on the mound where Clifford's Tower now stands. But these new defences were not sufficient to safeguard York and by September of 1069 a Danish and Norwegian fleet of two hundred ships anchored in the Humber. The invaders reinforced by an English host under Edgar the Atheling, captured, sacked and burned the city. They then retired to their ships and later, after the arrival of William withdrew altogether across the North Sea. William entered a completely destroyed York. The area between the Foss and the Ouse was laid bare but it did leave a clear building site from which soon emerged medieval York.

A modern visitor to York is immediately overwhelmed by the still pervasive medieval atmosphere of the city. The walls which still encompass two-thirds of the old town, the narrow, rambling streets, the towers and barbicans, the old inns and especially the recently restored gatehouses which almost challenge the great Minster as the true symbols and inspiration of the town, speak of that period of our history between the Norman Conquest and the establishment of the Tudors, when a walled town still seemed to be the only safe place to live. It is interesting to look at that period in terms of the four great gates of York and to see how the comings and goings through those gates underline the historic events of the four hundred years following the second entry of William the Conqueror into a devasted and still smoking York.

The expansion of York into the medieval city, still recognisable within the boundaries of the preserved and reconstructed walls, maintained the rough diamond shape of the old Roman fortress. It left the remains of Eboracum at the northern point of the diamond but now overshadowed and to some extent covered by the Minster and its administrative buildings. It incorporated in its southern half the buried remains of Saxon Eorforwic and Viking Jorvik under several layers of the rubble and rubbish of post-Viking York and the ashes of the burned city of 1069. The walls now appeared on the south-west side of the Ouse and enclosed the area of the old Roman Colonia. The total area within the walls after the Norman rebuilding was five times that of the original Roman fortress, but as in Roman Eboracum one main gate only, through which wheeled traffic could pass, was retained in each of the four walls. There were of course many postern gates only wide enough to allow a man on foot or a lightly loaded pack-horse into the city. But the posterns were liable to be closed when sufficient guards were not available and even likely to be completely blocked up in times of civil unrest or military threat. Of the four great gates of medieval York only Bootham Bar occupied the site of a Roman gate, the porta principalis dextra. Monk Bar in the north-east wall was near, but a hundred yards or so south-east of the Roman porta decumana. The south-west gate, Micklegate, was now across the Ouse and more than six hundred yards south of the most important of the Old Roman gates, the porta praetoria, already buried by then under the present St. Helen's Square. The fourth gate, on the south-east front of the city, Walmgate Bar, had moved out across the Foss river, along Collier, Fossgate and Walmgate from King's Square, the site of the Roman porta principalis sinistra.

All the gates of York have seen their full share of British history, have felt the tramp of armed men leaving for some desperate enterprise or the scurrying of defeated armies frantic to get back within the safety of the walls. Each of the gates has also carried its gruesome burden of severed heads, displayed to show in a harsh world that treachery, rebellion or just plain defeat could carry a hideous penalty. Bootham Bar and Micklegate would seem to have had more than their fare share of the limelight, but this was because Bootham faced on to the road to the ever recalcitrant North and towards Scotland. Micklegate, on the other side of the city, was the door through which the rewards and punishments and royal visitors from London entered the city. Walmgate and Monksgate were at the start of the roads to the North Sea ports and after the decline of the Scandinavian raiders and the end of the Danish connection they saw more of trade and honest merchants than of soldiers, at least until the Civil War. Even the merchant ships tended to bring their cargoes up the Ouse and directly into the city.

The word Bootham occurs in 1150 in the Anglo-Saxon word 'buthum', meaning in the twelfth century a fair or market held in the street. Outside the Bar and the northern walls lay Galtres Forest, referred to by Shakespeare in Henry IV, Part II, where the setting of act IV, scene 1 is given as 'Yorkshire, Gaultree Forest'. In 1405, Archbishop Scrope, one of the leaders of the rebellion against Henry IV, after preaching a seditious sermon in the Minster, attracted 20,000 men to his standard at York. They marched out through Bootham Bar and camped five miles north of the city in the forest. Expected help from the Duke of Northumberland did not materialise and the rebellion collapsed. Scrope and the other leaders of the rising were captured. After execution their heads were displayed above the gates of the city. An earlier

Archbishop led a more successful army out from Bootham Bar in 1138. Archbishop Thurston led the English troops north to defeat the Scots in the 'Battle of the Standard' at Northallerton. No doubt this example encouraged the later Archibishop to try his hand against Henry IV with disastrous results. Yet another militant churchman could also have inspired Scrope. In 1346, Queen Philippa, with Archibishop William le Zouch gathered an army in York and led it out through Bootham to defeat the army of the invading Scots of David Bruce at Nevill's Cross near Durham. The Queen captured the Scottish King and brought him back to York as her prisoner. Later she took him to London where she made a present of him to her husband Edward III.

The pattern of rebellions, wars and rumours of wars, especially with Scotland, repeated itself endlessly throughout the next century and it was always in York that the troops were collected for the march northwards. In 1481 occurred one of those incidents which demonstrates an eternal truth, 'no matter how motivated a soldier may be, a decent rate of pay helps to keep him that way'. Richard, Duke of Gloucester, had been appointed by his brother Edward IV to lead the English troops in the latest round of hostilities with Scotland. One Alderman Wrangwyshe, a merchant of moderate means but with immoderate ambitions, frequently of a military nature, attached himself to Richard and raised a company of 120 archers. Not only did he get each of the city parishes to contribute the men and pay for them but he also got himself appointed Captain for his recruiting zeal. Before they were marched off to battle the archers were gathered in Magdalen Chapel in Clifton, no doubt for an exhortatory sermon. The archers took what they probably saw as a last opportunity to organise a strike over pay. The City Council had agreed to pay the archers sixpence per day for twenty-eight days with an advance of fourteen days' pay. With an eye on their uncertain future the archers demanded their whole twenty-eight days' pay before they would march. The Lord Mayor had to give way. War was averted, however, and the company of archers marched back to an unforgiving York. The three ringleaders, who said in their defence that it was agreed . . . 'by the whole fellowship' (by a show of hands, perhaps) that anybody who took less than the whole money should 'repent it', were imprisoned for ten days. They were released when they said they were 'right sorry', and each of them found five sureties for 100 marks for their future good behaviour. The good citizens of York were not amused but there is no indication that they recovered any of their money. If they were sensible the archers would have spent the whole of the advance before returning.

As well as militant Bishops, York seems to have produced a most independent breed of Lord Mayors, willing to take on King or Rebel when sufficiently roused. After the death of Edward IV his two young sons were murdered in the Tower of London and Richard usurped the throne. He visited York in the same year, 1483, and gained the support of the city council. During the visit Richard was given a handsome present by the city. It is not clear if the sycophantic Wrangwyshe suggested the presentation but he certainly contributed. In August of 1485 when the Earl of Richmond landed at Milford Haven to raise a rebellion against Richard, the City of York raised 400 men to support Richard, whom they regarded as their legitimate King. Luckily, before they were irrevocably committed news was received that Richard had been killed at the Battle of Bosworth. The York contingent, still on the road, was hastily recalled and the City prepared to accept Henry Tudor as its King. Two years after the accession of Henry VII, Lambert Simnel and his supporters tried to win over York to their cause. The Mayor, William Todd and the Council stood firm for the King against the impostor Simnel. An attack on Bootham Bar was repulsed and a garrison of 4,000 men assembled at Micklegate. The rebels were defeated at Stoke, near Newark, and Simnel captured. Henry visited York in July where he knighted the Mayor who was subsequently moved to repair sixty yards of the city wall at his own expense. In the previous year (1486) Henry had married Elizabeth of York thus symbolically ending the Wars of the Roses. This event is commemorated in the entwined red and white roses in the great rose window in the south transept of the Minster.

Micklegate, compared with Bootham Bar, could be said, at least from the Norman Conquest, to be on the quiet if not the safe side of the city. It had its share of horrors during the dynastic Wars of the Roses and must have suffered more than a *frisson* when Lambert Simnel and his supporters were around the walls. There must also have been sighs of relief when the force sent to support Richard III marched back through the Micklegate without actually having fought against their future sovereign Henry VII. After Lambert Simnel, the Tudors without being heavily involved with York, did nevertheless add to its excitement. Henry VIII provoked the revolt known as the 'Pilgrimage of Grace' in 1539 by his dissolution of the monasteries. Aske, a leader of the 'Pilgrimage' who had entered York without opposition at the head of 20,000 men, was defeated on his way south towards London and sent back to be hanged at the Castle Keep. Henry, having presumably forgiven this lapse of loyalty by the city fathers, visited the city some four years later and stayed for twelve days. In the reign of Elizabeth the presence of Mary Queen of Scots in the north of England encouraged the Catholics there, led by the Earls of Northumberland and Westmorland, to rise and march on York. At this time York was the second city of England and to have secured it for the rebel cause would have been of great importance. The rebels were on Clifford Moor, just outside the city on 19 November 1569, but they retired to the north without gaining entry. The Earl of Sussex, Lord President of the Council of the North, raised a strong force in York and marched north from Bootham Bar to relieve Barnard Castle which was besieged by the rebels. After the suppression of the rebellion the heads of its leaders were displayed in the customary way, above the gates of York.

Further fears of a Catholic rising later in Elizabeth's reign, and the continuing danger of a Spanish invasion made the various parishes look to the state of their trained soldiers, weapons and armour. The Parish of St. Martin's, Coney Street, collected a rate of £4.15s. The town defences were also overhauled and in 1588 one 'Richard Lebb, loksmyth', was paid the sum of 3s. 4d. 'For the great loke and an iron slott for Walmgate Bar'.

In Stuart times, just before the Civil War, Wenham describes York and its defences as follows:

> The medieval walls are just over $3\frac{1}{2}$ miles in circumference and enclose an area of some 260 acres. From Skeldergate Postern to North Street Postern (via Micklegate Bar) and from Lendal Postern to Layerthorpe (via Bootham and Monk Bars) the walls were built on the Norman earth mound. From the Red Tower to Fishergate Postern the walls were much less formidable, being built on a lower, post-Norman mound. From Layerthorpe Postern to the Red Tower

there was a gap in the city walls, taken up by an expanse of nearly stagnant water known as the King's Fishpond. Seventeenth-century documents suggest that by that time the Fishpond was shrinking in size and gradually filling up; it is clear however, that during the siege (1644) it presented a considerable obstacle to the besiegers . . . Outside the city walls at the foot of the mound was the outer moat, varying in width and depth, and in most parts containing water. This was often choked with weeds and debris thrown over the wall and in hot weather was prone to dry up. However, between the Red Tower and Fishergate Postern the moat was generally filled with water at all times. As well as this inner moat there was an outer one at the foot of the mound inside the wall. It was mostly dry, was in some places filled up, and in others was used as an open drain or as a convenient dumping ground for rubbish. The walls were strengthened by the building at irregular intervals of small towers. Entry through the walls was by the four great gates or bars and by six smaller gates or posterns. All the bars were similar in structure, consisting of a gateway, closed by a portcullis and heavy wooden doors, and flanked and surmounted by a massive tower. Outside each gateway was an additional defence work — the barbican . . . Alongside Clifford's Tower was the bailey. Castle and bailey were both surrounded by a deep moat fed from the Foss. Access to the castle and bailey was provided by two drawbridges.[3]

Like most fortifications in time of peace, those in York had been badly neglected. The castle especially was in a ruinous condition but because of resolutions made in the so-called 'Second Bishop's War' (1640) against the Scots, many of the obvious deficiences had been made good by the time of the siege.

The story of York during the Civil War reflects the great dilemma of the time. Loyalty to the King, and a sense of honour fast disappearing in the rising tide of commercialism, fought against an emergent 'enlightenment' and middle class self-interest. However, when Charles I visited York in 1639 the city, like most of the surrounding countryside and small towns had no doubts about where its duty lay. The trainband of the city, 600 strong, drilled on Bishop's Fields which was situated between Old Thief Lane and the river. The King watched the trainband at their exercises from what are now the Museum Gardens, and very colourful they must have looked in their buff coats with silver lace, scarlet breeches, russet jackboots and a black cap with feathers. All this was no doubt to impress the King with the city's loyalty and indeed the impression was not false. After the King's estrangement from Parliament he moved north to Yorkshire again. This time loyalties were divided. He tried to enter Hull but the gates were shut against him and so in 1642 he retired to York where he set up his court. In York Charles raised a bodyguard of 200 troopers and 700 foot. This was construed by Parliament as an attempt to set up a standing army and was one of the precipitating factors in the armed hostilities that followed. On 16 August the King moved south from York and set up his standard at Nottingham. This was regarded as a declaration of war against Parliament and from then on there was no going back. York became the Headquarters of the Royalist Army. Operations were carried on from the city and all the prisoners captured in the minor battles and skirmishes round about were concentrated in York. The city was also the arsenal and store house for the Royalist Forces and the rebuilding and repair of the city defences was speeded up. In March 1643 Charles's brave and utterly uncompromising Queen, Henrietta Maria, entered York with 500 wagons containing munitions of war which she had obtained in the Low Countries. Much of the ammunition was stored in the Old Guildhall which had been rebuilt in the fifteenth century and survived for another three hundred years after the Civil War only to be destroyed by German bombs in 1942.

York held for Charles but the city was gradually invested by Parliamentary troops. During the winter of 1643, and before the investment was complete, all the Royalist troops had to be withdrawn into the city and billeted on the citizens because of the cold. The congestion, overcrowding and subsequent friction in the streets and taverns of the town can be well imagined. John Bellasis, the commander of the garrison, led a sortie of 3,000 men but this was defeated at the battle of Selby by the 5,000 strong Yorkshire Parliamentary Army under Lord Fairfax. After this Newcastle, who was commanding the Royalist Army of the North, ordered all the royalist forces in the North of England to retire into York, where he took over the command. Newcastle had been unable to hold up the powerful Scottish Covenanter Army which in alliance with the Parliamentary forces was advancing slowly on the city. By the end of April 1644 the city was loosely surrounded but Newcastle had meanwhile been able to send his cavalry to join the King's forces in the Midlands. The first phase of the siege saw the city invested by the Scottish Army, commanded by the Earl of Leven, numbering about 16,000 men, the Yorkshire Parliamentary Army led by Fairfax who had about 5,000 troops, and after 3 June the Earl of Manchester's Army of the Eastern Association arrived with a further 9,000 men including one Colonel Oliver Cromwell.

The River Ouse separated the Scots from Manchester's Army and so he built a bridge of boats across the river so that the two armies could co-operate during the siege. A little later Fairfax raised a mound on Lamel Hill and placed a battery on it to bombard the walls at Walmgate. Much damage was done to Walmgate Bar and an attempt was made to mine under the gate. A company of 'perdues', commandos, suicide troops or 'forlorn hopers' sallied out and brought in a soldier of the besieging army. The prisoner was 'thoroughly examined' in Clifford's Tower and eventually confessed that a mine was being dug and that it had reached the middle of Walmgate Bar. Sir Thomas Glenham, Military Governor of the city forced the besiegers to abandon their mine by mining above it and pouring water in on the miners.

On the 16 June a more successful attempt was made by the Earl of Manchester's men to blow their way into the north side of the city. A mine was exploded under St. Mary's Tower and an assault made on the great house called The Manor. The Manor, which is now called the King's Manor, was the headquarters and home of the Lord President of the Council of the North. When the mine under the Tower was fired about six hundred men broke into the Manor. After fierce fighting they were beaten back by the Royalist troops after having lost 50 killed and 250 taken prisoner. On 24 June a strong force from the garrison attempted a sortie but they were driven back in their turn losing 20 killed and 20 prisoners.

Newcastle wrote to the King for help. Earlier, in a letter to Prince Rupert, the King had said 'If York be lost, I shall esteem my Kingdom little else'. Despite the accuracy of this prophesy it was only after much hesitation that he ordered the Prince to move north to relieve York. On 29 June having crossed the Pennines with his army he sent a cavalry force forward to Skip Bridge, on the River Nidd about four miles from

York. Rupert probably intended that his cavalry would screen his movements round the north of the city but the Parliamentarians were convinced that he intended to attack directly from the west. To block this supposed attack the Parliamentarians raised the siege and concentrated their forces in the area of Long Marston. Rupert, however, moved his army of 8,000 foot and 6,500 horse, via Boroughbridge over the River Ure and Thornton Bridge over the Swale and down the east, or left bank of the River Ouse. By the evening of 1 July he was in the Rawcliffe, Clifton area and decided to give battle the next day. He sent orders into York telling Newcastle to join him and to start to move at 4 a.m. the next morning. Rupert's army crossed back to the west, over the Ouse on the bridge of boats somewhat carelessly left intact and unguarded by Manchester's troops when they left the city to concentrate at Marston Moor. Newcastle was clearly piqued by Rupert's order to join him, and in the circumstances he may have been right not to want to leave York without an adequate garrison. He may also have felt that there was no chance of a victory over the Parliamentary Army on this occasion or indeed that there just was not time enough to move his York garrison to the battlefield effectively in the few hours available. The Royalist Army from York did eventually arrive on the battlefield but they had not started early and were not in their allocated battle positions until four in the afternoon. The battle of Marston Moor started at about 7.30 p.m. and lasted until nearly midnight. The Royalist Army under Prince Rupert suffered a heavy defeat and the scattered and exhausted troops that survived retired on York. Newcastle made for Scarborough and sailed at once for the Continent. The defeated army began to arrive at Micklegate soon after midnight but at first only troops belonging to the original garrison were allowed to enter. Eventually the remnants of Rupert's army were let in. Whilst these remaining refugees and stragglers were still entering the city through Micklegate, Rupert was already leaving by Monk Bar, heading north to meet up with Colonel Clavering the new Colonel General of the Northern Army.

The siege of York was resumed on 4 July and by 11 July the Parliamentary Army was ready to storm the city but on 13 July Sir William Constable and Colonel Lambert spent the whole day in the city discussing the terms of its surrender. York capitulated on 16 July. The *Articles of Surrender* were generous to the city and included the following conditions:

1. That Sir Thomas Glemham as Governor of the said Citie shall surrender and deliver up the same, with the forts, Tower, Cannon, Ammunition, and furniture of warre belonging there unto, betweene this and the sixteenth of July instant, at or about the 11 houre thereof in the forenoon, to the said Generals (including Fairfax and Manchester).

2. That the Governour and all Officers and Souldiers . . . shall march out of the City . . . with their armes, flying Colours, drums beating, Matches lighted on both ends, Bullets in their mouths, and with all their bag and baggage.

. . .   .

8. That the citizens and inhabitants may enjoy all their privileges which formerly they did at the beginning of these troubles.

9. That the garrison that shall be placed here, shall be two parts of three at the least of Yorkshire men . . .[4]

On 16 July the road leading from Micklegate was lined for a distance of one mile beyond the city walls by the Parliamentary soldiers. The garrison which had sustained the siege since 21 April marched off towards Skipton leaving behind 35 pieces of ordnance, 3,000 stands of arms and much ammunition. Lord Fairfax was installed as Governor in place of Sir Thomas Glemham. The garrison was withdrawn in February 1646, after which only 60 men remained at Clifford's Tower.

The fortifications had suffered badly during the siege. Walmgate Bar was almost beaten down by the fighting in the suburbs around it and in the mining and counter-mining below it. Repairs also had to be carried out at Bootham Bar because of the fierce fighting there and also because buildings had been pulled down around the bar to clear fields of fire and to remove covered lines of approach to the walls. Monk Bar and the walls near it were also damaged. The last act in the Civil War was played out for York in 1648 when the Scottish Army was paid off, and no doubt much to the relief of the city, marched back to Scotland carrying with them the £200,000 *in specie* paid to the Receiver of the Scottish Army by the English Parliament. The money was counted by the Scots before they went, in the Old Guildhall used only five years previously to store the munitions brought in by Queen Henrietta Maria. It is said locally that it took the Scots twelve days to count the cash, but then they really were gone.

The aftermath of the Civil War in York as elsewhere, was a dislike of armies and garrisons of whatever persuasion, and this underlying tension simmered away in York for quite a long time. By 1687 relations between the garrison and the city seemed, at least on the surface, fairly cordial. We can read in the diary of the Garrison Commander, Sir John Reresby, on 3 February 1687 he . . . 'was accompanied with all the Officers of the garrison to Merchant Taylor's Hall where the returning and incoming Lord Mayors and all Aldermen . . . treated us to dinner very splendidly, where we debauched a little too freely'.[5] That it was only surface cordiality seems likely. Tension had arisen in the city over the pro-catholic policies of James II and loyalty to the King was certainly in some doubt. In the previous year Clifford's Tower, which had been restored after the damage of 1644, was again seriously damaged by an explosion and the roof was destroyed. This was possibly the work of supporters of William of Orange but it led to an increase in the garrison which must have raised tension still further. Sir John Reresby recorded on 16 August 1686, 'I received the King's order (signed by himself) to receive four companies of Colonel Oglethorpe's Regiment of Foot, and five of the Earl of Huntingdon's in York garrison, as also my own company, where they were to continue for the security of that place'.[6]

The garrison, by 1687, comprised ten companies of 500 men besides officers and this must indicate the anticipation of trouble. The daily guard of 80 men met in the Minster Yard between 9 a.m. and 10 a.m. every morning. They were then marched off to relieve the guards at all the gates and posterns. All the gates and posterns were manned during the day but the posterns were locked and left unguarded at night. At night, in addition to the main gates, there were guards at King's Manor, Sir John's official residence as governor, Skeldergate, North Street and Castle Gate. The 'taptoo' was beaten at 10 o'clock every night by five drummers, and by this time every soldier was supposed to be in his quarters. The soldiers were still normally billeted in civilian houses or inns and if they were found out of their quarters after taptoo by the military patrols they would be punished. The very large garrison, the surveillance and the billeting continued amidst bitter resentment until August 1688. In that month King

THE
ARTICLES
Of The
SVRRENDER
Of The
City of YORKE

To the Earle of LEVEN, Lord
Fairefax, and Earle of *Manchester*,
on Tuesday *Iuly* 16. 1644.

Together with an explanation of some part
of the ARTICLES.

LONDON,
Printed for MATHEW WALBANCKE,
July 23. 1644.

The Articles of Surrender.

James moved the York troops to Hull in order to guard the seaports and coast against an expected invasion by William of Orange. Two months later one company was sent back to York to form the nucleus of troops for Sir John Reresby's command which was re-forming. He called up the Militia and marched them into the city to reinforce his command, but this proved to be a mistake. A month later when an assembly of Yorkshire businessmen, meeting in the Guildhall, declared for William, the Militia went over in a body to their support. They surprised and surrounded Sir John's company of regulars, one imagines with some connivance on the part of the troops, whilst Sir John himself was arrested and held until the 'Glorious Revolution' of 1688 was an accomplished fact. Connivance, at least on the part of the troops if not the officers, seems likely since during the commotion the city gates were immediately secured by Lord Danby and placed under a strong guard so that no one could enter or leave the city. The next year saw 6,000 Danish troops under the command of the Duke of Wirtenburg quartered in the city. The Danes were en route for Ireland to help William of Orange against James II but it is unlikely that they were any more popular in the city than were the English soldiers a few years before.

York under the Hanoverian Kings was a peaceful place after the terrors and turbulence of the previous centuries. Micklegate Bar was partially restored in 1716 and in 1719 the front of Bootham Bar was rebuilt. The only military threat to the city came in 1745 with the Scottish rebellion in support of Charles Edward Stuart, Bonnie Prince Charlie. Although most of the Scots took no part in the rising, and the army in Scotland remained loyal to the King, Prince Charles Edward and his army, mainly composed of Highlanders, gained some initial successes. The establishment of the British Army in 1739 was down to 18,000 men compared to a French standing army of 133,000. Most of the British Army was serving abroad and by the seventeen-forties there were British regiments in India, North America and the West Indies. In Europe the war of the Austrian Succession involved British troops at the Battles of Dettingen in 1743 and Fontenoy in 1745, but after Fontenoy British troops were withdrawn from Europe to deal with the Scottish rising. Although elements of the rebel army reached as far south as Derby they were forced back into Scotland as the build up of veteran British troops began to be effective. Prince Charles Edward's army was finally and bloodily defeated at Culloden on 16 April 1746, but for a time the situation in York had looked serious. The people of York, like those elsewhere in England, had little sympathy for the Stuarts after two sorry examples, and even less did they want to be occupied by an army of wild Highlanders. At a meeting in the Guildhall in September 1745 it was agreed to raise four companies for the immediate defence of the city. In addition prominent citizens formed themselves into a city guard which remained under arms for about ten months. The four companies were gradually disbanded after about four months when it became obvious that the Scottish rising had spent itself and was on the defensive. It was clear too that the hard headed citizens had no desire to pay a shilling a day for the soldiers and two shillings a day for the sergeants once the crisis had passed. The last episode in this miserable story was seen in York when twenty-two rebels taken at Culloden, and sent back to the city for execution, were dragged on sledges from the castle to the race course where they were hanged in front of a fashionable crowd occupying the grandstand.

It is one thing to volunteer and to act freely over an issue, it is quite another, in Britain at least, to have an unpopular course of action imposed from above, especially when that action concerns the pocket of the citizen or his personal liberty. The people of York demonstrated the difference quite soon after their patriotic and spirited efforts to defend York from the Scottish rebels. New Militia regulations were enacted in 1757 and in the East and North Ridings they were regarded as oppressive and a grave interference with the liberty of the individual. On the day when the lists showing those qualified to serve in the Militia were handed in there was a riot in the city. 'Many yeomen, farmers and others, after drinking all the liquers in the town', gutted and pulled down Cockpit House, near Bootham Bar, then did the same to the house of a Mr Bowes and threatened to do the same to others. The rioters were eventually dispersed by the Lord Mayor and High Sheriff of the County by means of 'persuasive arguments and specious promises'. Similarly, when the notorious 'press gang' turned up in York in 1777 the Mayor was threatened with death if they were not withdrawn within three days. But again, under threat of invasion from France in 1782 the people of York mobilised speedily and loyally to defend the country from attack.

It seems that by 1720 there were some buildings for the York garrison in Coppergate. It is probable that there was a cavalry barracks and some military quarters but still the majority of soldiers would have lived in billets. At the outbreak of the war with France in 1793, which continued more or less unabated until the Battle of Waterloo in 1815, William Pitt inaugurated a great military building programme. Between 1794 and 1796 cavalry barracks were built at York at a cost of £25,000 to accommodate 21 officers, 240 NCOs and men and 266 horses. The Royal Coat of Arms that decorated the front of the officers' mess was carved in London in 'Coade stone'. It is said to be one of the best examples of its kind and now, beautifully restored, occupies a place of honour in front of the newly built headquarters of North East District in Fulford. In October 1795 three troops of Ancient British Fencibles, a regiment raised for short service only, marched into the new barracks which was to be continuously occupied by cavalry until the 15/19 Hussars were mechanised in 1939.

It was not until 1860 that the area of the barracks was further enlarged. Seven acres of land were then bought which, added to the purchase of 1793, made a barrack area of 19 acres. A 100 bed Hospital was built in 1860 and it was enlarged in 1872. Also in 1860 two troop and stable blocks were built and a barrack block and a block of soldiers' married quarters. The families' quarters' block contained 40 rooms and was meant to house 40 families. The officers' mess was extended on the site of the old hospital and a house for the commanding officer was built beside it. A further 35 acres was acquired in 1877 and this provided the site for the infantry barracks. At a total cost of £150,000 accommodation was provided for 60 officers, 1,100 NCOs and men, 92 married men and 16 horses. The barracks was shared by an infantry battalion and the Depot of the West Yorkshire Regiment. In 1951 Redford Barracks was renamed Imphal Barracks.

During the Victorian period the volunteer movement was stimulated by ill-founded fears of a French invasion. These fears increased after the Crimean War where our military unpreparedness had been clearly exposed and where another Bonaparte, Napoleon III, was involving France in a series of military adventures around the world. Regiments of riflemen, artillery and engineers were formed and by May 1861, 170,000 men had already enlisted for part-time service. The York City Rifle Volunteers were formed in 1859 and took for their motto the latin *pro aris et focis* (for our altars and our hearths). The volunteers, unlike the regular soldiers, were largely middle

Headquarters North East District and Coat of Arms

class and they were able to form a bridge between the army and the citizens and help to remove, to some extent at least, the anti-army prejudice which still lingered on in Britain. In 1881 the Volunteer Rifles became the volunteer battalions of regular Infantry Regiments following on the far-reaching Cardwell reforms of the early eighteen-seventies. As part of the great re-organisation and re-deployment of the army after the Crimean War, Headquarters North Eastern Military District was transferred from Manchester to York and occupied a newly built HQ block in October 1878. In 1905 this became Headquarters Northern Command.

When the headquarters moved from Manchester a new Ordnance Depot was built and occupied in 1888. Stores then arrived direct from Woolwich by sea, the ship being towed up river to the ordnance wharf by tug. This ship the *Princess* carried on a regular service from the Woolwich Arsenal until she was torpedoed and sunk during the First World War. After that the sea and river service to the Depot was discontinued and rail and horse wagons were used for some years after 1918. Although stores are now held in a variety of Sub Depots, RAOC Headquarters, Planning and Control and Accounts Branches continued to operate from the old buildings until June 1971. In the past several old houses had been purchased in York by the army, to provide accommodation for the Headquarters and its many branches. Bootham House was bought in 1882 to provide a house for the General Officer Commanding. In 1921 'Ousecliffe' was acquired and in its turn became Government House. Hollycroft House in Wenlock Terrace was purchased in the thirties. Fishergate House, a school built in 1837, was bought by the War Department in 1931 and Claxton Hall, a Dower House with 35 acres, in 1940. The occupants and use of these buildings have changed, sometimes quite often whilst they have been owned by the Army, but many were still in use, as we have seen, right up to the time of the massive rebuild of the Headquarters in Imphal Barracks in the late seventies and early eighties. The new buildings are shared with the Headquarters of 2nd Armoured Divison, recently re-deployed from Germany. At last, however, most of the HQ Branches and Services are under one roof.

From the middle of the nineteenth century, as we have seen, resentment at the presence of the military began to decline in York and elsewhere. The volunteer movement was not the only reason. The growing popularity of the monarchy and the vicarious excitements of an ever enlarging empire did seem to offer some recompense to the tax payer who, up to the Crimean War, begrudged the cost and distrusted the purpose of a standing army. This change of attitude can be seen clearly in York in the development of an institution known as Military Sunday which flourished in the city from 1885 until the outbreak of the Second World War. First conceived as a memorial to General Gordon after his murder in Khartoum, the great military parade and service in the Minster proved to be so popular that it was continued with much support for a further fifty-three years.

A visit to the Minster confirms the very real associations that exist between the military and the Cathedral. The King's Own Yorkshire Light Infantry Regimental Memorial Chapel is very prominent in the Minster and is obviously a place of pilgrimage for 'old comrades' and citizens alike. The stained glass in the memorial windows comes from the fourteenth century church of St. John Micklegate and commemorates the men from the Regiment who died in two world wars. As recently as May 1979 a memorial to the men evacuated from Dunkirk in 1940 was unveiled. In the previous year the York and District Branch of the Dunkirk Veterans Association had placed a 'Book of Remembrance' and a casket of sand from the Dunkirk beaches in the Cathedral. Under the memorial an inscription reads:

> Here, beneath the eighteenth-century statue of Christ carrying the Cross, created by the York artist, Richard Fisher, is a memorial to the men of the British Expeditionary Force who were evacuated from the beaches of France and Belgium in May and June 1940.

The memorial was unveiled by the Marquis of Normanby, Lord Lieutenant of Yorkshire. Even though the Military Sunday parades were not brought back after the last war the armed services still hold their parades and march to church on special occasions. At the Battle of Britain Parade and Service, in the Minster in September of 1985, in which soldiers, sailors and airmen took part, support and genuine affection for the services was obvious enough to guarantee that a large proportion of the citizens of York would welcome the return of Military Sundays.

The Yorkshire Gazette of the 6 June 1908 carries a report of Military Sunday of that year. It says almost everything that is to be said about the joys and tribulations of living in a garrison town and would seem to be a fitting note on which to end this description of York as a 'military town'.[7]

MILITARY SUNDAY

There are some few occasions in the year when the equanimity of the good, quiet, law-abiding citizens of York becomes disturbed, and perhaps foremost amongst these

Military Sunday, York Minster, 1908.

is that venerable institution, Military Sunday. It was a happy dispensation which ordered that, for this one day in the year, the soldier should be singled out for a profuse public recognition — an honour which in the highest sense he can justly claim because of the office to which he has been called. Moreover, it is well that for this annual occasion the soldiers should mass *en bloc* in the Cathedral of the city in which they are stationed to be reminded of their duties as defenders of the country.

In the matter of dimensions it is computed that last Sunday's crowd was the largest seen, if not in all the history of the institution, at least for a good many years. In every street, the bye-streets too, one had to edge one's way through a congested crowd.

A picturesque sight was the imposing march-past of the soldiers of the various regiments stationed at Fulford, each with its own band at its head. Each band played its martial air, and to the tune 1,600 soldiers measured their steps. A few mounted men cleared the way, then in lines several deep came the blue and yellow of the Lancers, the scarlet of the Infantry, the Artillery blue, the plumed Hussars, and the picturesque Border men from Strensall. It was all very grand, and provocative of a temporary, if not permanent, wave of patriotism amongst the onlookers. There was a clash of steel as the soldiers took their seats in the cathedral, from the pillars from which depended ensigns and flags. The historic edifice was crowded with people, some there for curiosity, some to hear the music of the bands, and some to reverently worship.

After the entrance of the soldiers came the slow and stately procession of the Lord Mayor and Corporation in their quaint official regalia.

It was an inspiring moment when the massed bands poured forth the haunting strains of Weber's *Euryanthe* but the greatest inspiration of the whole function was when we heard the choristers in the distance singing with beautiful expression the first verse of the appropriate hymn, *Onward, Christian Soldiers*. Then the bands took up the strain, and lastly in one grand throng the congregation, band and choristers gave forth of their pent-up sentiment in a hearty rendering of the final three verses . . .

The clergy in attendance were the Dean (Dr A P Purey-Cust), the Bishop of Hull (Dr R F L Blunt), the Chaplain General (Bishop Taylor Smith) . . . the lesson was read by Brigadier General Altham . . . The Chaplain preached a powerful sermon, in which he exhorted the soldier to 'Play the Man' and to see to it that neither the fruits of intemperance, impurity, nor gambling, nor any other cold, contrary wind which blew, should spoil the fulness, beauty, and fruitfulness of their lives.

After the final prayers, the congregation vigorously sang *Fight the Good Fight*, and during the collection time the bands gave a fine interpretation of Mendelssohn's *The War March of the Priests*, which they followed with *Ein Albumblatt*, a weird and pretty selection from Wagner. Then came Dr Naylor's famous fanfare introduction to *God Save The King*, and lastly the National Anthem, sung with all the force of expression which the congregation could muster.

Slowly the congregation filed out of the Minster and swelled the surging crowds in the street. Then the soldiers marched back to the barracks, and once more Military Sunday was over. The bands of course attended the evening service when the Cathedral was again crowded.

The offertories at the Cathedral, which were in aid of the military charities and garrison chapel, realised £91 0s. 7d., which is over £6 in excess of the amount obtained last year.

Bibliography

Some Military Associations of the City of York, A most valuable outline of the military history of York prepared by the officers of the Royal Army Educational Corps at HQ, North East District, York, 1972

A History of Roman Britain, Professor Sheppard Frere, Routledge & Kegan Paul, 1967

England Before the Norman Conquest, Charles Oman, Methuen, 1924

A History of the County of Yorkshire (City of York Volume), The County Books, Robert Hale, London

The King's War (1641-1647), C V Wedgwood, Collins, 1958

The Great and Close Siege of York, 1644, P Wenham, Roundwood, 1970

Royal Commission for Historic Monuments, Volumes on York, HMSO

The following museums are particularly recommended:

Jorvik Viking Centre, Coppergate, York
For the post-Roman and Viking history of York

The Yorkshire Museum, Museum Gardens, York
For Roman and Medieval antiquities

The Castle Museum, Tower St., York
Folk collections and reconstructions including one of the martial history of the City

The York Story, St. Mary's, Castlegate, York
Particularly good on the buildings of York

3

Edinburgh

PETER DIETZ

Auld Reikie! thou'rt a canty hole,
A bield for mony a caldrife soul,
Wha snugly at thine ingle loll,
    Baith warm and couth;
While round they gar the bicker roll
    To weet their mouth.
                Robert Fergusson, 1772[1]

WHEN HE was nine years old, in 1812, George Borrow followed his officer father and a party of soldiers into Edinburgh Castle and it must already have been one of the best known castles in British possession. Borrow himself says in 'Lavengro', writing about his early childhood and his arrival in the Scottish Capital, 'It is hardly necessary to say much about this Castle, which everyone has seen'. But nevertheless he goes on '. . . the Castle, into which everyone marched with drums beating, colours flying, and a long train of baggage waggons behind . . . was a garrison for soldiers. Two other regiments were already there; the one an Irish, if I remember right, the other a small highland corps. . . . We took up our abode in that immense building, or caserne, of modern erection, which occupies the entire eastern side of the bold rock on which the Castle stands. A gallant caserne it was, the best and roomiest I had yet seen, rather cold and windy, it is true, especially in the winter, but commanding a noble prospect of a range of distant hills . . .'[2]

That Edinburgh Castle was so well known even in the early nineteenth century was no doubt largely due to the increasingly popular works of Sir Walter Scott. But there was another reason for English awareness and for the mood of apprehension of the English soldiery as they entered the great fortress. Until the Act of Union in 1706, the Scottish Lowlands and the Border Country had seen continuous and bloody conflict between English and Scots. Even after the Union serious fighting broke out again on two further occasions and then, as in previous centuries, Edinburgh and its Castle was a main objective and a symbolic prize. Often the struggles saw the participants divided amongst themselves, with the English or the Scots aiding a faction on the other side of the border, hoping to gain some advantage by fishing in troubled waters. Even more in these circumstances the bitterness and lust for revenge that remained after the fighting was over would be projected towards the rival nation. From Roman times, and probably from long before, the history of relations between the people of the north of Britain and those of the south was written only in blood. Even after the Act of Union, which was itself called by many Scots 'The Great

Betrayal', the Jacobite risings of 1715 and 1745 were put down with a ferocity which nullified any hope of a genuine union but also indicated an almost irrational fear of the supposedly primitive and barbaric fighting men from the still scarcely known mountains of the north. It was more than a hundred years after the Act of Union before 'Victoria the Good' was able to bring together the Scots and the English into a fruitful and permanent partnership in which the best qualities of both peoples could be appreciated and accepted.

The tumultuous and frequently gory history of Scotland is reflected in the story of its major city and perhaps it was not entirely by chance that Borrow's father arrived in Edinburgh in 1812 with his English Militia Regiment to find not only a 'small Scottish Corps' but also an Irish Regiment esconced in the Castle. Divide and rule is a very old strategy.

George Borrow, who like Sir Walter Scott attended Edinburgh High School, very quickly found himself involved in the incessant brawls that took place between the school boys of the 'auld toon' and those of the 'new toon'. Living in the Castle as he did he automatically took his place in the ranks of the 'auld tooners' and seems to have enjoyed his part in the 'bickers' in one of which he reports that upward of a thousand boys were involved. The unruly boys of the city were not the only ones to brawl and riot as the colourful history of the City Guard will later make clear.

Edinburgh, unlike Colchester or York, was never a Roman town. Agricola with the Ninth Legion invaded Scotland in AD 81 and, having advanced as far as the Forth–Clyde line, stopped intending to establish a line of forts to protect his conquests and to make Stirling his northern headquarters. He planned to advance further north but was ordered to withdraw in AD 84. The Antonine Wall was built in AD 141 and after that Roman strategy tended to become mainly defensive. In AD 208 the Roman Emperor Severus, who had established his court at York, built a naval base at Cramond, now a pleasant suburb of Edinburgh. He pushed north as far as the Moray Firth but was never able to bring his Caledonian foes to pitched battle. After three years of inconclusive campaigning he was worn out and returned to York to die. Soon after this the Romans abandoned the Antonine Wall and for a further hundred years Hadrian's Wall became the northern frontier of the Roman Empire in Britain. By the end of the fourth century pressure all along the eastern frontier of the Empire, and increasing raids across the North Sea and over Hadrian's Wall into Roman Britain, brought about the Roman withdrawal from Britain. Fitzroy Maclean says in his *A Concise History of Scotland*, 'Thus Scotland only encountered the might of Rome spasmodically and never became a true part of the Roman Empire or enjoyed save at second hand the benefits or otherwise of Roman civilisation'.[3] However, it could be said that in establishing the Antonine Wall and holding it for even so short a time the Romans were instrumental in marking a difference between Lowlands and Highlands more than that of mere geography. This was to have important and sometimes tragic consequences, not least for Edinburgh, for more than a thousand years.

Edinburgh takes its name from the Northumbrian King Edwin. In the sixth century the Angles, who had established themselves in Yorkshire and in a separate, smaller Kingdom, Bernicia, to the north and east of them, combined to form the powerful Kingdom of Northumbria. Northumbria was strong enough to capture the British Kingdoms in southern Scotland and in 638 Edinburgh was taken. Edwin died in 632, five years after becoming a christian, but such was his reputation that his name was associated with 'the fortress on the hill' called in early gaelic Dineidin. Through the intermediate name Dunedin the modern name Edinburgh finally emerged when the first syllable 'Dun', meaning fortress, changed into the Old English for fortress 'Burh' and became the last part of the name. The Northumbrian rule in Edinburgh ended during the reign of the Scottish King Indulf (954-962). Gradually, through marriage and conquest, the Pictish Kingdom of the north, the Scottish Kingdom of Dalriada, the British Kingdom of Strathclyde, the Lowlands and Edinburgh were all united in a Scottish Kingdom. Lothian was gained for Scotland at the Battle of Carham in 1018 and when Duncan ascended the throne in 1032 his kingdom occupied roughly the area that Scotland does today.

After the Norman conquest of England in 1066 Edward Atheling of Wessex rose against the Normans but was defeated and had to flee with his sister Margaret to Scotland. They were wrecked on the Fife coast but were sheltered by Malcolm III of Scotland, grandson of Duncan. Malcolm had designs on the northern counties of England and saw in Atheling a possible claimant to the English throne and so he took Margaret as his second wife. The court of Scotland was kept at Dunfermline where Malcolm had his chief residence but he built a hunting lodge on the Castle Rock south of the Firth of Forth. He also built a chapel beside the lodge for his devout Queen, and the chapel, discovered and restored in 1845 to what is thought was its original form, is the oldest building in the Castle complex and perhaps in the whole of Edinburgh. Margaret died in 1093 shortly after hearing of the death of her husband and one of her sons at the Battle of Alnwick. The Castle came under heavy attack from the English but on a misty day her body was lowered down the steep face of the rock and taken by her surviving sons across the Forth for burial at Dunfermline. Through her piety and her experience of the Anglo-Saxon and continental courts where she had been brought up Margaret introduced a gentler, more religious and more civilised influence into the Scottish court. This first link through Margaret, between the Scottish and English royal houses, was to be typical of a relationship which persisted over the centuries. Through Margaret and her mainly Anglo-Norman educated sons, English became the language of the court and of literate people in Scotland. At the same time feudal land-holding and ecclesiastical organisation was introduced on the Anglo-Norman model into the Lowland areas of Scotland.

It has been said that St. Margaret's chapel on the Castle Rock was built not by Malcolm for his wife but by Malcolm's ninth son David, as a memorial to his mother. David I ascended the throne in 1124 and reigned for almost thirty years. He inherited his mother's piety, and if he was not responsible for the Castle chapel he was certainly responsible for the founding of Holyrood Abbey in 1128. The charter which David gave to the Abbey provided ample endowments and also provides the first documentary evidence of the existence of Edinburgh as a market town with its own merchants and tradesmen. Edinburgh gained its own charter as a Royal Burgh from Robert I in 1329 but as early as David's reign, two hundred years earlier, it had been recognised and regulated together with Roxburgh, Berwick and Stirling in the 'Laws of the Four Burghs'. David enjoyed a peaceful reign apart from the intervention in English affairs in 1135 when, despite his defeat at the Battle of the Standard at Northallerton, he achieved his objective, which was the acquisition of most of Northumbria, through skillful negotiation.

Edinburgh, being relatively near the border with England, was far more vulnerable in the Anglo-Scottish wars than any large English town and over the next two hundred years it was occupied, sacked and burned on several occasions. The Castle itself, recaptured from the English in 1314, lost and recaptured again in 1341 was afterwards destroyed to prevent it being used by the enemy but on both occasions it was rebuilt. In 1335 Edward III, after looting and then destroying Edinburgh, rebuilt the castle in order to maintain his domination of southern Scotland. The Scottish King David II attempted to invade England in 1346 but was defeated at the Battle of Neville's Cross and spent five years in captivity in England. He returned to Scotland in 1357 and started to build on Castle Rock the massive keep known as King David's Tower. Although the tower was not completed until after his death he lived there and administerd the country from the castle in the last years of his life. The walls of the tower were sixty feet high, and defended by cannon it successfully defied attack by Richard II of England although the town was ravaged. Again in 1400 the castle was besieged by Henry IV, but again without success and it was not until 1573, during Mary Queen of Scots' unhappy reign that the tower was battered to rubble by the English artillery of Sir William Drury who was supporting the Regent, the Earl of Morton against Queen Mary's party. The remains of King David's Tower were buried under the Half Moon Battery, built in the fifteen-seventies but parts of the original tower were rediscovered when the rock below the Half Moon Battery was excavated in 1912.

By the end of the sixteenth century improvements in the design of cannon and in explosives had sealed the fate of castles everywhere and it could only be a matter of time before even the strongest fortress had to capitulate in the face of competently handled siege artillery. But in 1457 a piece of ordnance arrived at the castle which demonstrated that artillery was already the 'Very Queen of Battles'. The magnificent siege gun, known as a bombard and affectionately called 'Mons Meg', was forged in the fourteen-forties, almost certainly at Mons, for the Duke of Burgundy. Another, and unnecessarily complicated explanation of the name would have it that the gun was made by a blacksmith at Mollance in Galloway who had a wife called Meg. The Mollance being shortened to Mons the cannon was called Mons Meg. Again it has been suggested that Mons was short for monster but both these latter explanations have been, dare we say it, quite exploded. Mons in Flanders was the great source of artillery in medieval times and the 'Great Gun' of nearby Ghent is very similar to Mons Meg. The first recorded instance of the gun being fired in Scotland, after its arrival as a gift to James II, was when it was used at the siege of Dumbarton by James IV. It was used in battle on several occasions after this and when the castle finally surrendered to Cromwell in 1650 the gun was referred to as 'The Great Iron Murderer called Muckle Meg . . .' which does indicate a certain success in battle. In 1681 the gun was fired off in honour of a visit to Edinburgh by the Duke of York. Unfortunately the barrel burst injuring several of the gunners. This incident was later commemorated by the Edinburgh poet Robert Fergusson in the Lines:

> Oh willawins! Mons Meg for you,
> Twas firing cracked thy muckle mowe!

After this accident the cannon lay dismounted and abandoned until after the Porteous riots in 1736 when the Board of Ordnance required all unserviceable guns to be collected together at the Tower of London. It stayed there until 1829 when Sir Walter Scott was able to take advantage of King George IV's recently awakened interest in Scotland and things Scottish to have the gun returned to Edinburgh. Almost as much fuss was made over the return of the great gun as was made over the celebrated visit of George IV to Edinburgh in 1822. Meg was escorted by a regiment of foot and three troops of cavalry, and led by a pipe band from where she was landed at Leith through cheering crowds up to the Castle. The cannon was at first displayed in the open close to St. Margaret's Chapel but recently it has been badly affected by weathering and has now been moved into the vaults of the 'French Prisons'. For all its age and chequered history it looks splendidly sleek and fat under its cleverly arranged lighting, for all the world like some great reclining Buddha, accepting pilgrims and homage as its proper due.

To return to the sixteenth century. In 1513 James IV, who had tried to act as a peacemaker between England and France, gave up the effort and decided to join in on the French side. In 1486 he had signed with England a 'Treaty of Perpetual Peace' but by 1513 Henry VIII had succeeded to the throne as King of England. James felt himself threatened by the bellicose young King and decided to strike first. He crossed the Tweed with the finest army ever raised in Scotland up to that time but within two weeks he had been killed at the overwhelming defeat of Flodden, and with him the flower of the Scottish nobility. Scotland was left in a state of anarchy and violence. James V, who ruled until 1542, died finally worn out trying to bring some order to his troubled kingdom, and was succeeded by Mary Queen of Scots who was one week old when he died. Henry VIII had wanted James V to marry his daughter in the hope of gaining control of Scotland but this came to nothing. Now another opportunity presented itself. A treaty of marriage was arranged through Arran, the pro-English Regent, between little Mary of Scotland and Henry's sickly son Edward. Henry wanted Mary to be brought up at the English court where he could control events but before this could be brought about she was carried off to Scone and crowned Queen of Scotland, while the Scottish Estates repudiated the treaty of marriage.

Henry, who was notoriously short-tempered, immediately ordered the invasion of Scotland. The instructions of the Privy Council to the English soldiers was that they were to 'put all to fyre and swoorde . . . bourne Edinborough towne, so rased and defaced when you have sacked and gotten what you can of it, as there may remayne forever a perpetuel memory of the vengaunce of God.' This brutal and stupid treatment of the Lowlands and Edinburgh in particular, which later came to be called, with bitter humour, 'The Rough Wooing', left an inevitable legacy of hatred and suspicion remembered whenever talk of a Union between the two countries was in the air.

The Reformation came much later to Scotland than to England and led to the drawing up of the 'First Covenant'. After the death of the catholic Mary Tudor and the succession of Elizabeth as Queen of England, negotiations were at last possible for the withdrawal of all English and French troops from Scotland. The growing power of the Scots Protestants and the weakening of the 'Auld Alliance' with the death of Mary of Guise, the Queen Mother, cleared the way for the Treaty of Edinburgh in July 1560, and for the ultimate victory of protestantism in Scotland. It was also at last possible, for some people at least, to conceive of a real union between England and Scotland. Although Mary Queen of Scots had repudiated her French connections after the death of her husband who had ruled France for one year only

Mons Meg.

as Francois I, she immediately became the centre of scandal, intrigue and suspicion, and when she returned to Scotland to take up her inheritance she was the object of every rebellion and disorder. By 1567 Mary was forced to abdicate and in the following year she fled to England for sanctuary where she was promptly imprisoned by the ever prudent Elizabeth. Mary was held under duress, with varying degrees of strictness for nineteen years during which time her supporters, with or without her knowledge and almost certainly without her agreement, plotted to put her back on the throne of Scotland. As a result of one of these plots Edinburgh Castle was seized by rebels and, as we have seen above, was only regained in 1573 by the Regent, Morton, and the heavy-handed aid of English siege artillery. When Elizabeth finally brought herself to authorise the execution of Mary in 1587 the Scots clamoured for war but Mary's son James VI, who had concluded an alliance with England in 1585, merely made a formal protest. James had long held ambitions regarding the English throne through his ancestor Mary Tudor, daughter of Henry VII, and was no doubt encouraged in his hopes by Elizabeth herself, influenced as she was by her powerful secretary Sir Robert Cecil, a friend and secret adviser of James. At Elizabeth's death in 1603 James became James I of England whilst remaining King James VI of the separate Kingdom of Scotland. The Kingdoms remained separate for a further one hundred and three years until in 1706 in the reign of Queen Anne, and despite some Scottish misgivings and noisy protest, the Act of Union finally brought the two countries into a close working partnership.

But before the Act of Union could really bring the two peoples together another century of bloodshed and bitterness had to pass. The friction was exacerbated by the high-minded stubbornness of the Stuart dynasty. Although neither James I nor Charles I of England were catholics they were equally determined that the Scottish Church should follow the English pattern. Charles especially, by the Act of Revocation in 1625, attempted to set the clock back in a way which was guaranteed to frighten and infuriate the Covenanters. On his visit to Edinburgh in 1633, when he came to be crowned, he was accompanied by the Archbishop of Canterbury. The coronation service was held in St. Giles which was made for the occasion the Cathedral of a new Bishopric of Edinburgh, and it was held with full Anglican rites. Most important of all in 1637 the new prayer book, designed as a compromise between the English Prayer Book and the practice of extempore prayer common in Scotland, provoked a riot on its first reading in St. Giles. The second Covenant which sprang from this agitation and unrest was inspired by the Earls of Montrose and Argyll who between them carried most of Scotland, but who were and remained bitter personal enemies. The Covenant, along with its complaint about unacceptable religious innovations, professed loyalty to the King, and in Montrose's case these incompatibilities brought about his downfall. After raising most of eastern Scotland for the Covenant he found that his conscience would not allow him to fight openly against the King, and even as the Royalist fortunes began to decline Montrose raised a motley army and carried out a brilliant campaign for the King in Scotland. By 1645 however, the Civil War in England had turned disastrously against Charles and after the Battle of Naseby it was only a matter of time before he accepted defeat. Charles surrendered to the Scottish Covenanting Army at Newark and as a condition of the surrender Montrose disbanded his army in Scotland and took ship to Norway. But the story in Scotland was not yet over. After the execution of King Charles his son was proclaimed King Charles II by Argyll.

Montrose not to be outdone, crossed to Scotland where his small force was easily defeated and despite his obvious intention to serve Charles II he was handed over to his enemies and, at Argyll's insistence, tried as a traitor to the King and executed with barbaric ritual. Cromwell invaded Scotland in answer to the arrival of Charles. The Scottish army was defeated and Charles again forced to flee to the Continent. Argyll contrived, incredibly to make himself acceptable to the new regime but after Cromwell's death ten years later and the final restoration of the monarchy, he was to his incredulous disbelief arraigned for treason and executed. His severed head was displayed on the same spike at the Tolbooth in Edinburgh from which that of his arch enemy Montrose had only lately been removed. Cromwell spent two periods in Edinburgh before his death and the restoration of the Stuarts. He lived in Moray House which had been built in 1628 by Mary, Countess of Home and, it is said, quartered his Dragoons in Holyrood Palace. He spent his time setting up an efficient system of military government which brought peace and tranquillity to the whole of Scotland, perhaps for the first time. Characteristically it was deeply unpopular everywhere and demonstrated yet again that people of spirit prefer to go to hell in their own way rather than to heaven under outside compulsion.

After the restoration Scotland still maintained its own military establishment and some of the oldest and most prestigious regiments of the British Army today first appear on the stage of history at this time. One of the first acts of Charles II after the restoration was to replace the English garrisons, stationed in Scotland by Oliver Cromwell, with native Scottish soldiers. In October 1660 he ordered a company of Guards to be raised in Edinburgh. In May 1662 four more companies were raised and the new regiment thus formed was called the 'New Regiment of Foot Guards'. In July 1666 George, Earl of Linlithgow was appointed Colonel. Independent troops of Dragoons had been raised in Scotland during periods of unrest and promptly disbanded when the threat abated. This regular fluctuation in the establishment was a regular feature of Scottish military life but in 1681 Lieutenant General Thomas Dalyell of the Binns formed the Royal Regiment of Scots Dragoons from some formerly independent troops of Scottish dragoons. The Regiment later became known as The Royal Scots Greys, and now, after its amalgamation in 1971 with 3rd Carabiniers, it is called The Royal Scots Dragoon Guards (Carabiniers and Greys). Records show that in 1683 it took 2,436 eils (1 ell = 45 ins) of stone-grey cloth, imported from England to completely clothe the Regiment. Another regiment which, whilst it was not raised in Edinburgh, nevertheless has great associations with the city and whose Regimental Headquarters and splendid Regimental Museum are now located in the Castle is The Royal Scots (The Royal Regiment), the First Regiment of Foot. The Regiment can trace its origins back to the mercenary troops fighting for continental rulers during the Thirty Years War. In 1633 Colonel Sir John Hepburn raised a Scottish regiment under warrant from Charles I for French service. It was placed on the British establishment at the restoration but it did not finally return to England until 1678.

Charles II died in 1685 and was succeeded by his Catholic brother James. James had as Duke of York acted briefly as Royal Commissioner in Scotland during the so-called 'Killing Time', when the Covenanters resisted the attempts of Charles and his royalist supporters to put the clock back, and inevitably paid the price of their rebellion. But after only three years James II was forced to flee to France and William of Orange, his Dutch, Protestant son-in-law, and Mary his daughter were proclaimed King and Queen of England and Ireland. In Scotland a Convention of the Estates showed a majority in favour of William and Mary and so in April 1689 they were also proclaimed King and Queen of Scotland. It could be said that the Estates were merely following the lead of England, as they had over the restoration of Charles II but it is difficult to know what else they might have done without plunging Scotland once more into anarchy and civil war. In the long run the majority of Scots were satisfied with their choice but in the short run, and especially in the aftermath of 'The Union', nothing appeared to be settled, only this time the boot was firmly on the other foot. With the accession of a staunchly Protestant King, and the 'Whig Ascendancy' in England, the mainly Lowland Covenanters were at a considerable advantage over their Highland fellow countrymen. The Jacobite risings which followed could be seen as a last stand for an older, more feudal but at the same time freer way of life, epitomised by clan loyalties, loyalty to the Stuarts who were seen as the only legitimate claimants to the throne of Scotland, and hatred of the oppressive foreign presence usually symbolised by the 'red coats', but often also by the black-coated, bible carrying Covenanters from the Lowlands. Not all the clans supported the Stuarts. Traditional clan enmities often counted for more than the wider issues, and in the risings of 1715 and 1745 Highlanders fought on both sides as indeed did some Lowlanders. But the thrust of the Jacobite risings came from the Highlands and was sustained by the majority of the Highland clans.

General dissatisfaction with the 'Union' and rumblings of discontent amongst the English Jacobites encouraged the supporters of James Edward, son of James VII of Scotland (James II of England), who had been promised help by Louis XIV, to declare against the Union and to proclaim James Edward, James VIII. Despite the rallying of twelve thousand clansmen to the cause and the early capture of Perth the opportunity to take Edinburgh was missed and support gradually slipped away. By the time that James Edward landed at Peterhead at the end of 1715 the situation was past saving. On reaching Montrose James Edward and his military commander the Earl of Mar slipped away by boat to France leaving a message for the Highlanders to shift for themselves.

The usual repressive measures followed. An attempt was made to disarm the clans but the more belligerent Highlanders handed in obsolete weapons and buried their more serviceable arms to use on another occasion which none of them doubted would one day come. General Wade was appointed Commander-in-Chief for Scotland and he commenced a ten year programme of road building intended to open up the Highland areas and to link the new strategic fortresses at Fort George, Fort Augustus and Fort William. At this time too, a number of Independent Highland Companies were formed into a regular regiment known as 'The Highland Regiment'. Its main duties at first were policing the Highlands which is no doubt why it was known colloquially as 'The Black Watch'. The regiment, at first numbered as the 43rd Foot, was renumbered 42nd in 1749 and finally in 1881 it was amalgamated with the 73rd (Perthshire) Regiment of Foot and renamed The Black Watch (Royal Highlanders). Although the high period of 'military dandyism' did not arrive until well into the next century all monarchs took a somewhat exaggerated interest in the dress of their soldiers and a dress as unusual as that of the new Highland Regiment had to be seen by the King for his approval. There is a nice story told in Carman's *British Military*

Uniforms (1957) of the men of the Black Watch performing a broadsword dance for the King on the occasion of their visit to the Palace and being rewarded personally by the King with gold coins, which they promptly handed to the doorman on their way out. John Kay, the famous Edinburgh artist (1742-1826) made a delightful etching of George, Fifth Duke of Gordon, when as Marquis of Huntly he was serving with the 42nd in Edinburgh Castle. The etching is dated 1791 but the dress is no doubt similar to that approved by the King. Three years later the Marquis of Huntly was given command of the 92nd (Gordon Highlanders) Regiment of Foot, raised by his father, the Fourth Duke of Gordon, in February 1794.

Although there was no great sympathy for some of the aims of the rising of 1715 amongst the Lowlanders it did unite the opposers of the 'Act of Union'. Most surprising of all was the planned joint rebellion of Jacobites and Cameronians who represented completely opposite religious view points. Edinburgh, as we have said, missed the dangers of an occupation by the Jacobite forces but an abortive attempt was made to capture the Castle by scaling the western slope near the sally port. The plot was discovered however and the scaling party, about one hundred men, mainly Highlanders, were forced to flee leaving four wounded behind who were made prisoners by the City Guard.

Between the risings of 1715 and 1745 the situation did not improve. Taxes on salt and malt led to outbursts of rioting in many Scottish cities and smuggling was turned to as a patriotic duty. The excise men became the scape goats for unpopular laws and in Edinburgh, unruly as ever, this led to an incident which further exacerbated an already tense situation. In 1736 two smugglers were apprehended and sentenced to death. On the Sunday before their execution they were brought, as was the custom, into the Tolbooth Church to attend public worship guarded by four soldiers. The two prisoners started to struggle whilst in the church and one of them got away and escaped to Holland, probably with the connivance of the worshippers and the city mob. The other prisoner was duly hanged in the Grassmarket without interference from the crowd although this had been expected. The Commander of the Guard at the execution was one Captain Porteous who had been commissioned 'in the field' for his courage during Queen Anne's wars. Porteous had been incensed earlier when fearing an attempt at rescue, the Provost and bailies had asked for the streets to be lined by some regular troops who happened at that time to be in the Cannongate. Angry at the suggestion that he could not control the mob with the City Guard alone he apparently drank too much at lunch before the execution. After the execution there was the usual growling and a little stone throwing. Eye witnesses insist this was nothing more than usual. Porteous, however, caused his evidently reluctant guard to fire on the crowd killing eight or nine and wounding many more.

This massacre of their fellow citizens outraged the ordinary people of Edinburgh and they were only appeased when Porteous was tried and condemned to be hanged. Porteous, however, had regularly played golf with certain influential townspeople who persuaded Queen Caroline, who was acting as Regent, to reprieve him. This so outraged the mob that a combination of feeling against Porteous, the Union and England led them to disarm the City Guard who had been called out to disperse them, burn down the door of the Tolbooth where Porteous was being held, and drag him to the Grassmarket where he was hanged from a dyer's pole. The City was severely punished by the Government especially since an investigation by the Scottish

ACT of COUNCIL

AGAINST

Throwing Stones, &c. at the Execution of Criminals.

HE Lord Provoft, Baillies and Council, with the Deacons of Crafts Ordinary and Extraordinary, taking to their Confideration, that the Peace and good Government of this City has been frequently difturbed and infulted, and many pernicious and fatal Confequences have enfued to the Citizens and Inhabitants thereof, by the moft infolent and illegal Practice of throwing Stones, Mud and other Garbage, at the proper Officers of the Law, City-guard and Common Executioner, when in the Exercife of their Duty and Office at lawful and publick Executions of Criminals, or in the executing of other lawful Sentences, or in the going to and returning from fuch publick and lawful Executions of Sentences upon Criminals or Offenders againft the Laws : THEREFORE, in order to prevent all fuch pernicious and illegal Practices in Time coming, and for the more effectual bringing to Juftice the Perfon or Perfons guilty of all or any of the aforefaid Crimes, DID, and hereby DO ENACT, STATUTE and ORDAIN, That the Perfon or Perfons who fhall be hereafter found guilty, or Art and Part of throwing Stones, Mud, Dung, or other Garbage, at the Officers of the Law, City-guard, or Common Executioner, or others lawfully convocated at fuch publick and lawful Execution of Sentences upon Criminals or Offenders againft the Laws, or in going to or returning therefrom, or fhall be found difturbing the Peace in any Sort upon fuch Occafions, fhall, upon their being convicted thereof, be whipt through the City by the Hand of the Common Hangman, and thereafter imprifoned for the Space of one Year : And for the better difcovering and bringing to Juftice fuch Offenders, the Treafurer for the Time being, is hereby appointed to pay to any Perfon or Perfons, who fhall difcover, or caufe be difcovered, any fuch Offenders, fo as they fhall be convicted of all or any of the aforefaid Crimes, the Sum of Five Pounds Sterling : And that none may pretend Ignorance hereof, DID ORDAIN thir Prefents to be printed and publifhed by Tuck of Drum through this City and its Liberties, and through *Canongate, South* and *North Leiths,* and that Copies be affixed on the publick Places in the ufual Manner. *Extracted,*

GEORGE HOME.

The Act of Council against throwing stones, etc. at the execution of criminals. Edinburgh, 31 August 1737.

Law Officers was met by a conspiracy of silence. The Lord Provost was disbarred from holding further office and the city was fined £2,000 which went to Porteous's widow. Measures to imprison the Provost, abolish the City Guard and dismantle the city gates were eventually abandoned after the unanimous protest of the Scottish Members of Parliament. Despite large rewards being offered none of the ringleaders of the Porteous lynching were ever discovered. Some of the mob were apparently disguised as women and one is said to have been the Earl of Haddington dressed in the clothes of his cook-maid. Sir Walter Scott gives an account of the lynching in his novel *The Heart of Midlothian*, which although it is presented as fiction is based on eyewitness accounts. He makes the point for the mob that they were executing a murderer already properly convicted in the courts and only saved from his just fate by a corrupt Government.[4]

When the second Jacobite rising came eight years later it is not surprising that there was popular support in Edinburgh and elsewhere for Charles Edward Stuart, grandson of James VII of Scotland and son of James Edward, the 'Old Pretender', who still lived in exile in Rome. The prosperous upper classes and professional people of Edinburgh and the Lowlands were much more cautious in their approach and even the support of the Edinburgh mob rarely extended to joining the Jacobite army or to accompanying Prince Charles on his march south. In the end it was again the Highlanders who provided the main force in the rising, and they it was who saw the affair through to the bitter end and took the consequences of the rebellion.

Charles landed on the island of Eriskay on 23 July 1745. His Highland army approached Edinburgh from the west on 15 September. Meanwhile, General Sir John Cope, who commanded the Government forces in Scotland, had moved north with his small army of inexperienced troops as far as Aberdeen, in the hope that the Whig clans of the north-east would come to his aid. The clans which had not joined Charles waited upon events and Cope, not wanting to be cut off completely, embarked his force and sailed south to Dunbar. Two regiments of Dragoons had been left by Cope to guard Edinburgh. These regiments together with a small force of volunteers advanced towards the rebel army but it was soon discovered that both horses and men were in a very poor state from lack of food and sleep. It was decided to withdraw to Leith Links where it was hoped to join up with Cope's force on its return from the north. However, before an orderly retreat could be made, a small reconnoitring party from the Jacobite army was mistaken for the main body and a headlong retreat, some said a flight, ensued. The government troops retreated at full speed past Edinburgh to Leith then to Musselburgh and finally to Prestonpans where order was fully restored. The fright and flight had started at Coltbridge, and the precipitate retreat was soon known as the 'Canter of Coltbrigg'.

From Slateford, Charles sent a letter to the City Council promising protection and the preservation of all their rights if he was peacefully received. There was much confusion in the city where indignation at Charles's demands vied with fear of the Highlanders. Apprehension about the reaction of the London government to what might appear to be another act of defiance in Edinburgh and the knowledge that Cope was near at hand finally persuaded the city to resist and the gates were closed to the Jacobites. This was to no avail, however, because a party of City Council Deputies, returning from attempting to arrange a suspension of hostilities, caused the gate at the Nether Bow Port to be opened to admit their coach. A party of Locheil's Camerons who were lurking near the gate rushed in, dispersed the guard and seized the city without a shot being fired. The Castle was not surprised however, and remained in government hands, defended with some spirit by the eighty-five year old Lieutenant General Joshua Guest. Allan Ramsay, who lived in 'Goose-pie House' near the Castle, had written several pro-Jacobite, anti-Union poems but he, like many other prominent citizens, nominally committed to one side or the other, preferred caution and absented himself from the city during its occupation by the Jacobites. Ramsay's house was used as a vantage point from which to fire into the Castle and the musket balls from the returning fire can still be seen embedded in its walls.

The state of ferment, excitement and confusion in the city immediately before its occupation by the Jacobites can be gathered from some of the eyewitness accounts that have survived. Dr Alexander Carlyle, who was twenty-three years old at the time, writes in his autobiography, 'on Sunday morning 15th September, the Volunteers rendez-voused in the College Yards before 10 o'clock to the number of about 400. Captain Drummond appeared at ten and . . . addressed us in a speech of some length, the purport of which was, that it had been agreed by the General and the Officers of the Crown, that the military force should oppose the rebels on their march to Edinburgh, consisting of the Town Guard, that part of the new regiment (of volunteers) that had got arms, with the volunteers from the country'.[5]

Whilst this mixed force was marched up to the Lawnmarket, Hamilton's Dragoons marched past them in the other direction to take part in the fiasco at Coltbridge. Carlyle goes on to say that the spectators began to think that at last some serious fighting was likely to ensue though before this moment many of them had laughed at and ridiculed the volunteers. In the Lawnmarket they did get a mixed reception from the mob in the street and the ladies. 'In one house on the south side of the street there was a row of windows, full of ladies, who appeared to enjoy our march to danger with much mirth and levity'. However, in marching down the Bow, a narrow winding street, the scene was different, 'for all the spectators were in tears, and uttering loud lamentations', This must have unnerved the volunteers who were probably none too steady anyway, for as soon as news of the 'Coltbrigg Canter' reached them many opined that 'it would be madness to think of defending the town, as the Dragoons had fled'. Finally, a horseman 'whom nobody knew' rode up from the Bow to the Grassmarket which the volunteers had now reached and told them the Highlanders were at hand and were 16,000 strong. That ended any serious attempt to defend the city.

Charles held court at Holyrood. He levied taxes and customs in Edinburgh and at the same time issued orders against looting or pillage and generally did his best to prevent injury or insult to the townspeople. He was not able to take the Castle although he tried to force its surrender by cutting off food supplies but even this embargo had to be called off when General Guest threatened that his guns would fire on the city. There was general relief when the Bonnie Prince left Edinburgh on 1 November despite the loss of income suffered by some landladies and the tears shed by some over-romantic young ladies. The Jacobite army advanced bravely into England where, as in 1715 the English Jacobites, whose numbers had always been exaggerated, failed to join the rising. Charles had been persuaded to avoid Newcastle where old General Wade waited for him with a small but growing army. Such was the intense feeling and real fear engendered in England by the Highlanders' invasion that an extra verse was written for the recently composed 'National Anthem', and it was sung every night at Drury Lane where it was greeted with loud applause:

> God grant that General Wade
> May by thy mighty aid
> > Victory bring
> May he sedition hush
> And like a torrent rush
> Rebellious Scots to crush.
> > God save the King.

But it was not to be General Wade who would save the Union. After reaching Derby by the beginning of December, without even a minor defeat, Charles was persuaded by his advisers of the very real dangers of going further south into a hostile country rapidly withdrawing veteran troops from the Low Countries. The long, slow and hungry withdrawal started towards the Highlands. But Scotland was now more openly opposed to the Jacobites. Many Scottish towns closed their gates to Charles. He won a last, indecisive victory over the English General Hawley at Falkirk but failed to follow it up. This was the beginning of the end for the Jacobite cause and despite some premature and ill-judged celebration in Edinburgh at the arrival of a garbled account of Culloden which gave the Highlanders victory, the truth was otherwise. Cumberland, son of George II, a fat, brutal but competent and experienced commander, withstood with his troops for the first time the previously irresistible wild highland charge, and then systematically shot the clans to pieces. After the battle he continued with gusto the butchery which made any future resistance to the Union an impossible romantic dream.

The City Guard which appeared in our story at the time of the Porteous Riots, and whose members were so easily dispersed by Locheil's Highlanders when they burst into the city, were an old and much hated institution found in most European cities from medieval times until modern police forces were established. They were charged with preserving public order and suppressing riots and street crime. They also acted as night watchmen and where necessary enforced curfews. In Edinburgh they came under the direct control of the Lord Provost who was their *ex-officio* commander. When necessary they could be increased to a strength of 300. They were usually discharged veterans and in Edinburgh the large majority of them were Highlanders. Quick to take offence and easily baited, Scott describes them, again in *The Heart of Midlothian*, as 'Neither by birth, education or former habits, trained to endure the insults of the rabble, or the provoking petulance of truant schoolboys, and idle debauchees of all descriptions . . . On all occasions when a holiday licensed some riot and irregularity, a skirmish with these veterans was a favourite recreation with the rabble of Edinburgh'.[6]

Scott goes on to say that the poet Robert Fergusson, whose disorderly way of life brought him into frequent contact with the Guard, 'mentions them so often that he may be termed their poet laureate'. An example:

> And thou, great god of Aqua Vitae!
> Wha sways the empire of this city,
> When fou we're sometimes capernoity,
> > Be thou prepar'd

> To hedge us frae that black banditti,
>   The City Guard.[7]

Scott also describes them as 'black savages with a cockade', but there can be little doubt that they were needed in the dark, narrow streets of the city. Quarrels broke out very quickly especially between Highlanders from rival clans, often over a refusal to give way and each in turn would attract a crowd of supporters. A 'bicker' would ensue, and as we have seen from George Borrow's account, these were still occurring at least up to the middle of the next century.

The Volunteers were hardly taken seriously in 1745 but as the century progressed and government interest in, and spending on, the Militia declined, certain volunteer regiments, like The Edinburgh Volunteers and The Leith Volunteers became fashionable in the city and increased in numbers and prestige. The 'Fencibles' also became an attractive alternative to the Militia for young men of spirit who did not wish to serve far from home. The Fencibles were troops raised in up to battalion strength for limited service, usually not more than three years, and with no obligation to serve outside a particular area. Both the Fencibles and Militia units begin to appear in the garrison records for Edinburgh Castle from about 1762 when the Sutherland Fencibles are shown to be quartered there. The list of Edinburgh Castle 'troops in garrison since 1660',[8] now largely completed by the staff of The Scottish United Services Museum, is a most valuable document. Interestingly it makes use of Paton's two volume edition of Kay's *Original Portraits*[9] to date and identify some of the regiments stationed in Edinburgh towards the end of the eighteenth century. The compilers of the record have also made use of details from a memorial in the dog's cemetery to date the probable presence of the owner's regiment. This entry was probably made slightly 'tongue in cheek', but the 'cemetery' is well preserved on the site of 'the low defence', and attracts much interest from visitors to the Castle. Whilst most of John Kay's military portraits are gently satirical they do give an accurate picture of the uniforms of the time, of the rather pompous and somewhat over-fed appearance of some of the burgher, volunteer officers. His street scenes, like the one reproduced as an end-paper to this book, give a particularly realistic impression of the bustling, tumultuous street life of the city in the eighteenth century.

By the second half of the eighteenth century much of the antagonism towards the Union was muted, at least for the businessmen and merchants, engineers, soldiers and statesmen who seemed to come disproportionately from Scotland to build, police and govern a fast growing empire. Life in Edinburgh continued to be turbulent and colourful but the garrison, whilst they were stationed in the Castle were rarely called upon to do more than put on a brave show for a royal visit or to celebrate the King's birthday in a loyal and appropriate manner and thus provide a good example to the city.

Fergusson again, and the birthday celebrations on 4 June 1772:

> Sing, then, how, on the fourth of June,
> Our bells screed aff a loyal tune,
> Our antient castle shoots at noon,
>   Wi' flag-staff buskit,
> Frae which the soldier blades come down
>   To cock their musket.[10]

Of course the fighting reputation of the Scottish Regiments was too high for them to be left for long in Edinburgh or anywhere else in Scotland. The first battle honour of The Royal Scots is Tangier 1680, The Royal Scots Greys claim Blenheim in 1706 and the Black Watch, Guadeloupe in 1759. After these the honours come thick and fast and by the time of the Napoleonic Wars at the end of the century there is no major campaign or important battle anywhere in the world, in which the British fought in which at least one Scottish regiment did not distinguish itself. Scottish regiments were prominent in India and in the Peninsula and their exploits at the Battle of Waterloo have entered into the mythology of the British Army.

The Napoleonic Wars brought changes to the Castle as to most other British garrisons, dockyards and ports. Prime Minister William Pitt set in train an enormous programme of barrack building in the early seventeen-nineties and the large new barracks overshadowing the Old Back Parade and dominating the Castle was built at this time. It was this 'Gallant caserne', that Borrow followed his father into in 1812, as we noted at the beginning of this account. It was probably the first time that many of the soldiers had been accommodated in barracks. Until about this time most soldiers were billeted out on unwilling householders or publicans very much at the expense of the army's popularity. The great victories of the Napoleonic Wars, and particularly the relief and joy felt at the final defeat of Napoleon at Waterloo swept the returning regiments up on a wave of popularity and gratitude and events in Edinburgh were typical of celebrations held all over Britain. A contemporary newspaper account of the return of The Black Watch to Edinburgh after Waterloo gives an idea of the popular enthusiasm.

> On the 19th and 20th of March the 42nd Regiment marched in two divisions into Edinburgh Castle from Haddington . . . Nothing could exceed the enthusiasm with which these gallant veterans were welcomed in every town and village thro' which their route lay. Early on the 19th vast crowds were collected on the streets of this city . . . the road as far as Musselburgh was crowded with people! and as they approached the city, so much was their progress impeded by the multitude, that their march from Piershill to the Castle (less than two miles) occupied nearly two hours. House tops and windows were also crowded with spectators; and as they passed along the streets, amidst the ringing of bells, waving of flags and the acclamation of thousands, their red and white plumes, tattered colours and glittering bayonets were all that could be seen of these heroes, except by the few who were fortunate in obtaining elevated situations. The scene, viewed from the windows and house tops was the most extraordinary ever witnessed in this city. The crowds were wedged together across the whole breadth of the street, and extended in length as far as the eye could reach; and this motley throng appeared to move like a solid body, slowly along, till the gallant Highlanders were safely lodged in the Castle.

The NCOs and privates were 'sumptuously' entertained at dinner in the evening in the Assembly Rooms and Sir Walter Scott was amongst the gentlemen who superintended the entertainment. Each soldier was also presented with a free ticket to the theatre. The 78th Highland Regiment of Foot (or The Ross-Shire Buffs), later The Seaforth Highlanders, arrived a few days later and 'a splendid fete in honour of the heroes', was given in Corri's Rooms on 3 April. This affair was for the officers and again is described by an eyewitness:

> The bands in succession played some most beautiful military airs, whilst the centre of the room, filled with all the beauty and fashion of Edinburgh, enlivened by the uniforms of the officers, seemed to move in a solid mass to the clash of the symbols and beat of the hollow drum. About 11 o'clock Gow was called for and his corps succeeded that of the 42nd. The light fantastic toe was soon upon the trip; and twelve sets were soon made up, which continued the merry dance until after 2 o'clock. In fact the *tout ensemble* was a scene quite enchanting.

From the evidence it is unlikely that Sir Walter himself wrote the accounts of the various celebrations but the reports do give an indication of the new feelings of pride and identity which the people of Edinburgh, and the Scots in general, had begun to have for their army. By the time the regiments had returned to the Castle, and the Volunteers stood down and the Fencibles, in part at least disbanded, the New Town of Edinburgh built on the open fields to the north of the Old Town and the Castle was almost completed. The New Town was built as an expression of the optimism, enthusiasm and energy released in Edinburgh by the coming of the Enlightenment and after the French Revolution and the Napoleonic Wars it seemed that an age of peace and prosperity had arrived at last. After the frantic military activity of the previous twenty years the so-called Second Enlightenment, of which Scott was the bright star, seemed in the words of Lord Cockburn to set Edinburgh 'above all other British cities except one, and in some things above even that one'. As the centre of gravity moved away from the Old Town, across the reclaimed and landscaped North Loch to the New Town and the Second New Town, the military hidden away in the Castle were forgotten. After the building of the vast new barracks in 1796 nothing more was really done to accommodate the Army in Edinburgh for over a hundred years. With the growth of the romantic movement the Castle became something to look at and to be cherished for its romantic and historical associations rather than as a place where soldiers lived and worked or as the Headquarters of the Army in Scotland. Some restoration work went on through the nineteenth century. The 'profile' of the Castle was improved and some early buildings like St. Margaret's Chapel were re-discovered and rebuilt in what was thought to be twelfth-century form. A more grandiose plan to 'Balmoralise' the whole of the Castle was mercifully resisted. In the end, with the restoration of The Great Hall and the Portcullis Gate, and the remodelling of some existing buildings to form the new hospital, a reasonably harmonious structure has emerged.

Queen Victoria's accession to the throne in 1837 and her lasting love of the Highlands only increased the essentially romantic view, taken from a comfortable distance, of the Army in Scotland as elsewhere. The Crimean war punctured this complacency for a short while. The courage and stoicism of the British troops, which included a Brigade of Highlanders as well as other Scottish regiments, compensated to some extent for the brave incompetence of the senior officers, many of whom had last fought forty years before in the Peninsula. The suffering and hardships endured by the troops in the Crimea stirred a sympathy which quickly disappeared in the heyday of Victorian prosperity and self-regard. It was not until just before the First World War that money could be found to build the first new barracks in Edinburgh

Craigiehall, Headquarters of the Army in Scotland.

since the eighteenth century. In 1913 work was commenced on a barracks designed to accommodate an infantry battalion and a cavalry regiment at Redford in the south-west suburbs of the city. The work continued throughout the war and was completed in 1919. The barracks were built to the highest standards both technically and visually. The style is 'Scottish Gothic' but nevertheless it presents a most pleasing appearance. It still fits well into the area in which it is built and provides a pleasant and appropriate foreground for the Braid Hills and the distant Pentlands. The Cavalry Barracks is now a listed building. Sadly, it now appears that the Army is giving up the Redford Barracks complex and will concentrate in a new barracks to be built on the site of a small barracks at Dreghorn nearby. A plaque at Dreghorn informs that the barracks there were built in 1940 but this is clearly wrong and it seems likely that they were built at about the same time as Redford.

Apart from the building of Redford Barracks the First World War has another most important public association with Edinburgh. Field-Marshal, Earl Haig of Bemersyde, Commander-in-Chief of the British Army in France for the last three years of the war, was born and had his early schooling in the city. Whilst he spent most of his working life away from his native city he was not forgotten there. When he died in 1928, after a ceremonial procession through London and a service at Westminster Abbey, his body was brought to Edinburgh where it was escorted by The Royal Scots Greys and the Cameron Highlanders to St. Giles Cathedral, where it lay in state. He is commemorated in the city by a splendid equestrian statue placed on the Castle esplanade. Many of his papers and a large quantity of Haig memorabilia have been given to the city and this is now safely lodged in the Huntly Museum. Amongst the more droll items in the Haig collection is a group of Toby Jugs depicting the allied leaders in the First World War including President Wilson, Marshal Joffre, Admiral Beatty and of course Field Marshal Haig. It may seem a little irreverent to include a pottery caricature of the great man in the museum exhibits but it does surely indicate the popular affection in which he was held by ordinary people all over Britain.

Before we leave Edinburgh and its many military connections there are two comparatively recent manifestations to be added to what has become largely an historical account. Something must be said of the move of the Army Headquarters from the Castle to Craigiehall and last, but in terms of co-operation and contact between the city and the armed forces, by no means least, comes the Tattoo. The Second World War affected Edinburgh as it did every other large town in Britain. Extra battalions were raised for the local regiments, although not on the scale of the First World War when the Royal Scots for example expanded to thirty-five battalions. Bombing raids on the city and on shipping in the Forth were commonplace and refugees, in and out of uniform, were seen everywhere. Members of the Polish forces who managed to get to Britain were concentrated in the Edinburgh area. Many of them settled in Edinburgh and the Lowlands and their presence is marked by the existence of a Polish Association with its own premises in the city.

Because of the expansion of the armed forces many extra camps and facilities were needed to house and train the newly raised units. Amongst the new camps set up in the Edinburgh area at the beginning of the war was one at Craigiehall near South Queensferry in the outer suburbs. Craigiehall is a fine 'William and Mary' mansion built in 1699 by the architect Sir William Bruce for the Third Earl, later First Marquis of Annandale. Major C. B. Innes, Black Watch, who has written the history of the house,[11] records that he found a splendid line in William Ballingall's book, *Edinburgh Past and Present* about Craigiehall, 'A handsome mansion, inviting to peace and retirement by the deep quiet and sage serenity of its aspect'. Major Innes remarks that things have changed since that was written in 1877. In the 1930s the house was converted into a Hotel and Country Club and apparently earned a somewhat dubious reputation for itself in that role. But in September 1939 its honour was saved by its being requisitioned by the Army. There is no record of the many army units which occupied the Hall, or the temporary huts which sprang up in the Park during the war but it is known that Gunners, Sappers, Signals personnel, ATS, and the Headquarters of an 'Ack Ack' Group were all there at some time. We do not know what they thought of the place but after the war the Army was anxious to retain it. It was clear that the Castle could no longer house all the branches and communications of a large headquarters and Craigiehall, conveniently near but in extremely salubrious countryside seemed ideal. The late John W. Oliver captured the spirit of the place as anyone who has served in the Headquarters will testify.

> Near the road where buses rumble
>   On their way towards the Forth
> Bearing crowds of much pressed travellers
>   To the ferry for the North,
> Amid the bowering woods and parkland
>   Stands a gracious, stately pile,
> Designed, If I remember right,
>   In good renaissance style;
> And by it gurgling as it flows,
>   Past woods, and fields, and rigs,
> The Almond pours its turgid streams
>   To Cramond's pair of brigs.
> A pleasant place to linger in,
>   And pleasant to recall
> Are the memories that cluster
>   Round the groves of Craigiehall.[12]

Since these lines were written the Forth Road Bridge has been opened, quadrupling the traffic on the road towards the north, and worse still, the main flight path of Edinburgh's Turnhouse Airport, which hangs directly above Craigiehall, now produces a continuous thunder of noise. But even so the Parkland, with its Headquarters building neatly tucked away inside the old walled garden of the house, and the married quarters with their breathtaking views of the Pentland Hills must rank as one of the most delightful military locations in Britain. And all this in the suburbs of Edinburgh. The pleasantness and convenience of its location must account for many of the visitors to the 'gracious, stately pile', but some visitors were not in a position to choose for themselves. Rudolf Hess is supposed to have been brought to Craigiehall for interrogation in May 1941 and in May 1945 Senior Wehrmacht and Luftwaffe Officers flew directly from Norway to negotiate the surrender of the German Forces in that country. They brought thirty suitcases with them, full of maps showing the disposition of their troops. A less happily remembered visit was that of Idi Amin, the tyrant dictator of Uganda. Amin, interested in all things military, visited the Headquarters whilst on a state visit in 1970. Invited to a 'Beating of the Retreat', he conspicuously

The Edinburgh Military Tattoo in progress on the castle esplanade.

failed to amuse the officers and their other guests by producing his small son in the kilt and glengarry of an Argyll and Sutherland Highlander.

It is appropriate to leave mention of the Edinburgh Tattoo until the end of this chapter.[13] We have stressed in many parts of this book how parades, ceremonial and military ritual have been important in building up an affectionate and proud relationship between the garrison of a military town and its private citizens. The tattoo is of course the supreme and most successful example of this use of military display. Tattoos are mounted in most places where the British Army serves and the Aldershot and Tidworth Tattoos and the Royal Tournament in London have become very big business indeed, quite apart from the excellent public relations which are established through them. Even so, it was an inspired decision to mount a military tattoo on the Castle Esplanade to coincide with the first Edinburgh International Festival in 1947. Originally conceived on a rather modest scale, the Tattoo has grown in scale and reputation so that now, set against the unique backdrop of the floodlit Castle, it ranks as one of the most outstanding spectacles in public entertainment staged anywhere in the world. Its value in bringing together an international audience, the citizens of Edinburgh and the armed forces of Britain and other friendly nations cannot be over-estimated. It has been said that the Festival has very little of real interest for the city itself but of the Tattoo this cannot be said. The Tattoo, despite attempts to increase the seating every year is almost always a sell-out and to an audience which, whilst strongly supported by visitors, is predominantly native. Scottish or foreign, it is impossible not to be moved by the setting, the colourful costumes and the stirring military music of the massed bands. The pipe music and especially the lament, traditionally played by a lone piper, high on the Castle wall is remembered and talked about all round the world.

The tattoo ends with the massed bands playing and the audience singing *Auld Lang Syne*. Many a cynical eye becomes a little misty at such a time, but nothing could be more appropriate to bring to an end this chapter on military Edinburgh than the original first verse of Allan Ramsay's *Auld Lang Syne*, written in Edinburgh in 1782.

> Should auld acquaintance be forgot,
>   Tho' they return with scars?
> These are the noble hero's lot,
>   Obtain'd in glorious wars:
> Welcome, my Vara, to my breast,
>   Thy arms about me twine,
> And make me once again as blest
>   As I was lang Syne.[14]

Bibliography

A Concise History of Scotland, Fitzroy Maclean, Thames and Hudson, London, 1970

Edinburgh, David Daiches, Hamilton, Edinburgh, 1978

Charles Edward Stuart. The Life and Times of Bonnie Prince Charlie. David Daiches, Thames and Hudson, London, 1973

Portrait of Edinburgh, Ian Nimmo (2nd Edition) Robert Hale, 1975

John Kay of Edinburgh, Hilary and Mary Evans (2nd revised Edn.) Harris, Edinburgh, April 1980

History of Craigiehall, Major C. B. Innes, Published by HQ Scotland (Army) Edinburgh, 1972

The Heart of Midlothian, Sir Walter Scott, The Waverley Novels, Nimmo, London, 1893

Lavengro, George Borrow, John Murray, London, 1851

There are many fine museums in Edinburgh but the Castle itself is a museum that must not be missed. Within the Castle walls are situated The Scottish United Services Museum, the museums of The Royal Scots Greys and The Royal Scots.

The Huntly House Museum on The Royal Mile is of particular interest because of its collection of Earl Haig memorabilia.

MILITARY TOWNS AND SEA POWER

4

Chatham

SUZANNE MARSH

For the casual visitor it would be hard to picture the Medway area of north-east Kent as a place of interest or somewhere worth a visit. With its skyline punctuated with chimney stacks, and its riverbank scarred by gantry and crane, it totally lacks the bucolic charm of the western part of the county or the historic splendour of Canterbury. The Medway towns have long been somewhere one bypasses quickly on the way from Dover or London following the ancient route of Watling Street or its contemporary motorway equivalent. Until recently only those with business in the area would have had cause to stop. That is not to say, however, that the area should be regarded as some sort of sleepy backwater; on the contrary it has always seen much activity both interesting and entertaining, and nearly always as a result of the close relations between the armed forces and the locality itself.

Since Tudor times Chatham has been associated with the Navy and more recently the Marines and the Army. Unlike other parts of Kent there has never really been an Air Force presence, although today there are links through the modern electronics industry which provides employment in the area. For most people 'Chatham' conjures up an image of the dockyard, with all the bustle and noise and smells one would associate with creation and repair of great 'ships of the line', now sadly all departed. Chatham has, however, also been temporary or permanent home to thousands of British soldiers in peace and war. The name is a little misleading since Chatham is just one of the small towns that line the banks of the Medway, all of which are or were in some way connected with the dockyard and with the military. Today these towns are linked by more than just their geographical location, they are linked by their martial and historical past, and although each has its own identity they can also be viewed as a whole made up from a collection of suburbs or districts. When formerly one talked of being posted to Chatham it was quite possible that Gillingham or Upnor was meant, and so it is today. 'Chatham' has become a sort of military shorthand which might quite easily stand for Chattenden or Brompton or of course even Chatham itself.

The scientific and geographical discoveries of the sixteenth century led on to developments throughout Europe during which trade was firmly established as the new cornerstone of western civilisation. Trade had to be protected and the evidence of this was nowhere more obvious than in the south-east corner of England where a number of dockyards was created to confirm and maintain Britain's position as a leading maritime nation. Chatham was just one of several yards dotted along the coastal inlets from London round to the New Forest, contributing to the growing prosperity of the country. The coming of the great sailing ships and especially the four-masted 'Ships of the Line' reinforced the importance of the Medway and provided its primary purpose and main income for the next 400 years. It also brought about the birth of Chatham as a garrison town.

The slow, wide River Medway is situated conveniently between Portsmouth and Deptford and it is reached easily overland from London. Troops could be moved from one base to another when threatened and the fleets from Chatham and Portsmouth could reinforce one another at sea with little delay. The Medway was seen to have a strong defensive capability and one which, in addition, afforded extra protection to the capital. By the middle of the sixteenth century the dockyard had become firmly established with permanent buildings and a semi-resident workforce. The growth of the Navy strengthened Britain's position with regard to the rest of Europe, but she was not alone in her ship building programme and enemy fleets could seek out and destroy where she was undefended. It was soon recognised that the dockyards at least must be protected and alongside the expanding dockyards there appeared a rash of *ad hoc* works for their support and defence. From 1539 onwards a whole series of castles, forts, bulwarks, blockhouses, palisades, spikes and towers sprung up along the banks of the Medway. These were permanently although not strongly manned and were meant to be reinforced by local volunteers when necessary. The Medway defences were then linked by a series of beacons which could give early warning to the rest of the country should invasion forces appear.

By 1559 the threat of invasion was even more serious and it was evident to everyone that the nation under Elizabeth was preparing for war. There was another crash programme of warship building, and it was recognised that in spite of the fortifications that had been built earlier, the dockyard was still vulnerable. It was agreed that a more efficient obstruction would have to be placed across the river from Chatham to Upnor. While the threat of invasion advanced or receded the dockyard at Chatham came to be accepted as the foremost in the country and provision was made for it to be permanently garrisoned. This was in addition to the new defences along the river banks. Fear that the Spanish might sail up to Rochester or Gillingham and fire ships at anchor so greatly perturbed many of Elizabeth's senior advisers that a commission was set up to look into the situation. This included Walsingham, Burghley, Howard, Drake, Frobisher and Hawkins who suggested that a chain be placed across the river from Upnor to Chatham to act as a boom preventing hostile ships from gaining the upper reaches of the river. The chain was held in position by five lighters, secured to piles on one side and a series of wheels on the other. By this means it could be raised or lowered in order to allow access to the dockyards. In the event it was never tested, but the existence of the Spanish fleet was a real threat and more than justified its existence.

The West Country always claims Drake as one of her sons. This is not entirely fair because although he was born near Plymouth he spent most of his formative years in the dockyard at Chatham. After falling out with his original Tavistock parishioners Drake's father became the incumbent of Upchurch, Kent, and was responsible for the spiritual wellbeing of the dockyard. The family lived on one of the Hulks moored at Chatham as have many others since then. From 1549 until he was apprenticed at twelve years of age to the master of one of the small boats which plied between the channel ports, the young Drake spent his time learning about the sea and seamanship from the dockyard at Chatham and not Plymouth as is popularly supposed.

The Civil War divided loyalties in the Medway, reflecting opinions across the country. The towns of Rochester and Chatham, which had co-existed amicably for so long found themselves on different sides, Chatham was with the Parliamentarians while ecclesiastical Rochester supported the King. Quite early in the conflict, stealing a march on the Royalists, Roundhead soldiers seized Rochester and its Castle without a fight, supposedly while its garrison was away harvesting and its Captain playing bowls. Ever prudent, the defenders of Upnor Castle surrendered to the Parliamentarians as well and it appeared by the end of August 1642 that the Civil War was to all intents and purposes over in the Medway. However in 1648 there was an upsurge of anti-puritan rather than pro-Royalist feeling in other parts of Kent. This inflamed some lingering feelings of discontent among the dockyard workers who roused themselves sufficiently to seize Upnor Castle again and dislodge the surprised garrison. However, the rising was never a serious threat and was swiftly dealt with by Halifax who marched from London, dispersed the rioters and promised to redress some of their grievances. After that Upnor was turned into a prison for Royalist officers.

With the exception of Rochester Castle and Fort Amherst, which is currently undergoing restoration, Upnor Castle is the only other structure specifically designed for the protection of the Medway, still standing today. Like the other two Upnor is also a protected 'Ancient Monument' and one where it is possible to spend a quiet hour, gazing at the river and contemplating past glories. Although few ships use the Medway today compared with former times, the ones which do, show something of what it must once have been like. Upnor is an ideal spot from which to look up at Chatham and pick out the sights, the covered slips, the wharves, the old imposing waterside buildings and the outline of Brompton Barracks dominating the skyline. Sadly, the dockyard is barely functioning today but it is not difficult to imagine what a bustling hive of activity it once was with all the great ships riding at anchor, where today only a single barge or coastal vessel passes by.

Upnor village is itself well worth a visit as it has remained more sylvan than much of the surrounding Kent countryside, and although only a small village it is well served by two public houses. The castle itself has an interesting history and was built between 1559 and 1567 specifically to protect the dockyard. According to official documents the original building was smaller that the current one, consisting primarily of a water bastion surmounted by a guard house and accommodation for its defenders. This water bastion is still much in evidence and visitors can see how effective it should have been in protecting the waterfront and the castle itself. Unfortunately, much of the building stone for its construction was removed from Rochester Castle wall, but as Upnor Castle is not very large the vandalism was not too great. As the Chatham dockyard grew in importance so Upnor was correspondingly enlarged, until by about 1600 it had reached its present shape and size. This involved the addition of a palisade, gatehouse and drawbridge topped with several large guns. The whole fortification was manned by gunners and reinforced in an emergency by soldiers and local volunteers. Although during the Civil War it changed hands several times, it was essentially a peaceful posting and neither it nor its defenders appeared to suffer any real damage.

It is ironic that the only time the castle was called upon to defend the dockyard — to fulfil the function for which it was designed — it failed miserably. This was during

A visiting party being conducted by ferry from Upnor Hard, 1958.

the famous Dutch raid of 1667. Relations with the Netherlands has been far from good and there had been many clashes both diplomatic and at sea. Britain had, however, inflicted a notable defeat on the Dutch at Lowestoft in June 1665, where both fleets had fought bravely and there were many losses on both sides. After the Dutch withdrew the British Admirals believed that there would be no further confrontation for some time. The fleet was laid up at Chatham and the guard was lowered.

One of the most lively and entertaining descriptions of the dockyard at this time is by the diarist Pepys, who made frequent visits in his capacity as a junior member of the Navy Board.[1] Pepys records how all was not well with the administration of the yard and how he had misgivings about many matters there. Whether he brought his fears to wider notice is not known, but certainly nothing was done. At the beginning of June 1667 the Dutch fleet under Van Ghent and de Ruyter put to sea again and surprised the very much depleted British fleet which was forced to retire into the Thames. This humiliating defeat was made the more so by the fact that many of the Dutch ships had their crews supplemented by discharged or disaffected British seamen who, in some cases were owed up to two and a half years back pay by the British Admiralty. Problems with finance meant that not only was there no pay but all aspects of defence, apart from ship building experienced severe restrictions. London had just suffered the ravages of the plague and the Great Fire and was in the process of being rebuilt by the city merchants who strongly resisted additional taxes.

On 10th June the only partially completed fort at Sheerness had to be abandoned after a surprise attack by the Dutch who then occupied it. On the 12th the invading forces sailed up the River Medway and attacked the English ships defending the chain between Gillingham and Hoo. This chain was not the Elizabethan one formerly at Upnor but a later one which was lost in the subsequent engagement with the Dutch. It was not realised that the Dutch had actually landed at Gillingham until the next day but overnight there was panic in Chatham where a frantic but futile attempt was made to thwart the Dutch by sinking three ships in the harbour mouth. Reinforcements were hurriedly summoned to man the shore batteries. An eight-gun battery was speedily improvised in Chatham churchyard which still remains as a commanding position today. On the 13th the Dutch continued into Chatham Reach destroying several ships and capturing the *Royal Charles*.

Samuel Pepys, who arrived in Chatham a few days after the Dutch withdrew, describes the raid in his diary:

> 30th June. Lords Day to Chatham, and here I was told in all the late attempt there was but one man they knew killed on shore; and that was a man that laid upon his belly, upon one of the hills on the other side of the river, to see the action; and a bullet came and took the ground away just under his belly, and so was killed. Thence by barge, it raining hard, down to the chain; and in our way did see the sad wrecks of the poor Royal Oake, James and London, and several other of our ships by us sunk; and several of the enemy's whereof three men-of-war, and that they could not get off and so burned. We did also see several dead bodies lie by the sides of the water. So to the chain, and there saw it fast at end in Upner side of the river; very fast, and borne upon several stages across the river and where it is broke nobody can tell me. I went on shore at Upner side to lok upon the end of the chain; and caused the link to be measured, and it was six inch and a quarter in circumference. They have burned the crane house that was to haul it tought. It seems very remarkable to me, and of great honour to the Dutch, that those of them that did go on shore to Gillingham, though they went in fear of their lives and were some of them killed, and not withstanding their provocation at Scelling, yet killed none of our people nor plundered their houses; but did take some things of easy carriage and left the rest, and not a house burned; and which is to our eternal disgrace that which my Lord Douglasse's men, who came after them, found there plundered and took all away. And the watermen that carried us further did tell us that our own soldiers are far more terrible to those people of all the country towns than the Dutch themselves.

The castle itself was hardly damaged even if it had not proved equal to the task of defending the dockyard. As Pepys commented:

> The Dutch made no more of Upner Castle's shooting than of a fly . . . Upner played hard with her guns at first, but slowly afterwards, either from the men's being beaten off, or their powder spent.

Although the castle was left untouched its humiliation was complete and the following year it was converted into a magazine for ordnance stores. In 1827 it became an ordnance laboratory. Upnor Castle has however maintained its military connections and in 1872-3 there were attempts to forge a permanent link with Chattenden when a 2 foot 6 inch gauge railway was built between the two. Today of course the link remains as strong as ever. Anyone sailing by can still see soldiers training on the river banks as they have done for the past two thousand years, from the time that the Romans came to Kent.

The close shave afforded by the Dutch in 1667 brought about a complete re-examination of the Medway defences as part of the overall protection of London itself. In 1668 it was decided that there should be a permanent garrison of 1,000 foot soldiers in Strood, Rochester and Chatham. These were to be reinforced by troops of horse based at Gravesend, Maidstone and Sittingbourne plus the militia from Kent in times of crises. A major series of fortifications was again embarked upon, together with the accommodation for the new garrison. The importance of the dockyard remained, and while the rest of England awakened slowly to the beginnings of the industrial era, Chatham was already full committed to the dominance of the workshop and yard.

The forerunners of the modern Royal Marines were founded in 1664. A draft order for the raising of two Marine regiments was presented to William III in 1694 and five companies were quartered at Chatham. In 1755 a permanent body of 5,000 marines was established with the title 'The Marine Corps' and was distributed in three 'Grand Divisions' between Chatham, Portsmouth and Plymouth. The marines maintained this close connection with Chatham until the nineteen-sixties. The dockyard meanwhile continued to consolidate its position of pre-eminence among the Royal Dockyards, its stability guaranteed by the permanent presence of so many troops close by. In 1759 a momentous event for the dockyard was the laying of the keel for the *Victory*. This marked the beginning of yet another upsurge in naval building which this time lasted for more than fifty years. The *Victory* was launched in 1765 but she was not actually commissioned until 1778, when she eventually took part in the battle of Ushant. Marines formed one fifth of the *Victory's* complement as they did with all the 'ships of the line', but the seamen were mainly pressed men. Launch Day itself was a great event with Pitt, later Earl of Chatham, and other ministers arriving from London. Chatham was fêted in a day of feasting, fair and military spectacle, the precursor for many similar festive occasions to come.

1801 again saw the country stirred by the threat of invasion, this time from Napoleon, but only a few years later the Navy was once again in decline. In 1797 even the *Victory* was considered to be no longer required and had been laid up in Chatham destined to become just another hulk. By 1803, however, the recommissioning of the *Victory* had been ordered and this was completed in time for her to become Nelson's flagship at Trafalgar. Nelson, like Drake, was another vicar's son who had spent part of his youth at Chatham, living with his uncle in the dockyard. After Trafalgar the *Victory* was not left to rot as she had been in 1797 but was sailed to Portsmouth where she remains today as a proud memorial to the Navy of Nelson's day.

At the beginning of the nineteenth century the Medway towns underwent another period of intense military expansion. The first and most evident example was the building of the circle of forts which eventually ringed Chatham and the vulnerable dockyard. This new spate of building started initially as an expansion of the protective system devised during Tudor and Stuart times against the Spanish, French and Dutch. At the time of the French wars an inner defensive line was constructed but a second, outer ring was added later in the century.

The fortification of the Medway towns was a long-standing preoccupation of the military planners, but equally it concerned many people who considered it their duty to curb the planners and rearmers by starving them of funds. Whenever the direct threat receded wrangling immediately took place over cash and resources for the fortification and defence of the area. The need to defend the dockyard area was obvious from the moment of its establishment but this made no difference. For three hundred years all manner of military works, bastions, batteries and bulwarks were erected and dug along both sides of the muddy, slow, meandering river from Rochester to Sheerness, but having to fight for finance they frequently fell into disrepair and when the next crisis or invasion threatened they had to be hurriedly repaired or replaced. Of the more permanent works many eventually served quite a different purpose from that originally intended. As we have seen the only installations ever to face hostile action, Upnor and Sheerness, both failed the test, but the need for some defensive system was still considered vital. From Napoleonic times onwards the series of permanent forts that was planned and erected provide an interesting insight into the then current strategic thinking. They also mark a surprising commitment to defence spending at the beginning of the century when many British soldiers on the Continent were not being paid at all. Of the inner ring of forts around Chatham and the dockyard Forts Pitt, Clarence and Amherst were the most important.

Of the main forts, Clarence and Pitt, little now remains. All were built on the high ground commanding the river and the populated area of the city and dockyard. Fort Clarence, completed about 1812, was positioned so that it overlooked both the dockyard and Rochester Bridge. Fort Clarence hardly had a glorious history, and almost from its completion it was found to be redundant and turned into an insane asylum. By 1846 it was degraded even further and converted into a prison for the convicts who provided labour for another bout of military expansion in the area. The history of Fort Pitt, on the other hand, is rather more noble as befits a fort named after the great architect of the victory over Napoleonic France. Completed by 1819 it features in the early pages of Dickens' *Pickwick Papers* as the site of the proposed duel between Dr Slammer and Mr Winkle. Described by Dickens as a 'trench' and a 'fortification', it is probable that he played there as a child. Initially it provided accommodation in its casemates for about 540 infantry and gunners. Strategically Fort Pitt was in a stronger position than Fort Clarence as it was designed to defend Chatham from the south as well as from the river. In addition it was intended to form part of the defences of London as it commanded the road from Deal and Dover to the Capital. It was believed that an invading force would have to confront Fort Pitt and its defenders or else advance via Maidstone and risk leaving the whole of the Chatham garrison in their rear. Even though not completed until 1819 the building was used from 1814 to house convalescent soldiers. From 1824 it became an invalid depot with accommodation for 172 inmates whom Queen Victoria is reported to have visited on at least four occasions. Fort Pitt became a general hospital before the Crimean War and served as one again during the First World War. Eventually with better medical facilities provided elsewhere the military gave up Fort Pitt and it was converted to educational purposes. With so many military doctors in the area it is not surprising that Dickens should choose two of them for his protagonists in *Pickwick Papers*, Dr Slammer of the 97th stationed at Chatham, and his second Dr Payne. It is even possible that the young Dickens, as a child, would himself have been treated by one of their number during the time when his family was connected with the dockyard.[2]

Gun drill in operation using eight-inch guns at Fort Amherst, circa 1860.

Fort Amherst, the third of the principal fortifications was started about 1756, far earlier than the other two. Situated directly overlooking the dockyard, above Chatham churchyard, it provided the ideal vantage point from which to view the sailing-ships which came up the Medway in the summer of 1985 for the start of the 'Tall-ships' race. It is a pity that the fort did not exist in 1667 when the Dutch paid their 'courtesy visit' to the Medway. Amherst was designed as a permanent structure of brick and masonry, set into the chalk hillside. It was initially expected to house 130 guns and their crews. Although like forts Clarence and Pitt, Amherst was never really tested in its envisaged role, it remained in continuous military use until the Second World War. Without visiting the fort it is difficult to visualise how extensive was the area it eventually came to occupy. Within the hillside overlooking the town and river there were initially six sections, either batteries or bastions, all linked by a warren of tunnels. The building did not take place all at once. Amherst, along with all other works in the area fell victim to the vagaries of the treasury over the years. All the same the fort does provide a fascinating illustration of eighteenth and early nineteenth-century military fortification and the style and tastes of the military engineers of the time. Preserved within the hilltop, Amherst was not considered suitable for anything other than military purposes and, unlike the other forts, it was not converted to civilian use. Although it never had to defend the dockyard it did serve a useful purpose in that it provided a valuable training and exercise area within which the gunners could practice unhindered, and from where they could fire off the noonday gun.

By the twentieth century advances in military technology had made the defensive line around Chatham obsolete and the Channel coast at Dover was where the real front line was now perceived to be. Amherst was still important in other ways however and during the First World War her caves and warrens served as temporary accommodation for troops and supplies *en route* for France. During the Second World War it served the local community as a shelter. Sensible use was made of its elevated position and light anti-aircraft guns were installed on the 'Lines' and spigot mortars were mounted in the fort itself. The interior of the fort was taken over by the Civil Defence organisation for their local headquarters. It is interesting to see today the original chamber, which could be sealed against poison gas, restored to its wartime condition. Amherst was used by the Civil Defence until the nineteen-fifties as a training area and for exercises. After that it was sadly allowed to fall into disrepair although it has never been entirely forgotten. There are still many people locally who remember playing, as children, in its murky chambers and maze of tunnels. Today, Fort Amherst is again involved with the local community although not in a military capacity. A group of dedicated workers, both amateur and professional, is carefully restoring the fort and its surrounding ramparts, turning it into an interesting attraction for the Medway towns and for visiting tourists. Because of their enthusiastic and painstaking work it is now possible to take a guided tour within the fort to see for oneself what it was like to be a soldier in the fortress garrisons in the past. The restoration is being carried out in an imaginative and sensitive way and is providing jobs and training for many unemployed people in the area who have been sorely distressed by the closing of the dockyard. Much of the work is sponsored by the Manpower Services Commission. It seems to be a model of its kind and could well be imitated with advantage elsewhere. Happily, the link with the garrison continues in the form of a consultancy and physical help is provided when it is required.

Several writers have recorded their recollections of the Medway region during the nineteenth century but none so vividly as Charles Dickens. Although surely familiar, it is still worth repeating his lively description of the four towns, Stroud, Rochester, Chatham and Brompton from the *Pickwick Papers*:

> 'The principal productions of these towns', says Mr Pickwick, 'appears to be soldiers, sailors, Jews, chalk, shrimps, officers and dockyard men. The commodities chiefly exposed for sale are marine stores, hard-bake, apples, flat-fish and oysters. The streets present a lively and animated appearance, occasioned chiefly by the conviviality of the military. It is truly delightful to a philanthropic mind, to see these gallant men staggering along under the influence of an overflow, both of animal and ardent spirits, more especially when we remember that the following them about, and jesting with them, affords a cheap and innocent amusement for the boy population.'

Of course we can see that the above description is not without its hidden barb and he does not mention at all the all-pervading aura of dirt and cement dust which characterised the district.

As a child Charles Dickens lived with his family in Chatham from 1816 to 1822. The family lived at first in some comfort at number 2, Ordnance Terrace, later re-numbered 11, until declining fortunes forced them to move to 18, St. Mary's Place. His father John, although patently unable to manage his own family finances was employed in the dockyard pay office. Most of his biographers agree that the happiest years of his childhood were those he spent in and around Chatham. This is the more likely when one considers that he moved back to the area, to Gad's Hill, when success and wealth meant that he could have made his home anywhere. Whatever he may have thought of the area it cannot be denied that events he witnessed and places he visited while he lived in Chatham keep recurring in episodes in his books and essays. We have seen how he portrays the two doctors and Fort Pitt, and many other encounters from this time appear in his works although some memories were obviously painful to him.

Most English-speaking school children have been directed at one time or another to Dickens's stories as an illustration of social conditions in early nineteenth century England and more particularly of how these conditions affected children. The stories are made particularly poignant by the knowledge that they were based for the most part on Dickens's own childhood experiences and observations. The young Pip's departure on his journey in *Great Expectations* was supposedly based on Dickens's own departure from Chatham to London, while the haunting meeting with Magwitch the convict, in the marshes, undoubtedly stems from his seeing convicts from the hulks around Chatham. The ostracism experienced by the family as John Dickens propelled them ever more rapidly towards the Marshalsea debtors prison imprinted itself strongly on the young mind. He very keenly felt the fall from grace, from a position of relative affluence to one of penury. His observation of the social hierarchy in the town is quite revealing; he tells us that 'dockyard people of upper rank don't know people of lower rank', but will converse only with the aristocracy of the garrison, the Colonel and the senior officers.

Henry Coxwell, in his book *My Life and Balloon Experiences*,[3] published by W H Allen in 1889, records his childhood memories of Chatham. Coxwell was born in Wouldham on the Medway in 1819, and lived for some time on HMS *Colossus*, one of the Hulks, with his family. He tells of his time in the Marine barracks where he attended the elementary school for the sons of officers, superintended by a sergeant. One of his more distressing memories was watching the weekly floggings, when up to 200 lashes might be administered in front of the assembled garrison. Later, after moving to Gillingham he attended the 'Higher School'. Here he describes the pupils as a mix of 'Military element, the naval boys and a fair contingent of commercial lads'. His description echoes Dickens's own of the type of people who lived in the district.

Coxwell recounts how on one occasion there was a lively confrontation between his own friends and 'the wild half-ragged boys of Brompton, who were mostly soldiers' sons'; hostilities, to be sorted out by mutual consent on the next holiday. He takes up the tale:

> As it happened, we were the first on the ground, and no time was lost in taking possession of an earth-work, or rather a clay work not long thrown up by Col. Pasley and his Engineer Detachment.

With some delight Coxwell tells of the sound thrashing meted out to the soldierly lot. There were, it would seem, even lower forms of life than the sons of soldiers in the area and he tells how in 1827 it was necessary to carry firearms for fear of highway robbery if travelling from Rochester to Gillingham at night. He recalls other later visits to the 'Lines', when he went to watch some of the early balloon ascents, occasions which influenced him profoundly. Chatham played a significant part in the history of ballooning and it eventually became the centre for army balloon experimentation. From 1882 there was a military balloon school and a factory in the old St. Mary's Barracks until it was transferred to Aldershot in 1890.

Apart from the visit to Fort Pitt by Mr Winkle, the other main event in 'Pickwick' associated with Chatham is the 'Grand Review' upon the 'Lines'. This is a finely described incident which makes one think that Dickens probably returned to watch similar events later in life. The 'Lines' were used for such events throughout the nineteenth century and they were always very popular. The 'Lines' which are still accessible, on the high ground between Gillingham and Brompton were at that time occupied by the Army, either as a tented camp or for manoeuvres. On the particular occasion that Dickens describes, he says the whole population of Rochester and the adjoining towns turned out to watch. On a similar occasion in 1848 so many tried to attend that the roads were completely blocked and many people had to be turned away. In 'Pickwick' the actual programme of events was as follows:

> The manoeuvres of half a dozen regiments were to be inspected by the eagle eye of the Commander-in-Chief; temporary fortifications had to be erected, the citadel was to be attacked and taken, and a mine was to be sprung.

From contemporary accounts we can see that this was no different from many other such occasions. Dickens treats us to a colourful account of the start of the proceedings, the splendour of the officers and the efficiency of the troops, and how all is nearly brought to grief when the 'companions' find themselves between the two opposing factions, to be extricated only just in time. Dickens, who clearly enjoyed such spectacles lets Snodgrass proclaim, slightly tongue in cheek,

> It is indeed a noble and brilliant sight; to see the gallant defenders of their country drawn up in brilliant array before its peaceful citizens.

The 'Lines' were the subject of an uneasy truce between the military and the local population who had always considered that they had equal rights in the ground. Much of the fortification and building which took place during the late eighteenth and nineteenth centuries was considered to be an incursion and an inconvenience by the local people who threatened the local Commander with death if they were prevented from playing cricket there as in former times. They also complained of falling into the newly opened ditches at night. The local population always considered the 'Lines' as a freely available recreational area where at the very least cricket and horse racing might take place, and where entertainment could be found at the expense of the soldiers.

In 1848 *Jones Woolwich Journal* describes 'Grand Siege Operations at Chatham', and shows how the demonstrations were still as popular as ever with an estimated 35-40,000 spectators converging on the garrison. The scale of the exercise must be appreciated. It was not like the set piece demonstrations and reviews of today but rather more in the manner of exercises on Salisbury Plain with defensive positions and a nineteenth century type of attack and counter-attack, with movement and muddle and overwhelming confusion. Such events were always popular with foreign royalty as well as with Queen Victoria and her family and many official visitors descended on Chatham every year to add to the general sense of festivity for the local people. The visits were made even easier when a direct rail link was opened between Chatham and London avoiding the longer route via Woolwich and the bank of the Thames. Entertainment is still provided locally in the form of the traditional 'Open Days' which are held every year during the summer months.

Chatham and Woolwich have shared many things in their military past. Both garrisons were inaugurated as a response to the needs of their respective dockyards. They continued these links through the Gunners, Marines and Sappers since they might easily serve, or have served in, either station, and the The Royal Military Academy of Woolwich served both. These were honourable links but there were more questionable although equally important matters which concerned both areas. The first of these was the use of the prison Hulks which were a notorious feature of both Thames and Medway and the second was the effect of the Contagious Diseases Bill and the disturbance it caused among the civilian population of all garrison towns in the eighteen-sixties.

The first records of the use of obsolete vessels as prisons in Britain date from 1594 although very little is known about these early instances.[4] The use of Hulks as prisons began on a large scale when the wars with America and France provided very many prisoners of war and at the same time prevented the transportation of felons to the Colonies. It was also commonplace for ships no longer regarded as sea-worthy to be used as extra accommodation at Chatham and the other dockyards for the personnel working there. Even the *Victory* could not escape this ignominious fate and for a short period at the end of the eighteenth century herself served as a hulk. The use of such ships, not considered suitable as accommodation for marines or soldiers, as floating prisons was considered to be both logical and economic. Even as late as the nineteen-seventies HMS *Maidstone* was used as an internment centre in Northern Ireland but ironically in this case, the accommodation was not considered to be of a high enough standard for IRA terrorist suspects and so the British Army used it instead. Conditions on the Hulks, even by nineteenth century standards, were appalling and the mortality rates from sickness and disease were notoriously high. At the time of the Napoleonic wars it is recorded that the Hulks held Danes, Swedes, French and Americans, and amongst the Medway Hulks the ones most frequently mentioned were the *Canada* for men, the *Euryalis* for boys and the *Hercules* which was used as a hospital or for isolation. Attempts to escape were sometimes made but they were surprisingly rare, perhaps because the prisoners were always manacled when they were ashore. Dickens's portrayal of Magwitch in *Great Expectations* and his meeting with Pip in the marshes at Christmas was quite unlike the usual attitude of local people towards the convicts. There is a story, however, which is probably apocryphal, that the present-day residents of the Hoo Peninsula are the descendants of those convicts who managed to escape and gained sanctuary there. When the new Chattenden Barracks was being constructed towards the end of the last century a small graveyard was found, reportedly for Napoleonic prisoners who died in the Hulks moored at Upnor.

Part of the justification for the floating prisons was that they provided the labour for much of the early nineteenth century expansion of the dockyard and for most of the dirty and unpleasant jobs within the Arsenal at Woolwich. Groups of convicts would have been a common sight along the banks of the Medway and the Thames and it is certain that the young Dickens would have seen them often at work in Chatham dockyard. Once the prisoners were removed from the Hulks and installed in permanent prisons it became another garrison task to provide a guard for them. In 1841 there were 3,625 prisoners on all the prison hulks in England but during the eighteen-fifties the Victorian social conscience brought about a review of the whole system and by 1857 they were no longer using Hulks as prisons although they were still used for some time longer by the Army and Navy.

In early Victorian terms it is possible to see the use of the Hulks as necessary for the development of the dockyard and the Chatham defences; the practice was no worse than many other aspects of Victorian life but this cannot be said of the Contagious Diseases Acts of 1864 and 1866.[5] The Bills were introduced with the laudable intention of protecting the armed forces from venereal disease which was reaching epidemic proportions in the garrison towns and seaports. Medical advances since the Crimean war, coupled with a more efficient system of gathering statistics brought a new awareness of the devastating effect that epidemics were having on the fighting men. Because of a hypocritical unwillingness to deal with the men involved all the misguided and vicious provisions of the Acts appeared to be directed against women. In 1866 the application of the Act was extended to cover eleven garrison towns including Chatham. Enforced by the police the intention was to identify and compulsorily treat all infected habitual and occasional prostitutes thus hopefully reducing the incidence of disease among the forces.

Although statistics indicate that the number of reported cases did decline the Act was not an overwhelming success. Control over enforcement was highly inadequate and it seems that the police took to themselves powers far beyond the intentions of the Acts. Not surprisingly, many military doctors were reluctant to treat the women sent before them, while it was said that even to be seen talking to a soldier was in some areas sufficient for a woman of whatever social status to be branded a 'Queens Woman', or as Florence Nightingale called them 'War Office Prostitutes'. Opponents of the Acts, of whom there were many, maintained that totally blameless women were being wrongly accused and their reputations and even their lives ruined. The Act was unpopular in all the garrison towns where it was enforced but reaction was particularly strong in Rochester and Chatham. It was rescinded after a few years largely as a result of work by the Quakers and Josephine Butler the famous prison reformer, but not before it had managed to create misery for guilty and innocent alike in the naval and military towns. Parliamentary critics of the Acts were able to say that for the short time they were in operation, Britain had for the first time in its history a system of licensed and state regulated prostitution.

As Chatham and the Medway was once the heart of the British Navy it is now the home of the Royal Engineers. To some local diehards this might be regarded as the final invasion. From the earliest times, and certainly since the existence of the Roman Army, engineers, sappers and miners have been an important element of the military forces. Similarly, in the British Army while these 'specialists' have always played an important part they have only existed as a corps since 1787. Today it would be hard to imagine the Medway without the Sappers and their familiar activities along both banks of the river. These activities on the water and land have always entertained local people and visitors alike, but it must be added, not always intentionally.

It is easy to see how the first permanent garrison came into being in response to the needs of the dockyard. The garrison expanded because of Britain's participation in the Continental wars of the late eighteenth and early nineteenth centuries and later because of the growing professionalism of her forces which required newer and better buildings and more specialised training facilities. From the middle of the nineteenth century, across the whole country, there was a rush to build new barracks and cantonments and Chatham's expansion was part of a nation-wide programme. Few of these early buildings are still standing in Chatham but to list them chronologically, they were first, the 'Upper' and 'Lower' barracks, built between 1757 and 1758 for the infantry of the garrison. These were officially known as Chatham Barracks, but also variously referred to as 'New', 'Infantry' or more recently, 'Kitchener Barracks'. Soon after this in 1784, the 'Royal Marines Barracks' was completed. From then on there was always a Marine detachment in Chatham until the nineteen-sixties when sadly they, and the Royal Navy, withdrew from the area. 'Brompton Barracks', now the Royal School of Military Engineering, formerly known as the 'Artillery Barracks' was built between 1804 and 1806. 'St. Mary's Casemates' constructed by French prisoners captured during the Peninsula War of 1807-12 was later used as married soldier's accommodation and finally in 1844 as a powder magazine. Construction continued in the 1820s with the expansion of the Engineer Barracks and the Marine Hospital. The Naval Barracks, on the other hand was not ready for occupation until 1903, meanwhile naval personnel remained on Hulks such as HMS *Pembroke* which gave its name to the Barracks.

Although the modern corps was created to meet the need for a professional force of engineers during Wellington's Peninsula Campaign, the Sappers were not designated as Royal Engineers until 1856, when they settled in Brompton Barracks and have remained ever since. As early as 1812 a Royal Warrant was issued for the creation of an establishment for the:

> Instruction of the Corps of Royal Artificers or Sappers and Miners, and the Junior Officers of the Royal Engineers in the duties of sapping and mining and other military field works.

Colonel Charles Pasley the first Commandant set up the forerunner of the existing school of military engineering in the half-empty Artillery Barracks. He was a strict task-master and his daily orders which can be seen in the Corps Museum make fascinating reading. His system was for everyone to start off on the same basic course and to progress upwards. As each stage was mastered wages would be increased. Those who failed would have to repeat the course. 'Drummers not yet grown' were to remain on the lowest level. Pasley was an innovator in other ways and remedial courses in mathematics were also introduced. Discipline was strict and there were parades three times a day, excused only if the soldier was attending classes. The orders also record that on one occasion at least, 200 lashes were administered for insolence, although it was more usual for an offender to be fined or incarcerated in the 'Black Hole' for seventy-two hours. Today's wrong-doers will be glad to know that the location of this 'Black Hole' has been lost in the mists of time. The 'followers and families' of the men at the first Engineering School were, it seems a rather 'light fingered lot' and Colonel Pasley had to post orders to the effect that 'women' found stealing fascines, an easily burned engineering store, would be turned out of barracks, while those sharing the fire would be stopped two days' pay. Along with the early students, women were part of the complement of the establishment. This was usual in the British Army where there were always several women officially 'on the strength',

General Gordon's statue outside the Royal Engineer's H.Q., Brompton
Barracks, Chatham.

not of course as forerunners of the WRAC, but as washerwomen and general domestic
helpers. Their life was precarious at best and although supposedly married to one of
the soldiers they could be put 'off the strength' for quite trivial reasons.

The first real married quarters were not constructed until 1856 when four were built
for sergeants and forty-two for other ranks. Below the rank of sergeant the married
quarters would consist of one room per family. Since that time there has been a vast
expansion of living accommodation on both sides of the river and at the same time
standards have increased so that each accommodated family can expect the number
of living and bedrooms recommended by local government regulations and each will
have their own kitchen and bathroom. A far cry from the nineteenth century when,
because of the appalling lack of space, conditions were minimal but even so, nowhere
as bad as conditions on the Hulks. HMS *Hood* was still being used for accommodation
as late as 1879.

Even though dominated by the dockyard, as we have seen, the river has never been
the sole preserve of the navy. From the earliest times the soldiers have spent many
happy hours there 'messing about in boats', bridging or barging or just blowing things

up, and one of the main attractions for the Sappers in Chatham is the proximity and availability of the river. The first 'military boat-bridge' in the area was *in situ* from 1804-18, although there were undoubtedly earlier examples elsewhere, like for example the bridge over the River Ouse at York during the Civil War. The Medway 'boat-bridge' is supposed to have spanned the river from the dockyard to Upnor and like other ferries and barges to have eased communications for the entire garrison. Ferries existed on the river for many years, and there will be many still serving soldiers who will remember the daily crossings from Upnor Hard to Thunderbolt Pier, on cold, grey, winter mornings on their way to lectures or classes on the other side of the river. Built in 1883 for the use of the 23rd Mining Company RE, it was possibly named after the Sapper badge or more likely, after the nearby Hulk of HMS *Thunderbolt*. It is said that it stands very near the spot where HMS *Victory* was built. After the ferry how prosaic today's bus-run seems!

Another aquatic pastime frequently indulged in by Sappers past and present is bridge building. These bridges should not be confused with the more permanent 'military boat-bridge' or the more solid stone built variety, but are generally the more familiar pontoon, Bailey or modern motorised type made famous by Sapper 'Open Days' everywhere. These swiftly erected and dismantled constructions were just as popular during the last century as they are today, and there are in existence early photographs of visiting ladies daintily picking their way dry shod across the Medway complete with bustles and parasols. Of course more serious training did take place along the river banks and in the marshes where the earliest instruction in underwater mine warfare took place over one hundred and fifty years ago. Perhaps the most dramatic demonstration took place in 1857 when Sappers proceeded to demolish the old Rochester bridge. Needless to say this was at the invitation of the authorities since a new bridge was to be constructed on the site. It was a task no self-respecting Sapper would let pass and it was set about with much enthusiasm by the RE Establishment under Colonel Sandham, watched by the ever curious and long suffering local population supported by the National Press. There have been few occasions as dramatic since then but the garrison and the local community have coexisted more than amicably. The garrison is proud to hold the Freedoms of Gillingham, Chatham and Rochester on Medway. These formal links provide the framework for the co-operation, mutual support and affection which is common to all military towns and which makes them, despite some obvious disadvantages, pleasant and interesting places in which to live.

Bibliography

Samuel Pepys Diary, (New Edition) Ed. Latham & Mathews, Bell and Hyman, London, 1970

My Life and Balloon Experiences, Henry Coxwell, W. H. Allen, London, 1889

Brochure of the Royal Arsenal, Woolwich, Wesley Harry, Ministry of Defence, PR Department, March 1984

The Novels of Charles Dickens, especially *The Pickwick Papers*

5

Plymouth

ROBERT SADLER

OF THE three great naval bases in the South of England, Plymouth, Portsmouth and Chatham, Plymouth is in some ways the most interesting from the military point of view. Naturally, the Plymouth of today is dramatically different from the Plymouth of nine centuries or so ago. Like London it has grown and has gradually merged with other townships nearby. Thus Plymouth eventually merged with Dock (or Devonport as it became known in the nineteenth century) and with Stonehouse. The biggest change took place in 1914 as a result of administrative reorganisation when Plymouth was amalgamated with the neighbouring towns and this account of Plymouth does not attempt to deal with Devonport or with Stonehouse in any great detail.

Lying in a small boat within ten feet of the shore on a hot summer's day in twenty feet of water with a two knot current rushing past it is possible to imagine that little has changed in the Hamoaze in a thousand years. Then, on looking up, Brunel's great bridge and the new suspension bridge can be seen. Close at hand there lie a Royal Naval Depot Ship, two destroyers and a frigate. In the distance beyond Drake's Island can be seen Renney's breakwater and beneath all this flows the River Tamar.

The Tamar almost severs Cornwall from England. Its valley has been drowned like those of the Cornish south coast rivers and that of the River Dart, thus creating a deep estuary. Joining it is the estuary of the River Plym and at the junction of the two is the peninsula on which Plymouth grew up.

Seventy-five miles away lies Land's End at the tip of the South West peninsula. Across the sea to the south lies Brittany, about ninety miles distant. Two hundred miles away overland lies London.

Apart from some copper mines in the Callington area, long since worked out, there is little to account for Plymouth's growth in importance except its location by an extensive deep water anchorage. Across the Channel from Brittany, Falmouth offers an extensive anchorage but one that lies near the end of a peninsula, fifty miles further from London. Fowey and Dartmouth offer deep water anchorages but of limited size and they lie in narrow steep sided valleys that have hindered urban and port development. The nearest deep safe anchorages to the east of Dartmouth lie many miles away.

So the great deep water estuary of the Tamar offers the best haven between Falmouth and the Solent and although Dartmouth was a early rival to Plymouth it did not have the same potential. R. A. J. Walling summed up the position succinctly when he wrote:

The *raison d'être* of a community of a quarter of a million in this neck of the country still lies in its harbours, dockyards and naval establishments. Thence sprang the most brilliant episodes of its history and many of its most famous men.[1]

In the days of the small early settlements there was an Iron Age Fort at Sutton Pool (probably used for local defence) but Plymouth was not a Roman garrison town. Rome after all was concerned primarily with the territorial domination of the country so her garrisons were established with that end in view. The land of West Barbary (or Cornwall) was poor so that although the Romans settled in parts of Cornwall they saw no need for a garrison near the mouth of the Tamar.

Right up until the Middle Ages there was a good road from London only to Exeter. However, the marauding that took place as Rome's power declined, culminating in the Norman invasion and subsequently in the Middle Ages, clearly led to an increased perception of the importance of the sea.

At the time of the Domesday Book the King kept various manors for strategic reasons: King's Tamerton dominated the Saltash crossing, Sutton commanded the head of the Sound, and Maker dominated the mouth of the Tamar. The first known record of the name Plymouth occurs in the Pipe Rolls of 1211.

Plymouth was first used as a naval base in 1296 and 1297 when naval expeditions were launched from there. Henceforward, Plymouth's location at the mouth of the English Channel determined its future as England emerged as a sea power. However, for some three centuries after this it was important from the naval point of view as an assembly place for fleets rather than as a port in its own right. The Cattewater and Mill Bay provided limited security; even when vessels were of small size they were subject to surge as the ocean masses moved up the Channel in bad weather and they were exposed to the south-east. At first, therefore, Plymouth grew in importance as much for reasons of territorial home defence as for naval reasons.

Plymouth was repeatedly raided by corsairs from Brittany in the second half of the fourteenth century. Edward had ordered defences to be erected about 1374, but they were not very effective. The raid of 1403 was carried out by a fleet of 30 ships with 1,200 foot soldiers and the guns of the castle, firing granite cannon balls were virtually powerless. So too was the garrison which was unable to prevent the Bretons landing and sacking part of the town, though after a brisk fight the Bretons were repulsed. The English responded by raiding Brittany with four thousand men. The Bretons then in turn attempted to raid Dartmouth but were unsuccessful.

The comparatively undefended state of the port had led to vociferous complaints each time it was raided. By 1400 its population was exceeded in size only by London, York and Bristol and when the raid of 1403 took place Henry IV ordered a wall to be built around it, although the inhabitants were not satisfied. They were at this time subject to the jurisdiction of the Priors of Plympton. The Prior of the day had been instructed by Edward III to ensure that Plymouth could defend itself but his efforts had been inadequate and as the town grew the system of local government became manifestly outmoded.

In 1411 the inhabitants of Sutton Valletort and Sutton Prior sent a petition to Henry IV asking for the right to levy dues and tolls for defence purposes. The King replied with unusual despatch. He sent a message requiring the townspeople to negotiate with the Priors but it took twenty-five years or so for an agreement to be reached. In 1439, a significant date in the history of the church, a further petition was submitted that was approved in full without amendment. Plymouth was incorporated by Act of Parliament, the first town to be treated in this way.

From its outset the Corporation had special powers for it took command of the castle, and made each of its four wards responsible for defending one of the castle's great towers with the mayor being in overall command in the north-east tower overlooking the harbour. The Corporation provided the guns and ammunition for the fortifications, maintained the ramparts on the waterfront, fortified St. Nicholas' Island (later Drake's Island) and maintained sentries and warning beacons to watch the sea.

As far as Plymouth was concerned, the dissolution of the monasteries led to the final disappearance of local influence by Plympton Priory, but feelings ran high in Cornwall for the old church and led to the Western Rebellion in 1549. The main body of the Cornishmen marched into Devon to attack Exeter, but a subsidiary force was detached which invested Trematon Castle near Plymouth and then moved on to the town, but the attack was unsuccessful and the Cornish were defeated by Lord Russell after he had relieved Exeter. The Corporation sent men into Cornwall to pursue the rebels.

In the Middle Ages the garrison of Plymouth consisted of all the male inhabitants capable of bearing arms. As late as 1572 the Corporation ordered that every inhabitant should have in some convenient place in his house 'a good black bill or a clubbe'. This arrangement was not particularly satisfactory. In 1599, for example, Lieutenant Edward Dodington, fearful of a Spanish invasion, kept his militia, the Plymouth companies, at 'Stand to' all night. But the inhabitants would not garrison the fort on Drake's Island and Lieutenant Doddington complained that many inhabitants had fled with their belongings rather than leave them unprotected whilst they were on garrison duty.[2] Nevertheless, from that time to the twentieth century there has been a strong tradition of local territorial defence. A town militia with the mayor as Major Commandant was in existence in 1717 when civic records include items of expenditure on drums and silk sashes.[3] Worth notes that by the second half of the eighteenth century, in 1779, there were two corps. The men of one corps clothed themselves and had no pay and the other was paid and clothed by the Government. The more strictly Volunteer Corps eventually increased to six companies and a strength of 350. They must have made a gay picture when on the march for they had uniforms of red turned up with yellow and their helmets were covered with yellow material.

Towards the close of the century the Plymouth Horse was formed – a body of the most respectable tradesmen. Then there were the Sea Fencibles, two hundred and fifty strong, mostly drawn from Custom House officials, a rifle corps of about fifty men, and a small body of cavalry drawn chiefly from butchers. Stonehouse and Dockyard each had two independent companies and when the Treaty of Amiens was signed with the French in 1802 the total force included nearly 1,500 men.

During the Napoleonic Wars the volunteers were often billeted in public houses and were immune from the Press Gang so that they had little difficulty in gaining recruits but they were disbanded after the war in 1815. During the long peace that followed the regular army was run down in strength so that when the Crimean War broke out most of the regular units of the garrison had to go abroad leaving the South Devon militia to help man Plymouth garrison. Many of the militia had volunteered

A map of Plymouth and the surrounding area, 1643.

for service in the Crimea when the Government decided to reinforce the garrison with mercenaries drawn from different European countries known as 'Jagers'.[4]

The Jagers quickly showed themselves to be ill disciplined and had to be moved to a camp at first on Maker Heights on the west side of the Sound and then after terrorising the villages of Millbrook and Cawsand to the east side of the Sound at Bovisand, then uninhabited but later to become a coast defence site. Finally they mutinied against their own officers and were disbanded.

Fears of an attack by the French led to a revival of the local militia. The Dockyard artillery volunteers were reformed and a rifle corps was established that in 1859 became the 2nd Battalion The Devonshire Regiment which subsequently became the 5th Battalion The Devonshire Regiment TA. The artillery volunteers eventually became the Devon Heavy Brigade of Coast Defence Artillery.

It is interesting to note that during the 1939-1945 war the 16th Battalion of the Devonshire Regiment was concerned with the defence of Plymouth and the 17th Battalion (drawn almost entirely from Dockyard workers) was concerned with the defence of the Dockyard and Devonport by that time part of the City of Plymouth. Both battalions were initially Home Guard units.

Until the seventeenth century, England's political and military energies had been directed towards the Continent, but for some time it had become increasingly obvious that a naval base was necessary in the West Country. Dutch and French sea power and the attractions of trade with the New World brought matters to a head. Perhaps because of his origins it was William of Orange who finally initiated plans to begin the extensive works that were necessary. The first work on the new dockyard began in 1691. The site chosen lay on marshy ground some two miles from Plymouth on the Hamoaze. The water on the Devon side was seventy feet deep and the anchorage was almost completely landlocked. By that time further growth in the Cattewater area was virtually impossible, particularly because until Renney's breakwater was built in the nineteenth century it was subject to Channel surge and was exposed to the southeast.

In fifty years Dock was half the size of Plymouth. Intense rivalry grew between the two communities stemming from the jealousy felt by the inhabitants of Plymouth at the extent of the Crown's investment in the new Dockyard. The new community was inevitably rough and violent. However, by 1800 Dock was larger than Plymouth and by 1820 its population totalled 35,000 compared with Plymouth's 21,500. It was the wars with France, the American colonies and subsequently the United States that led to this growth. From the middle of the eighteenth century the Dockyard dominated the economy of Plymouth. It brought with it the seamen; it employed Dockyard workers; it produced ropewalks and sailmakers' lofts, victualling yards, foundries, coopers' yards; and, of course, the depot ships and the naval barracks, the Royal Navy Hospital and the barracks for the Royal Marines. When the railway era came a special spur was laid to the naval arsenal. Great warships were built and launched there. In the 1890s an enormous extension to the Dockyard was built which made Devonport the largest of Britain's naval bases. By 1914 some warships could truly be described as Plymouth ships since they were built by Plymouth men and mostly manned by them.

In the 1914-1918 war the following vessels manned from the Plymouth port division were amongst the Royal Navy's losses: four battleships, one battle cruiser, five armoured cruisers, five light cruisers, three monitors, four armed merchant cruisers, fifteen destroyers, twenty-five submarines and seven sloops.[5] The economic effect of all this upon Plymouth and indeed upon the area as a whole needs little further comment.

Of course the naval presence affected local political and social life as well as the economy. All the great admirals and some of the country's most distinguished soldiers became familiar figures in Plymouth. For instance, no connection could have been more intimate than Plymouth's connection with Captain Edward Pellew, subsequently Lord Exmouth. In 1796 the *Dutton*, a transport with 400 soldiers and a large number of women and children aboard, went ashore on the rocks below the Citadel. All were in imminent peril for the ship was dismasted and she was listing to seaward when Captain Pellew and a midshipman who were watching from the shore managed to board the ship, take charge and organise the rescue operation. Pellew and the midshipman, Mister Edgell, stayed until everyone on board had been safely got to land. Pellew was then twenty-nine years of age and his exploit won him immediate fame and popularity. He subsequently became Commander-in-Chief Plymouth.

Similarly, Admiral Benbow, who died at sea in a naval battle in 1702 when his two subordinates deserted him, was a great favourite. Then there was Lord Anson who brought prizes, money and prisoners to Plymouth. All three of Captain Cook's voyages started in Plymouth and Captain Bligh of HMS *Bounty* was born there. Amherst was appointed C-in-C Plymouth during the last years of the American War of Independence. Captain George Edgcumbe, subsequently the first Earl of Edgcumbe, was with Amherst in the action at Cape Breton Island in 1758 and was naturally well known in Plymouth. Keppel was tried by court martial for his conduct of operations off Brest in 1779, was completely acquitted and became a popular hero. Indeed the dockyard shipwrights lit bonfires in his honour. Nelson, when Vice Admiral stayed in Plymouth in December 1800 and January 1801 whilst his flagship, *San Josef* (captured by Nelson in the battle of Cape St. Vincent) was refitted. Emma bore him a daughter there. Admiral Sir James Saumarez fitted out an expedition to Algeciras in Plymouth: although this was unsuccessful he subsequently defeated both the French and the Spanish fleets so the Plymouth townsfolk fêted him riotously. His popularity continued through the wars and during his period in office twenty years later when he became C-in-C Plymouth. The list is endless.

In the eighteenth and nineteenth centuries some of the leading artists in the country came to the area. Sir Joshua Reynolds was born at Plympton on 16 July 1723 and whilst a guest at Mount Edgcumbe he completed his first portrait. He subsequently settled in bustling Plymouth Dock where he painted members of the Kendall family and, it is claimed, many of the naval officers at Dock. He certainly painted the Commissioner of the Dockyard, Philip Vanbrugh. Although Reynolds subsequently settled in London he was followed by other painters who were attracted both by the quality of local society and by the setting.

Between 1818 and 1832 officers of the Royal Navy were mayors of Plymouth no less than six times, and of course Sir Francis Drake and Sir Richard Hawkins (Sir John Hawkins's son) were amongst Plymouth's most notable mayors.

The importance of the Navy to Plymouth and its impact upon it has lasted down to the present day. To take one or two further instances to make the point: when a local pleasure boat sank in the Sound in the 1960s HMS *Iveston* sent divers down to look for it; when ratings with local connections were commissioned their promotions were reported in the local newspaper. As recently as 1967 10,000 Naval recruits lived in Plymouth for six months during their training.[6]

The defences against sea-borne invasion already referred to began to be developed early in the fifteenth century when Leland described 'the strong castle quadrate having at each corner a great round tower' (the area outside the castle's site is still known as the Barbican). The possibility of Spanish invasion subsequently re-emphasised Plymouth's strategic importance and a fort was established in 1590. Some bases had governors under the Lord Lieutenant of the County. Thus, when Richard Hawkins was Mayor, Richard Grenville was in charge of the defences and subsequently Sir Fernando Gorges was the first Governor of Plymouth's Elizabethan fort.[7]

No account of Plymouth as a garrison town would be complete without reference to its history in the seventeenth century. Charles I declared war on Spain in 1625 and assembled an army of 10,000 men in Plymouth. Unfortunately when the fleet came in it brought the plague. There were insufficient provisions to feed the troops who first began to plunder the countryside and then fell prey to the plague so that eventually either through hunger or sickness many could not carry their muskets and a quarter of the civilian population of Plymouth died.[8] Much the same story was repeated in 1626.

Plymouth's position in the Civil War was remarkable for whereas almost the whole of the West Country stood for the King, Plymouth supported Parliament from the outset of the conflict. No other town in the west had a democratic system of government and it was a staunchly Protestant town whose beliefs were reinforced by the stories brought back by seamen when they returned from their encounters with the Spanish.

The Plymouth garrison consisted of men who were citizens rather than soldiers. When the King called upon Sir Jacob Ashley, the Governor, to advise him and to become a major general in his army, the Mayor, Thomas Ceely, took over as governor without protest from the garrison, until Parliament sent Colonel Ruthven, later Lord Grey de Ruthven, to command Plymouth and the young Sir Francis Drake, a descendant of the famous admiral, raised the Plymouth Horse.[9] By the time the Royalist forces under Sir Ralph Hopton had begun to besiege the town it was ready for them. Both the forts on the Hoe and on St. Nicholas' Island (later Drake's Island) were controlled by the Corporation. In consequence, supplies could always reach the town by sea. In an era of short-range weapons control of these forts meant that the Corporation could control the sea approaches to Plymouth. To the east and to the west the town was protected by two large river estuaries. To the north there was the crumbling town wall. Right up to 1645 the Corporation was at work strengthening the defences and at one stage the garrison was built up by sea to a strength of 9,000 men. The Elizabethan fortress walls had deteriorated and in 1620 the gates had been removed so that in 1643 it was necessary for the walls to be repaired, the gates to be replaced, ditches to be dug and ramparts with wooden stockades to be built.

Dissidents were few but the town was shaken by the defection of Sir Alexander Carew, commander of the Forts on the Hoe and on St. Nicholas' Island. Fortunately his garrison realised his intentions and he was arrested. After a year in prison in London he was executed. Had he been able to arrange the fall of St. Nicholas' Island the town would probably have fallen. The importance of the sea to the beleaguered townsfolk was demonstrated when Prince Maurice's campaign in the west began. He delayed his arrival outside the town in order to capture Dartmouth but the delay enabled five or six hundred men to arrive at Plymouth by sea from Portsmouth.

When Prince Maurice eventually launched his attack with a strong force he took Stamford Fort but with considerable difficulty. Indeed all that his success did was to strengthen the resolve of the Corporation and of the townsfolk at large. They signed a Solemn Vow and Covenant pledging, amongst other things, to defend Plymouth, Stonehouse, the Fort and the Island to the last, and to give no part of them into the hands of anyone without the consent of both Houses of Parliament.

Three weeks later, on 3 December, 1643, the defenders won their greatest victory, the Sabbath Day Fight, which was commemorated by Freedom Day. The ridge upon which it was won became known as Freedom Fields, a name which has become widely known through the Freedom Fields Hospital. A further, though not as important, battle took place on 20 December and the Royalists were again defeated.

This ended Prince Maurice's campaign. The town had suffered severely. The train bands had stood firm and the inhabitants stood up well to their trials but the town was short of both food and water. The sea again came to their help with a 'run' of pilchards, and mullet, which was easily caught in baskets.

After Prince Maurice left the field the Cavalier operations were carried on at first by Colonel Digby and later by Sir Richard Grenville. At the start of the Civil War, Grenville was a Parliamentarian and actually took part in discussions in London about how best to defend Plymouth, but he changed sides and eventually undertook the blockade of the town so that it is not surprising that he was regarded with anathema by the townsfolk. Meantime, Essex and his Roundhead Army ventured into Cornwall and were soundly defeated. The King tried to persuade Plymouth to surrender but the town stood firm, reinforced by remnants of the Roundhead Army from Cornwall. In September the defenders had 150 guns, 400 cavalry and 2,000 infantry to defend four miles of fortifications. In addition they had the help of sailors from ships in the Cattewater.

Curiously enough the town had to withstand only one serious attack from the large army outside its defences. Charles attempted to turn the line from Stonehouse to Pennycomequick without success. Grenville was then left in charge and although he was paid considerable sums for his services was ineffectual.

In January 1645 he attempted a general assault but he was defeated. He made a further attempt without success and that was the end of his efforts. In January 1646 the siege was raised. Plymouth had withstood three years of siege, a vital factor in the final victory of Parliament. The inhabitants and the garrison shared hardship to a degree that they were not to experience again for three hundred years. That is not to say that Plymouth was totally united against the King but the dissidents were few and mostly uninfluential and the train bands were particularly exemplary in their behaviour and general discipline.

R. A. J. Walling has drawn attention to the remarkable part played by the Corporation: 'The Mayor was not only Chairman of the Committee of Defence which had responsibility for the maintenance of troops, the raising of the train bands and the preservation of order, but he had an active share in matters of policy.' Indeed, as he goes on to point out, the Corporation was not only a very wealthy body responsible for the defence and administration of one of the major ports and cities in the kingdom but it had, what was for the time, the very remarkable experience of being an elected

The Citadel today and the Cattewater beyond as seen from Plymouth Hoe.

body. It had then and it has continued to have the support of men of great ability amongst its members.[10]

After the restoration of the monarchy in 1660 Charles II decided to strengthen Plymouth's defences partly because of the competition with the Dutch at sea and also perhaps because of the need to ensure the Crown's supremacy in Plymouth. On 17 November 1665, the King signed a warrant to the Earl of Bath, Governor of Plymouth, and others ordering a new 'Citadel' to be built. For centuries since that time it has been the effective centre of the Plymouth garrison. Significantly a house for Plymouth's Governor was built within the Citadel. But when the Dutch wars ended in 1674 the fortifications had been only partially completed. The Powder Magazine was not completed until 1727.

When James II was deposed in 1688 and William of Orange sailed into Torbay with 500 ships, the Earl of Bath sent an officer to assure him of the loyalty of Plymouth garrison but many officers of the garrison were arrested for protesting their continued loyalty to James II.

Sir John Ligonier, later Field Marshal and Commander-in-Chief, was Governor from 1752-1759 and it was during this time that the fortifications were modernised and reached their most elaborate form of development. They remained the same until 1888 when developments in armaments led to the feeling that if the Navy failed to prevent an invasion there would be little point in further resistance. All the outer works were then levelled and in 1936 Madeira Road was built through part of the double wall.

There is an interesting story about the Citadel and Plymouth's defences in general during the American War of Independence. A man who claimed to be a Spanish Count named Parades (there was some doubt about this: it was claimed he was really a pastry cook) offered his services to the French who were anxious to secure details of Britain's defences. He was asked to visit the ports and dockyards and to recruit agents.

It is claimed that he visited the Citadel in 1778 without difficulty and warned the French Minister, M. de Sartine, that Admiral Byron was leaving for America and that Admiral Kepple was to follow. However, the French distrusted the reports and did not attack. Parades subsequently obtained full plans of the Dockyard and fortifications and took them to France. When he returned he was accompanied by another agent to check the account he had taken to France. As the ship arrived it was visited and the two agents were arrested. Parades subsequently claimed that he bribed the examining officer with £1,500 to release him. Whether the story was true or not he was soon back in France where he proposed that a force of 4,000 men, ostensibly bound for America, should invade Plymouth which could easily be taken by surprise attack. Instead, the French combined with the Spanish fleets, embarked 30,000 men and sailed for Plymouth. They entered Cawsand Bay where they anchored on 6 August 1779 with sixty-six sail.

Plymouth was in an uproar. Old guns were brought out and sited along the shore, a boom was put across the Cattewater and thousands of French prisoners-of-war were marched into the country. However, a sudden storm forced the enemy fleets to put out to sea where they met HMS *Ardent* with a convoy of merchant ships. After an exchange of shots the British ship surrendered in the face of overwhelming odds. Fortunately for British pride Admiral Sir Charles Hardy, with a small fleet, then met them and the enemy promptly withdrew. Parades (unjustly) was discredited and M. de Sartine, the French minister, lost his office.[11]

From 1895 onwards much of the accommodation in the Citadel was rebuilt, starting with the present Officers' mess, and in 1899 it became a station for units of the Royal Artillery and has remained so ever since. It was between 1899 and 1957 the headquarters of the fixed defences of Plymouth under various titles. Until 1923 there was a regiment of the Royal Garrison Artillery stationed there but with the reorganisation of the Gunners at that time the unit became a Heavy Regiment. Shortly after the oubreak of war it became the Coast Artillery Training Centre responsible for training officers and men for coast artillery defence. In 1946 the Coast Artillery School moved down from Llandudno and joined the Coast Artillery Training Centre which from then on consisted of 47 Coast Regiment and the Coast Artillery School under the Commandant, Coast Artillery Training Centre.

In 1956 the Coast Artillery was disbanded and the Citadel was empty for a couple of years until 42 Field Regiment RA was stationed there. In 1962 it became the permanent station for the Commando Regiment RA which supports 3 Commando Brigade Royal Marines, and 29 Commando Regiment are still at the Citadel.[12]

There were, of course, substantial fortifications. In 1783 the Citadel had 95 guns (ranging in size from great 32 pounders to 4 pounders), another 159 pieces of artillery were in batteries around the Sound and St. Nicholas' Island had 29 guns and two mortars. However, these gradually became unserviceable until the 1860s when there seemed a possibility that France would invade and these fortifications were reviewed and replaced. It is hard to appreciate the intensity of feeling that led to the creation

Citadel Gate, built in 1670.

of Palmerston's 'follies'. The defences were inspected thoroughly and were found to be sadly out of date and generally inadequate. An elaborate and expensive plan was proposed that envisaged all-round defence with 622 guns and a garrison of 2,550 men.[13] This was drastically pruned and although forts were built on the landward side of Plymouth (Palmerston's follies) they were never properly equipped. Batteries were, however, fully established at Tregantle Down, Whitesand Bay, Polhawn, Rame Church, Penlee Point, Cawsand, Maker Heights, Picklecombe Fort, Garden (at Mount Edgcumbe), Mount Wise and Lower Mount Wise, Staddon Point, Renney Point, Fort Bovisand and Plymouth Breakwater.

Some of these batteries remained operational until after the Second World War. At the outset of the Second World War, Plymouth was protected by six 9.2 inch guns, six 6 inch guns and eleven 12 pounders.[14] Staddon Point Battery had its guns replaced in 1850. It remained in use in the Second World War with four 12 pounder guns in an anti-torpedo boat role. It was connected with Fort Bovisand that had nine 9 inch guns and fourteen 10 inch guns in the late nineteenth century, and which was used for plotting and range finding in both World Wars. Before Penlee and Renney Batteries were built, Plymouth Breakwater Fort (completed in 1870) was protected by four 5 inch thicknesses of Armour plate, fourteen 12.5 inch guns and four 10 inch RML guns. Renney Battery, armed with 9.2 inch guns, was in use in both World Wars and was the principal practice battery for Coast Artillery until 1956 when the Regiment was disbanded.

Stanley Goodman, secretary of the Old Plymouth Society, has described work done by Major K. Hitchins of Crownhill, Plymouth, who commanded batteries on Drake's Island and other places. He has excavated the remains of an 1870 12 inch RML, made the traversing carriage and cradle and put it back in its original emplacement, where it is now fired once a year:

> All the Steelwork was fabricated by our City Engineer in his blacksmith's shop and carried across to the Island by Navy Helicopter — too big to go through the main defence entrance port. Three other RML's we hope to mount in due course.[15]

So far as the Service presence is concerned it has mirrored that of other military towns in the British Isles (with the exception of the garrison towns in Northern Ireland). The British Army of the eighteenth and nineteenth centuries was comparatively small and so was the Army element of Plymouth garrison, Inevitably, the Royal Navy was in truth both the Senior and the dominant Service. The Plymouth Division of the Royal Marines was established in 1755, along with those for Chatham and Portsmouth. They were quartered in Plymouth around the Barbican and they occupied Stonehouse Barracks in 1783.[16]

The size of the regular army element was gradually strengthened so that by the outbreak of the First World War there were normally two or three infantry battalions in the garrison, including a Highland regiment. By 1939 they were generally housed in Raglan Barracks (north and south), Plumer and Seaton Barracks. Mr Goodman, Secretary of the Old Plymouth Society, remembers the 'Plumer brick buildings in a long line from the Barracks and Officers' Mess buildings on Fort Austin Avenue down to a garrison church on the roadside at Crownhill'.[17] Plumer Barracks was 'built so far as I can discover about 1910. It contained a large officers' accommodation building (used latterly as a Magistrates' Court), a small garrison church, a three-storey barracks on a site adjoining the Officers' accommodation and a whole series of things that can only be described as hutments containing motor transport, horses and a few guns. It is difficult to guess what the purpose was'.[18] Seaton barracks was 'a Hore Belisha rebuild of hutments. Granby barracks in Devonport housed the RASC and the horses for the Raglan people.[19] Raglan Barracks was built during the Crimean War of 1854-1856 inside the hurriedly constructed Devonport lines as a consequence of the French scare of the time. The barracks was intended for and used for infantry regiments designed to have a defensive role in conjunction with the accelerated fort building of the time. It went out of use after the Second World War and was demolished in 1969 to be replaced by military and naval housing.

The outset of the Second World War seemed to augur well for Plymouth. Every development or peak in our national history has been paralleled by a sudden increase in Plymouth's population; enemy airfields seemed far away and the activity in the dockyard was generating jobs and wealth. Unfortunately, as France collapsed the enemy was quickly within easy striking distance and the Plymouth Blitz followed. Anti-aircraft guns were in short supply throughout the country so that the Government experimented with such devices as the PAC (Parachute and Cable).

On 11 July 1940 Plymouth was defended by a mere 18 heavy anti-aircraft guns (from 56 (Cornwall) HAA Regt RA), a figure that compared with 6 for Weymouth, 36 for Bristol, 44 for Portsmouth and 43 for Southampton. The defences of Plymouth and Weymouth were both intended to be supplemented by supporting fire from those warships that were in harbour. By August 1940 the defences of Plymouth and Falmouth had been supplemented by 24 barrage balloons and in Plymouth's case by 28 anti-aircraft guns. However, the build up of guns was short-lived and by 11 September there were only 26 anti-aircraft guns. There was also a smoke screen and this deterred three raiders carrying the Fritz-X guided bomb (a 3,100 lb armour piercing bomb) and two were subsequently shot down.[20]

Of course anti-aircraft guns were an ineffective means of defence against enemy aircraft. It has been estimated that it took 3,700 rounds of ammunition to bring down one enemy aircraft. The anger and hurt felt by some of the inhabitants at the destruction of Plymouth comes poignantly through some lines written by the Secretary of the Old Plymouth Society some forty years later:

> AA defences were pitiful and almost non-existent (the fall of France was not foreseen and it had not been expected that the town would be attacked). HMS *Belfast* in Jennycliffe Bay in Plymouth Sound provided most of the defensive noise by firing her 6 inch into the sky. The noise comforted the citizens but had no other effect. I do not know of any hits obtained by AA. There was a near miss on a Sunderland flying boat trying to land in the Sound with a distinguished passenger on board but that could hardly be counted. There was a Balloon Barrage over the town manned by the Auxiliary Air Force or AA Command.[21]

56 (Cornwall) HAA Regiment went to India in March 1942 and was replaced by 116 HAA Regiment. Meantime the coastal defences were strengthened and emergency batteries set up.[22] In January 1941 Plymouth garrison numbered 6,533 all ranks (including the Coastal Artillery Training Centre's 1,959 all ranks),[23] but by July 1941, 566, 567 and 568 Coast Regiments had been established there. Unfortunately, a small dossier (held by the Imperial War Museum) intended for pilots of the Luftwaffe makes it clear that German Intelligence knew exactly where the coastal defence batteries were sited.

There were of course some light anti-aircraft defences. Lieutenant Colonel Jim Bawden recalls a day in 1941 when he was an artificer sergeant. The Army workshops in Plymouth were responsible for the maintenance of all anti-aircraft equipment in the Plymouth and East Cornwall areas. Some of the equipment was naval and was sited on the Barbican. It included the Vickers 2 pounder mark VIII (or the 'Chicago Piano'). One of the more sophisticated weapons of the time it included an elaborate hydraulic system designed to prevent the weapon firing on particular arcs in order to avoid destroying parts of the ships on which the gun was normally mounted. The hydraulic system of a particular gun was leaking and Artificer Sergeant Jim Bawden's services were called upon to repair the weapon. In order to do this he had to climb down into a well below the gun. The job completed, he emerged from the well and grabbed a conveniently dangling rope to swing clear. To his horror he heard gunfire and saw tracer rounds crossing the bay and the breakwater and, fortunately, over the Short Sunderland flying boats that were moored there. It took him a moment or so to realise that the rope he was dangling from was firing the gun. He subsequently discovered that it had been temporarily rigged by a Royal Marine Sergeant to permit manual operation whilst the hydraulics were out of action.

By 1943, the whole of the south west of England was becoming an armed camp. Considerable American forces were stationed at Crownhill where they occupied both Seaton and Plumer Barracks, and also at Stonehouse where they occupied Raglan Barracks. They took over the Old Admiralty House at Mount Wise and 'they had an important naval advance base in the Cattewater where they occupied almost the entire frontage from Sutton Pool to Laira Bridge'.[24]

In the months before the D-Day landings the Americans manned light anti-aircraft guns (LAA) at strategic points. Subsequently, the Vth and VIIth Corps of Omar Bradley's 1st US Army embarked from Plymouth to take part in the D-Day landings. Other countries were also represented in Plymouth at the time. For example, Coastal Command Operations were mounted from Mount Wise and the Royal Australian Airmen who served there had a distinguished record. Plymouth (Devonport) was the main depot of the Polish Navy during the war and the Poles were accommodated initially in a depot ship, the *Glydnia* in the Hamoaze and later in Stoke Barracks.

Although the Navy took over a further substantial part of the water front in the immediate post-war years to permit dockyard development, the post-war years also saw progressive reductions in the size of the garrison. Nevertheless, HMS *Drake* continues to provide accommodation (£2,000,000 was spent on renovations in 1967) for the crews from ships being repaired and to act as a holding unit for those about to leave the service. The Engineering College at Manadon still exists and there is still a Flag Officer Plymouth. But the number of HM ships using the port is greatly reduced and so, consequently, is the shore-based establishment. Plymouth Dockyard is being civilianised and RAF Mountbatten has largely lost its fleet of small boats, only a small service element of twenty-five men being left.

As far as the Army element is concerned the reorganisation of the defence structure and the ending of National Service has led to a radical transformation. The Coastal Defence Regiment was disbanded in 1956 and the guns were removed from the Plymouth batteries. The Devonshire Regiment was amalgamated with the Dorset Regiment in 1967: and the creation of United Kingdom Land Forces was followed by the disappearance of much of the old Command structure, including Devon and Cornwall Sub District, the Plymouth Headquarters of which closed in 1968. The Royal Marines occupy the Citadel and Stonehouse Barracks and the Army units that remain in Plymouth's garrison are there in a support role for them. It is striking that when the new TA establishment was published in the 1960s its strength was 350, a figure that tallied with the Plymouth volunteer force of 1779.

Inevitably, there has been some loss of contact with the inhabitants as a result of the reduction in size of the garrison and the emphasis on regular forces as opposed to conscript and part-time forces, but Plymouth's relations with the garrison have generally been amicable, concerned and mostly coloured with intense pride.

Of course there have been brawls and in the eighteenth century there was the hated Press Gang.[25] Public House signs reflect Plymouth's association with the Services, particularly along the waterfront. Names such as the Barbican and the Parade stem from earlier usage. The Royal Navy Hospital was completed in 1760 and was placed under the command of a Post Captain in 1795. A military hospital was opened in 1794. A feeling of compassion for sailors led to the creation of Miss Agnes Weston's Sailors Rest, in Devonport, subsequently destroyed in 1941.

In the two years before the First World War the Chamber of Commerce and similar organisations made concerted attempts to bring the Territorial Army up to strength. Meantime, a campaign was being waged to unite the Local Government authorities of Plymouth, Stonehouse and Devonport. The local Government Board conducted an inquiry into the merits of the rival campaigns. In the last few days before the outbreak of the First World War the Plymouth Corporation with magnificent timing called the Commander-in-Chief Plymouth and the General Officer commanding the garrison to give evidence. They both said they preferred in the event of war to deal with one local authority rather than three. Amalgamation followed forthwith.

There have been repeated examples of the feelings of the local inhabitants, too many to list in any detail but the following may serve as a few instances. When Plymouth men of the 2nd Devon Battalion went to South Africa during the Boer War the town's people raised the money to buy them a maxim gun and they formed a machine gun company. When the Duke of Cornwall's Light Infantry (which had been stationed in Plymouth) embarked it was pouring with rain and the crowd intermingled with the marching troops and held umbrellas over them, while householders along the way burned Bengal lights. When HMS *Exeter* returned from the Battle of the River Plate against the *Graf Spee* she was given a tremendous reception. She had been built in the Dockyard and her crew had mostly been drawn from Plymouth. People lined the Sound and Hamoaze to cheer her. The feeling of pride and involvement was manifest.

When the Germans repeatedly attacked the city during the Second World War 400 of the dead were buried in a mass grave. In seven nights of bombing nearly a thousand people died and the flames could be seen turning the night sky a ruddy red from near the Land's End in Cornwall, but the City continued to play its part as the great arsenal and naval base that it had been for so long.

The feeling of the City for the Services was clearly demonstrated yet again at the time of the Falklands emergency when Dockyard workers, sailors and soldiers combined to despatch the requisite task force with appropriate speed. Ironically, the impact of the emergency upon the mass of the inhabitants in the centre of the City was perhaps most clearly seen in the deserted bars in the public houses and small hotels; their clientele had gone elsewhere.

What of the future? Britain's role as a world power has been dramatically changed, and the nation is beset by economic problems. Many people argue that we should concentrate our energies in support of NATO, with inevitable effects upon the balance and equipment of our forces but there are others who feel that this might put us at the mercy of any nation that decided to tweak the old lion's tail.

But the geographical position of Plymouth remains. It will always dominate the mouth of the English Channel. At any point less than the total devastation of the country by nuclear war, its factories and its dockyards must continue to ensure its military significance. For this is a town that looks to the future. Whilst it is intensely proud of its past and the fact that its name has been given to some forty Plymouths all over the world, little physical evidence remains in Plymouth itself to remind us of its history as a military town. Hardly a scrap of the Civil War fortifications remains; bones, musket balls and cannon shot have been found but that is all. Some of the Royal Citadel remains and some of the forts built in the nineteenth century, but the combination of time and the German air raids in the 1940s have wiped out most of

Clarence Yard, shortly to join the private sector like the flats and marina in the background.

the visible relics of the past. The colours of the Devonshire regiment are laid up in St. Andrew's Church. A poster in the Elizabethan House shows part of the war graves in the cemeteries at Ford and Western Mill. Like all the graves maintained by the Imperial War Graves Commission they are impeccably kept to a standard pattern. As in the great military cemeteries in Brookwood in Surrey, in Flanders, in Singapore, in Berlin, and in Hongkong, to name only a few, there lie friend and foe alike, men and women from the Commonwealth and from allied countries — all together at peace at last.

To the people of Plymouth, with their awareness of their past, the following lines written by Sir Henry Newbolt seem as meaningful as they were during the Second World War:

> Drake is in his hammock till the great armadas come
> (Captain, art tha sleepin' there below?)
> Slung between the round shot, listening for the drum,
> And dreamin' arl the time of Plymouth Hoe
> Call him on the deep sea, call him up the Sound,
> Call him when ye sail to meet the foe:
> Where the old trade's plyin' and the old flag's flyin'
> They shall find him ware and wakin' as they found him long ago!

Bibliography

Plymouth: A New History, Crispin Gill, David & Charles, Newton Abbot, Vol. II, 1979

History of Plymouth, R. N. Worth, William Brendon, 1980

It Came to Our Door, H. P. Twyford, Underhill, Plymouth, 1945

From the Lower Deck – the Old Navy 1780-1840, Henry Baynham, Hutchinson

Time to Finish the Game, A. M. Hadfield, Phoenix House, 1964

The Story of Plymouth, R. A. J. Walling, Westaway Books, 1950

Blitz on Britain, Alfred Price, Ian Allen, 1977

Coast Defence of England and Wales 1856-1956, Ian V. Hogg, David & Charles, Newton Abbot, 1974

The Royal Citadel, C. W. Woodward, pamphlet, City of Plymouth Museums & Art Gallery

6

Woolwich

SUZANNE MARSH

WOOLWICH has a military history which stems from Roman times, and since then all manner of service personnel and establishments have been associated with the town, but none spring to mind so readily as the Arsenal, the Royal Artillery and the Royal Military Academy. Until the eighteenth century, Woolwich was a relatively unheard of village with a small dockyard, overshadowed by Deptford and the City. Emerging unscathed from the Civil War pre-industrial Woolwich was described by a later biographer as a 'pleasant watering place',[1] and it is not hard to imagine how it must have been: with an attractive river front, topped by the woods and heath of Charlton and Shooters Hill. Woolwich did not begin to figure prominently in the Nation's defences until the Dutch sailed up the nearby Medway and destroyed the British Fleet in 1669. The panic stricken authorities, realising that there were no adequate defences for London, hurriedly despatched Prince Rupert to Woolwich to see to its fortification. The site of the first emergency defences became know locally as 'Prince Rupert's Walk' and took the form of a raised wall along the river bank able to support up to sixty guns. Much to everyone's relief these first temporary measures were never put to the test and after the crisis a more permanent military enclosure, 'The New Carriage Yard', was developed alongside the dockyard on the Warren site in 1697. This roughly triangular riverside complex eventually became known as the Arsenal.

Although initially physically integrated into the body of the Arsenal, The Royal Military Academy and the Royal Regiment of Artillery Barracks should be viewed as separate and important institutions in their own right. While it should be remembered that for many years they co-existed virtually under the same roof their development was quite separate even though they benefited from one another's proximity. So much has happened in Woolwich since the eighteenth century that to record it all would do none of the individual events justice. A more representative and more lasting impression can be gained by picking out a few events of importance and viewing them separately.

There has been much written about the Royal Arsenal. Some works have been historical, some antiquarian and some personal memoirs; all have been equally fascinating. There was obviously something about the place which appealed to the child in so many of us. Whenever there was a demonstration of some new pyrotechnic or projectile like Congreve's Rocket or Mallet's Mortar, people would flock for miles to see it. Before the nineteenth century the Arsenal was rather like a village within a town and until it was enclosed in 1778 people could enter at will whether for business or merely to see the sights. It is claimed that by 1774 the buildings extended over 104 acres and about 500 people were employed there. Later the covered area extended into the marshes eastwards to Plumstead and the number employed increased to thousands.

The Royal Arsenal, late eighteenth century.

The architecture within the old Arsenal is a subject worthy of a book in its own right. Each phase of building from the earliest in the seventeenth century reflects the fashionable style of the time. To take just one example, the Royal Brass Foundry, completed in 1717 along with several other buildings, was designed by Sir John Vanburgh. Unfortunately many of the older buildings were neglected until the Crown Agents stepped in and some restoration has now been set in hand. Today the Arsenal is a restricted area, but there are proposals to create a museum in one of the historic buildings and to open it again to the public. When, and if this comes about students will find in the Arsenal a microcosm of our architectural, military and industrial past.

It is not surprising that the Arsenal had its greatest effect on the district during times of international crisis. The Crimean War saw a period of reorganisation and growth within the Arsenal itself and as many as 10,000 men and boys were employed within its sheds and factories. There were experiments with countless new forms of artillery and it must have been a paradise for inventors as all sorts of new shells were tried; they filled them with cayenne pepper, with chloroform and with 'cacodyle', described as a 'most virulent contrivance for poisoning the air'.[2] There were plans for filling shells with liquid iron, and one should not forget the 'Great Mallet Mortar' with its three foot diameter shell weighing 200 lb. The projectile sank so deep into the mud that some contemporary wags claimed it had gone to Australia. Even though it may have sounded as if 'Heath Robinson' was in charge many serious and important munitions were developed and gratefully received by the nearby Gunners.

Many of the staff and officials actually lived within the walls of the Arsenal, together with their families. Their children found it a wonderful place to live and several of their recollections appear in *The Woolwich Story* by E. F. E. Jefferson published by the RA Printing Press, Woolwich, in 1970. Here is a description of what it was like to be living there in 1900:

> For the children, living in the Arsenal was almost unadulterated paradise as, during the silent hours when the factories were closed down, as they were in peacetime at 5.40 p.m., we had the whole place to ourselves with narrow-gauge trucks to ride on, canals and bathing pond to fish in for tiddlers and log piles to float upon, trying to avoid a soaking process. There were also stacks of wood seasoning in the yard and upon these we used to climb and have feasts of peanuts, dates at 1d. a pound and lemonade. The river front, over three miles of it, was a great magnet as we used to try to board the various War Department steamers if there was no one to stop us. On Sunday evenings in the summer 'T' Pier was a favourite gathering place for the residents to watch the steamers and barges and particularly the pleasure boats, *Eagle*, *Southend Belle* and the rest, returning from Southend, Margate and Yarmouth. During working hours in school holidays, there was always much of interest to be seen, for we youngsters had entrée to many of the factories where we watched the various processes in the making of bullets and cartridges, the manufacture of steel for the shells in the foundry and the huge blast furnaces for making the parts of naval guns. Outside the Central Office there was a grassy bank and in the Spring there was a profusion of crocuses in many colours which spelt in Latin: 'We make thunder' — reminder of the guns made there and of the continual noise of proving them at the butts on the marshes.[3]

During the Boer War the Arsenal and Woolwich responded to the need for increased production once again as they did also in 1914. By 1915 men, boys and women were making and filling all types of shells, manufacturing and repairing guns, carriages and mountings not to mention assembling and filling ammunition boxes. Contrary to popular belief the use of women in armaments was not new. There had been women and girls employed in the cartridge factory from the Crimean War until 1872 when boys were used instead. During the Great War the presence of women was not accepted with equanimity by the men even though there was a shortage of man-power and there was considerable opposition to what was called 'dilution of labour'. Boys from the secondary schools were encouraged to do voluntary clerical work during their holidays receiving ten shillings per week. A soldier's wife might expect to earn about two shillings per day, while a soldier's pay was only one shilling and four pence.

The very nature of the work carried out at the Arsenal made it a dangerous place and even in peacetime accidents were a constant threat. During wartime this danger was heightened by the threat from enemy action. From May until September 1915 there were several Zeppelin attacks and then in June 1917 Gotha raids began. Fortunately only about six bombs fell inside the Arsenal itself although the frequent

Mrs Lloyd George's visit to the Arsenal, 1918.

warnings had to be taken seriously and there was constant disruption. The town and barracks suffered more from these attacks and in comparison with the disasters at Silvertown and Chilwell, Woolwich suffered remarkably few casualties.

During the inter-war years the Arsenal underwent several changes of fortune which meant that when rearmament was started again in the 1930s and the country began once again to think about preparation for war, it was already in full production. During the Blitz in 1940-41 the Arsenal along with the rest of London took its share of enemy bombs with well over 100 workers killed. But even the menace of the flying bombs did not halt the vital war effort for long.

The first official Academy was established in Tower Place in The Warren in 1721, in what is now the Officers' Mess. By all accounts its academic standard was low and its achievements meagre but it did mark the first state organised military education in this country. Very little is known about the first Academy. It would seem to have closed for a while for in 1741 the *Gentleman's Magazine* announced that 'An academy is ordered to be built at Woolwich for instructing the gentlemen belonging to the train of artillery'. Although there was probably little formal, structured teaching it is known that money was allocated for mathematical instruction for gunners and engineers and for the teaching and practises of ordnance. The academy of those early years hardly seems to have been somewhere one would have willingly consigned anyone let alone the pampered sons of gentlemen. Conditions were harsh and insanitary and discipline was slack. Cadets had to provide much of their own food and other comforts. Places were secured by nomination and vacancy. There was initially no age specified and cadets as young as twelve or as old as thirty were often admitted. Once there, instruction might continue for as long as five years or more, contrasting very favourably with the short, sharp shock of present day Sandhurst.

In 1850 the Academy moved to larger premises outside the Warren, but in 1778 it is recorded that there were 100 cadets in a building intended for 40. The Academy had begun to improve its academic standards during the 1760s under the influence of the Marquis of Granby, who reorganised the classes and the entrance requirements. The position of the cadet has always been a difficult one. Brigadier Hogg in a lecture on 'The Shop' as the Academy was soon called, quotes an eighteenth-century French professor who describes the average cadet as 'almost an officer and not quite a gentleman'.[4] This attitude was echoed in 1930 when General Wagstaff said, 'The GC is a type of his own. He is not an OR soldier nor is he an undergraduate. He is really a 6th form schoolboy'.[5]

The cadets were not always well behaved and there were numerous occasions when cadets were either individually or communally 'gated' for acts of violence. A particular favourite was the nearby Charlton 'Hornfair', an annual festival held locally, repeatedly attended and wrecked by the 'young gentlemen'. This event was put out of bounds for the cadets but they still 'visited' it every year, usually with disastrous consequences. In 1846, for example, their behaviour was so bad that several were sent down and all leave was stopped. Somewhat naively the Governor appears to have expected the cadets to inform upon one another, threatening severe punishment for those failing to do so. It seems that few cadets took much notice of such entreaties and continued their acts of vandalism almost unhindered. Appeals to their better nature also failed, as this letter from the records of 1778 shows:

> The Lt. Gov. expects that henceforward no GC will be guilty of ever attempting

to open or spoil any of the desks or drawers of the Inspectors, Professors or Masters, or of any other Cadets, or even attempt to take anything out of them under the name of smouching as they may be fully assured such base and vile crimes will be pardoned no more.[6]

Even one of the famous 'old boys', General Gordon, who attended the RMA in 1848, proved a less than perfect student. His persistent pranks and bad behaviour led to his being banned from Woolwich Common and on one occasion being rusticated.

For many years one of the highlights of the year for the garrison, the cadets and the townspeople were the RA Races which took place on the common until the 1860s. The usual course was 'Once round and a Distance' and the judges' post was the RMA. When eventually it was moved to Eltham, the cadets were forbidden to attend. They showed their displeasure, however, by dismantling a nine pounder gun and throwing it into the canal. This resulted in all being gated and some sent down. Although the races were never reinstated the cadets managed to introduce some equestrian pleasures of their own. In *Woolwich Story* we are told how in the 1890s the cadets used to return to 'The Shop' at the beginning of each session from the nearby Arsenal Station:

> . . . The cabbies had a hectic hour or so, relief from the usual tedium. All the cabs are hired out at once and there is an extra tip for the first to pass through the Academy gates, for there is betting on the race. It does not do the horses, the drivers or the vehicles any good but there is usually ample time for recovery when they are once again on the rank.[7]

Needless to say the cadets were charged twice the going rate for this escapade, but there is no record of anyone complaining.

The appearance of the cadets in town was always an occasion for remark; drill and uniform combining to make the most of unpromising material. The discomfort of wearing 'blues' and the insistence on short hair seems positively relaxed when compared with the requirements of the eighteenth century. In 1798 the regulation hair style demanded a four-inch queue or tail. Cadets whose hair did not conform were instructed to grow it, and anyone who cropped his hair was degraded until his hair reached the regimental length. A year later the required length was even longer and any GC whose own efforts failed to produce the required amount had to be supplied with false tails by the Academy hairdresser and was forbidden to leave the grounds until it was long enough. Happily by 1801 queues were no longer fashionable and even hair powder made optional.

During the early part of the twentieth century a frequent and popular sight in the Woolwich district was that of cadets bicycling in their smart uniforms and jaunty pill box hats. Cadets were permitted outside the Academy 'to visit relatives' at the weekends. It is probably just as well that there is no record of how close those relatives had to be. The cadets were seen outside 'The Shop' on other occasions, in formations practising 'bicycle drill'. 'The Shop' responded to the demands of the Great War in many important ways, but one in particular was of considerable interest to the local civil population. In 1916 a familiar landmark, the clock, had its chimes stopped ostensibly in order to prevent Zeppelins from finding out that they were over a populated area at night. It continued nevertheless to show the time and it is recorded as being the first clock to show daylight saving in Britain.

The history of the Royal Artillery is long and honourable and it would not be possible to do it justice in the short space available here. In Graham's *The Story of the Royal Regiment of Artillery*,[8] he says that the first two companies of artillery were formed at Woolwich in 1716. Captain, later Lieutenant General William Congreve founded the Royal Military Repository in 1778 as a school of methods of mounting and dismounting ordnance. Congreve's name is of course more widely known in connection with armaments but he should also be recognised for his involvement in the production of standard military procedures and the creation of drill.

Today the most obvious manifestation of the Royal Artillery presence in Woolwich is the large barracks facing the common. With its buildings bearing the names of battles and honours from all over the world it is hard to picture its small beginnings in the Warren. Although little is left to remind us, Woolwich was for many years also garrisoned by Marines, Sappers and Miners and many others, and they too played an important part in its development. There were obviously clashes and conflicts between the various corps, but on the whole they seem to have co-existed side by side amicably enough with each section absorbed by its own particular aspect of military life. Probably the most significant feature of the whole garrison complex has been its successful integration, not only in the smooth inter-action between service and professional life but also in the integration of the garrison with the community. The town and the garrison have always intermarried, and to pursue the metaphor, Woolwich can truly be said to have been the birthplace of the Gunners and it is still their home. While the Sappers and Marines have moved on and the Arsenal and 'The Shop' have closed the Gunners remain, and still continue to play an active role in the everyday life of the town.

Rather than relate the military advances and achievements of the garrison, although these should in no way be underestimated, it makes a change to look at the way the town reacted to the presence of the military and how the two accommodated each other. As has been seen with the cadets at 'The Shop', the townspeople had quite a lot to put up with from the military. However, they were entertained in return by lavish displays and spectacular reviews performed by the assorted soldiery on numerous occasions. Due to its proximity to London, Woolwich has always been a popular place for visits from the reigning monarch and other visiting dignitaries. Other Londoners also took ready advantage of Woolwich's easy access by river and later by rail, and it was a popular venue for excursions and trips. There were many Royal visits recorded, but Queen Victoria and her family took a particular interest in the garrison. There were several 'Royal' cadets at the RMA. Prince Arthur, Duke of Connaught, was there in 1867 and Prince Louis Bonaparte, The Prince Imperial, was a cadet in 1872. After his tragic death in Zululand in 1879 it was via the Arsenal that his body was brought back to England for burial. His coffin was landed at the Arsenal steps and lodged in state in one of the guard-houses before being transferred to Chislehurst for interment. One particularly memorable occasion for the garrison and the town was the series of festivities to mark the accession of Victoria to the throne in 1838. The event is recorded in several places but 'The Records of the Woolwich District' give the most concise and detailed picture. There was a parade around the entire borough including the Arsenal and the Barracks, and at all the major stopping points the good news was proclaimed. The 'Records' tell us that the parade was led by a detachment of Horse Artillery, and included the Artillery, Sappers and Miners and Marine bands, not to mention other Soldiers, all the town officials and the Kent Militia. Then a few days later on the 5 July almost the entire contingent of European Royalty assembled in London for the celebrations, descended on Woolwich.

> July 6th, 1838 — Yesterday a grand review and sports took place at Woolwich. The coaches which ply between London and Woolwich discharged loads of passengers and from every direction carriages, equestrians and pedestrians poured in. There could not have been less then 100,000 persons present.
>
> . . . The firing commenced on the practice range in the marshes by a discharge of thirty twelve-pounder rockets at a target. The company visited the mechanical wonders at the Arsenal, and then proceeded to the Common, where the Artillery went through the manoeuvres of attack and retreat, and several rounds of cannon were fired . . .
>
> . . . On the side of the line that fronted the barracks, and from the lawn of which the Common-ground is divided by a ditch and a brick wall, the pressure was very great. Several persons were sorely bruised. A splendid breakfast was afterwards served in the mess-room. About 800 guests sat down. The toast of 'the Queen' was announced to the multitude by a salute of cannon fired by officers exclusively, the men being all engaged at dinner, which was served to them and their families in number 4,500, on the barrack-field. Then followed the old English sports; and at night there was more feasting and a splendid show of fireworks. The affair has caused a great stir at Woolwich, and no accommodation could be obtained at any price.

What a splendid event it must have been, not only a spectacle but also an illustration of the interrelationship and goodwill which existed for the most part between the garrison and the town. Not quite so grand, however, was the Queen's Jubilee which was spoiled by an untimely storm. The preparations had been extensive including a concert to be performed by both the garrison and the town children. Later there was to have been an *al fresco* celebration but this all had to be cancelled with the exception of the 'military families' who were able to use the Repository Field area which had been covered in for the occasion. The whole was to have been rounded off by a military band concert and a firework display. All was made good in 1900 when the Queen made an official visit to the Herbert Hospital to visit the wounded recently returned from South Africa. This occasion saw the arrival of the Royal train having come across country from Windsor to the Arsenal station. All the Royal family were in fact frequent visitors to Woolwich where they used to board the Royal Yacht for trips farther afield.

The garrison made its physical presence felt in other ways, some beneficial and others less so. It might be reasonable to assume that the nature of the hazardous works and experiments carried out in the Arsenal might offer a certain degree of danger to the town. But in fact, although there certainly were explosions and accidents on the site it presented no real danger to the town itself. It might even be suggested that the reverse was true as the military were constantly being called upon to put out fires in the town; this task most frequently falling to the Sappers and the Marines who were most experienced and happened to live closest. Without a doubt the town is dominated by the Barracks, the Academy buildings and the Arsenal to this day and the whole Borough reflects its links with the military.

Not only do the names of the Public Houses emphasise their patronage but the street names also give some indication of their former contact. It is said that when the Red Barracks was originally built it could be seen up to twenty-five miles away in Essex. Nowadays the skyline is dominated by the Queen Elizabeth II Military Hospital which replaced the old 'Herbert' and serves the local community as well as military personnel and their families.

In addition to the recruits and other single soldiers serving in Woolwich there were many men with their families. The local census returns and parish registers show just how dispersed throughout the community the military really was. It is mentioned in the local records that the retirement of many Marine officers during the 1880s and their settlement into the Shooters Hill area, greatly enhanced the district. Sadly the relationship was sometimes placed under a considerable strain, especially after the Peninsular War when many men were discharged or pensioned off and returned home idle to their families in Woolwich, falling victim to cheap alcohol and disease. As might be expected such large numbers of disgruntled men sometimes caused problems. Eighteenth-century conditions of service were far removed from those of the twentieth century, discipline was arbitrary and floggings frequent. The Naval mutiny of the Nore of 1797 is well recorded, what is less well known is that one year later the soldiers at Woolwich tried the same thing, expelling their officers from the barracks and claiming 'more pay and less drill'! Their uprising was not serious and even while protesting they carried on with their garrison duties. Surprisingly the Government set up a commission of enquiry and the soldiers managed to achieve concessions on every point of grievance.

Serving soldiers were originally allowed to camp out on Woolwich Common, where they built mud huts for their families. Later, after the peace of Amiens, brick ones were built, known in the records as the Duke of York's cottages. These were not built at Government expense but by private charity. They were eventually demolished after a particularly bad outbreak of diphtheria among the garrison children in 1875.

As with all garrisons, the 'wives' have always been an important factor in Woolwich history. Although few would have gone as far as General Belfield, the Commander in 1777, who suggested that the wives of absent officers might move into vacant rooms in the newly built barracks. He maintained that it would thereby help to keep out the damp. Not surprisingly others were more sceptical and his idea was never implemented. For the most part the official attitude to the wives of Woolwich was the same as that of the rest of the Army. There were the usual quota of official camp followers, and other permitted wives, chosen by lot and 'on the strength'. These were allowed to accompany their husbands when posted overseas, and for them life was passable, even if it would not seem so today. For those left behind it was far from tolerable as they were without status and without any means of support. Certain of the Woolwich families connected with the Army used to provide financial assistance for as many of the Army families as possible, in order to purchase the passage for them to join their husbands. As the regiment could be absent for up to ten years this would appear to be a worthwhile and humane act, however the more worldly might also point out that the greater the number of wives accompanying their husbands the fewer that remained at home to require Poor Relief. One wonders whether some of the soldiers might have preferred their wives to have stayed in Woolwich as this typical little Victorian verse from 1848 implies . . .

Lines

Addressed to Soldiers on Foreign Service who neglect their Wives and Families at Home.

Behold, stern Winter now appears in sight;
Adieu, fair Flora, and your beauties bright;
· · ·
But, oh, there's worse than winter's icy hand
Now pressing sadly on our favour'd land,
Grim Poverty its death-like gloom has cast,
And human beings fade beneath the blast.
See yonder matron, sorrowing all alone,
On her the bitter blast has sadly blown;
Deprived of all that sweetens mortal life,
We here behold the absent soldier's wife.
She meets the winter with increasing dread,
While her poor children cry aloud for bread.
Say, can fam'd Woolwich, with its grand display,
To such a bosom one soft charm convey?
Nor can the Thames, whose waters sweetly flow,
Do ought but tend to aggravate her woe;
On it she saw the stately vessel move
That bore away the object of her love,
Whilst she remain'd her troubles to bemoan,
Robb'd of her husband, happiness, and home!
· · ·
Natives of Woolwich, I appeal to you,
I ask you, friends, is not my statement true?
Does it not hard upon your income press,
So many soldiers' families in distress?
· · ·
You unkind husbands are you not to blame?
While you can take the fatal glass in hand,
And seem quite happy in a foreign land;
Regardless of your families' great distress,
And never sending them the least redress.
· · ·
If soldiers can their families neglect
What may our country from such men expect.[9]

There were sad wives of another type to be found in Woolwich as well as those 'abandoned'. These were the ones who had returned to Woolwich from far away exotic places for the sake of their children, leaving their hubands behind in the sun. These wives lived a far from exciting life in drab lodgings, just waiting for the time to pass.

Again, in *Woolwich Story*; Jefferson provides us with a lively description of what life must have been like in the 1880s. Even on ordinary weekends soldiers were not allowed to 'walk-out' unless properly dressed in their 'regimentals'. What a bright and cheerful place Woolwich must have been with each regiment sporting a different coloured uniform, watched over by the scarlet-capped military police. Jefferson also reveals some acute observation of the soldiers' smoking habits. He tells how their matches were always stored in their headgear, no matter whether 'Busby' or 'Pill box' and that the 'Woodbines' or 'Weights' were always tucked between the middle buttons of the tunic as it was a great crime to spoil the shape of their outline. He goes on to show why the display was so important . . .

> And neither do the girls go singly but generally in twos: for there is safety in numbers. They cannot resist the uniform but they have to be careful whether it be a trip over the ferry to Victoria gardens or a nice long walk to Hanging Wood lane just over in Charlton. At a shilling a day the 'rookie' infantryman has not much to spend but, bless you, the girls do not expect it, unless they are the designing ones; and they go for the Cavalry or Horse Artillery at one shilling and fourpence a day, or for the man with a stripe or two.[10]

Living in Woolwich provided entertainment for the ordinary civilian children apart from the more formal parades and reviews. For example, in 1908 the 1st Woolwich Scout Troop was formed at the Wesleyan Soldiers' Home. So much 'returned' Boer War supplies and other 'surplus' kit was provided for the boys that they and countless others all over the country, resembled diminutive veterans of the South African war, and indeed continued to look like it for many years. Their staves came from the Service Corps Carpenters' Shop while the Engineers provided maps and compasses and a sergeant who taught drill and 'knotting and lashing'. The garrison warden provided two bell tents, and other camp equipment. When they had their first official inspection the military police controlled the crowd, but it appears they had a far harder task controlling it when there was an official visit from Buffalo Bill at around the same time.

During the nineteenth century Britain was faced by a demand for a whole range of political and social reforms. While many measures were passed, these appeared to many people to be too slow and too few. One of the manifestations of this desire for change was the 'Great Charter'. The six points of the Chartists were considered positively revolutionary at the time although all (except annual elections) seem quite reasonable today. The final Chartist upheaval took place in the early summer of 1848. The actual signing of the charter had always been an issue of some contention especially as Queen Victoria, the Duke of Wellington and Mr Punch were all seemingly prevailed upon to sign it! Even George McDonald Frazer's 'Flashman' claimed to have signed it several times.

During April and June of that year it was the intention of the Chartists to present their great petition to Parliament as the climax of a great procession that would form up at Kennington, south of the River Thames and, some feared, within striking distance of the great Arsenal at Woolwich. So concerned was the Government of the day that the Iron Duke himself was called out of retirement to advise and to co-ordinate and control the defences of London. Large numbers of Special Constables were enrolled and the Military Pensioners were called up from Chelsea and Greenwich. The Cavalry, Guards and other infantry in London were prepared as were the Kent garrisons including Woolwich.

The Duke of Wellington was convinced that the key to controlling such large numbers in the city was to hold the open spaces, thus ensuring the mobility of his troops and at the same time preventing large crowds from gathering. Consequently the Cavalry and Guards were held ready but out of sight in their barracks which, with commendable forethought had for the most part been built on the edges of the larger London parks. The Pensioners were held in reserve at the Tower of London. On Sunday 9 April, the Sappers and Miners from Woolwich were sent to the Bank of England to put up breastworks and barricades of sandbags. The Duke's plan was to avoid provocation by keeping the troops in reserve and to allow the police to maintain contact with the procession. This plan was followed.

However, it was decided to supplement the London troops with artillery from Woolwich and more marines and infantry were called in from Chatham and Dover.

According to *The Kentish Independent* for the week beginning 10 April 1848, an entire regiment of Artillery was assembled on Woolwich Common for inspection by Lieutenant General Sir Thomas Downan before they left for London. All went well with the inspection of the regiment and its equipment and the General had expressed himself well pleased with their turn-out when there was a near fatal accident. One of the officers' horses bolted and he was almost trampled to death when it threw him in front of a galloping troop of Horse Artillery. Shortly afterwards the Field Train Department at Woolwich was ordered to prepare five more batteries for immediate departure for the Capital. The *Kentish Independent* again records:

> An order was received at Woolwich on Monday evening from the Master General and Board of Ordnance directing the Commissary of the Field Train Department to prepare for immediate service, five field batteries consisting of three nine pounder brass guns, and one twenty-four pounder brass howitzer to each battery, with carriages, ammunition, waggons, and acoutrements complete. The Artillery were engaged on Tuesday under the direction of Mr Young the Commissary in packing the batteries, which were complete at five o'clock in the evening, ready at a moments notice to be removed to Ireland or to the Metropolis, as occasion may require.

The batteries are subsequently reported as arriving in Central London and dispersing to their allocated positions. What the paper does not relate, but the *History of the Royal Regiment of Artillery 1815-1853* does, is that the batteries were so out of practice that one of the troops only managed to reach as far as Hanging Woods on the edge of the next village. There the road begins to climb up towards Blackheath, and the troop was unable to make it up the hill; their gun stuck fast, and they were unable to go any further.[11] History does not name the unfortunate troop, merely telling us that their gunners, drivers and officers had to be withdrawn and another troop substituted. In the event the day passed off quietly enough and all the troops were returned to their barracks untested. What would have been the outcome if this early example of Military Aid to the Civil Power had been put into effect can only be surmised and perhaps it is fortunate that it was never necessary. Certainly there were fears that Chartists or other agitators would try to influence the troops in their stations all over Britain. It was said that there were police reports on subversive talk from soldiers including a party of 12 Scots Fusilier Guards who signed the Charter and said that they would not fire on the people. These unfortunate twelve were supposed to have met in a public house and were overheard by the landlord who reported them.

Orders were published banning the civilians from military canteens and in Woolwich in particular contact between soldiers and civilians was reduced as much as possible. The Arsenal was also considered to be a likely target for Chartist attack and civilian guards were increased or replaced by the military under the control of an officer and the whole area completely closed to the public. There were several reports of suspicious characters loitering near the wall, but there are no reports of sabotage or of anyone being arrested inside the Arsenal or nearby. A far more serious threat was posed by a disgruntled public, denied access to their favourite free entertainment, and many complained loudly to the Arsenal authorities and to the local press to have the ban lifted.

Shipping artillery horses for the Crimea.

The piers at Woolwich have themselves borne witness to a long association with the military. Built and extended during the nineteenth century by Sappers and convict labour from the nearby Hulks, countless numbers of young men embarked from them to fight for their country overseas. Woolwich saw them leave for the Crimea, for India and for South Africa, and for the very many theatres of the First and Second World Wars. Many people in Woolwich still remember the sight of troopships alongside the Arsenal loading and unloading men and equipment. For the Artillery, as for the Marines and the Sappers, even though Woolwich was their home their most important adventures happened away from the garrison. It would never do, however, to lose sight of the role which Woolwich played in their support and nurture.

Perhaps the most lively descriptions of life in the garrison early this century come from Ruby Ferguson, daughter of the Chaplain to 'The Shop' before the First World

War. In her book *Children at the Shop* we can experience all the excitement felt in the town (at least by the children) and what Edwardian life was like for the military and town alike. The event she describes below is believed to be the departure of the Gloucesters for India in 1910:

> Through the town streets we went, running beside the column, and the traffic pulled out of the way into the side turnings. You felt you were part of it, that it wouldn't be the same unless you were all in it, a solid mass of people laughing and waving and making a big thing of it. The soldiers liked it too, they couldn't help liking such a send off, showing them how fine they were, how much their country cared. Sunshine and noise and clamour and fun. Union Jacks waving and the ring of their boots on the paved street, and the sense of being important, and the anticipation of a voyage and a landing and a wider life. Sunshine to see them off, and hotter sunshine still to come. They carried their sixty-pound packs as though they were feather pillows. They owned the town today, they owned half the world, they were the British Army.[12]

Bibliography

The Woolwich Story, E. F. E. Jefferson, The R.A. Printing Press, Woolwich, 1970

Children at the Shop, Ruby Ferguson, Hodder and Stoughton, London, 1930

Records of the Woolwich District, Vincent, at the Woodlands Local History Library, London Borough of Greenwich

The Royal Arsenal, Woolwich, a brochure by Wesley Harry, printed for the Ministry of Defence, PR Dept. March 1984

The Story of the Royal Regiment of Artillery (6th Edition), Brigadier C. A. L. Graham. DSO., R.A. Institute, Woolwich, 1962

THE NEW MILITARY TOWNS

7

Aldershot: Home of the British Army

PETER DIETZ

UNLIKE most of the other towns described in this book Aldershot has always appeared to be a place dominated by military personalities. That is not to say that York or Edinburgh have not produced famous men nor have they necessarily lacked strong men able to stamp their mark on local history. This book is full of colourful characters inhabiting all of the fortresses, garrisons and military settlements which we investigate, but in these other towns there is almost always an exterior reason for their existence. Usually the location of a military town has a geographical origin or some politico-strategic consideration dictates the necessity for a permanent garrison. The strategic *raison d'être* for the existence of Aldershot Camp cannot have been so overriding as that for York or Chatham or even Rheindahlen but the whims and pleasures of powerful men seem to have dictated the course of Aldershot's development to a greater extent than in most other military settlements.

The necessity, in the mid-nineteenth century, for a training area where large military formations could be exercised could have been met in a number of other places. That the selected area should provide a concentration zone between London and the south coast, across the likely invasion routes might still have indicated a different location perhaps to the south or south-east of London. However, in 1852 the Duke of Wellington, Commander-in-Chief of the Army since 1815, finally died, leaving the position of respected advisor on all things military to his good friend Albert, the Prince Consort. Albert had many interests. As an educated man he was concerned with the arts and sciences, with commerce, with learning and with the proper defence of his adopted country. Like many continental rulers he had taken a dilettante interest in military matters but from the time of his arrival in England, in February 1840 for his marriage to Queen Victoria, this interest became more serious, almost to the point of obsession. He was met at Dover and escorted to London by the 11th Light Dragoons commanded by Lord Cardigan. Cardigan was already known to the general public, and especially the London public, as a martinet, a military dandy and a notorious duellist, but all this would be forgotten by the fickle crowds in the glory of the 'Light Brigade' charge at Balaclava, which he led. But even at his most controversial

Cardigan had a reputation as a 'good soldier' and an efficient trainer of cavalry at least in their somewhat stilted parade ground manoeuvres. In October 1839, the Duke of Wellington, as a guest of Lord Cardigan, saw the 11th at exercise and was very impressed. It was no doubt this exhibition which led him to select Cardigan and his regiment to escort the Prince. Cardigan made good use of his opportunity. The Prince became Colonel-in-Chief of the regiment, and its name was changed from 11th Light Dragoons to the much more prestigious 11th (Prince Albert's Own) Hussars. On the change of designation a new uniform was naturally called for and the Prince who again, like so many European rulers, took a great interest in military finery, was no doubt called upon to advise and approve. The final result must have been magnificent. They wore overalls of cherry colour, jackets of royal blue edged with gold, short coats worn as capes swathed with braid and gold lace, and fur hats adorned with brilliant plumes. *The Times* reported: 'The brevity of their jackets, the irrationality of their headgear, the incredible tightness of their cherry-coloured pants, altogether defy description . . .'. Cardigan paid for most of this display himself and he was estimated to spend at least £10,000 a year of his own money on the regiment. It is just possible that he also spoke to the Prince about more serious military matters.[1]

In any event the Consort began to take a more professional interest in the Army, and under the tutelage of his friend Colonel William Knollys, he attended battalion field days in Hyde Park and became quite proficient in the minutia of training and tactical exercises. So successful was this instruction that the Great Duke himself, towards the end of his life, begged Albert to take over from him as Commander-in-Chief. The Consort, always the target of jealousy and suspicion, wisely refused, but he did continue to take a profound and informed interest in things military. The death of Wellington allowed many schemes for more efficient training and even for some degree of army reform to be taken out of the pigeon holes to which they had been consigned during his lifetime. In 1852, just before Wellington's death, a training camp had been set up at Chobham where, on the open heathlands, battalion exercises could take place in reasonably realistic conditions. Chobham was only a few miles from Windsor and Prince Albert was a regular visitor to the camp. The Prince was familiar with the vast manoeuvres which took place on the Continent where the interests of the Army took precedence over the rights of landowners and the protests of a servile peasantry. He was easily convinced that a larger exercise area was required where formations up to brigade or even divisional strength could be trained.

The problem assumed some urgency after the *coup d'état* of Louis Napoleon in December 1851 and even more so after he was proclaimed Emperor Napoleon III of France in 1852. The British Generals, and certainly the more senior ones most of whom, including the new Commander-in-Chief Lord Hardinge, had fought the French with Wellington in the Peninsula and at Waterloo and recognised no other enemy, were going through one of their periodic and usually groundless invasion scares. A concentration area not too distant from London and the Channel Ports which could also be used for advanced training suddenly seemed desirable and attainable with royal support. Without the Iron Duke to pour scorn on the idea of a French invasion or to oppose any kind of military innovation Lord Hardinge and his staff took to their horses and began to scour the countryside for a likely site for their grand camp. We do not know what alternative sites were reconnoitred but Hardinge, after staying for several nights at the Red Lion Inn at Aldershot, and after thoroughly exploring the area, wrote to Prince Albert recommending Aldershot as a site for a permanent camp for the Army. In a detailed memorandum he put forward a plan for the purchase of ten thousand acres which he believed local land-owners would sell at £12 an acre. He pointed out to Albert that by using the railways, another of the Prince's advanced ideas, it would be possible to concentrate a large military force on the site and, what may have been more important for Albert, it was easily accessible from London.

The Prince Consort could see that the next war was likely to be against the Russians and not the French and he pressed the Government to proceed with the camp at Aldershot at all speed. One hundred thousand pounds had already been allocated for the camp when war was declared in March 1854. Albert immediately urged the War Office to 'strike whilst the iron is hot, you can now ask Parliament for anything you want'. In the then prevailing atmosphere of war fever and patriotic self-sacrifice there could be no opposition to a centre where the troops could be properly trained for 'modern' warfare. The War Office was quick to take advantage of a mood in the country which would allow them to make up for the complete neglect of the armed forces ever since Waterloo. Starting as orderly rows of tents rather in the style of the classic military camp, the Aldershot heathland was quickly transformed into a wild shanty town. Twelve hundred huts of wood and brick were erected in the midst of a quagmire of unmade roads and tracks constantly churned and fouled by the hundreds of horses hauling materials on the site. The plan of the camp, obscured by the construction yards and the labourers' shanties and shelters, resembled so we are told, a mixture of the contemporary Californian gold mining boom town and the sordid railway construction camps which sprang up and disappeared overnight in the first great period of railway building. To make matters worse the winter of 1854 was reckoned to be the coldest of the century, and as with the construction of the Headquarters camp at Rheindahlen almost exactly one hundred years later, the exceptionally severe weather caused chaos and delay. As an aside, one wonders if these battles with the elements are an essential part of the legend of every great construction programme, incorporated into the mythology in order to emphasise the titanic nature of the enterprise. Be that as it may, whilst labourers were laid off and forced to move into the nearby towns and villages in order to keep warm, cavalry had to be sent from Aldershot as far as Bristol and elsewhere to put down unrest caused by the very cold weather and an unprecedented rise in the price of coal to two shillings and threepence a hundredweight.

Before Lord Hardinge's descent on an unsuspecting Aldershot it was a small village nearly four miles from Farnham with three 'gentry' families, a few farmers and two inns, the Red Lion patronised by the General and his staff and the Beehive. Happily, both inns survive albeit in reconstructed form. In 1850 Aldershot had a population of less than one thousand souls. Over the next hundred years the population was to increase more than thirty fold but the military presence has dominated the town from the time the first tented camp appeared on the low hills to the north right up to the present day. When the camp in the near future completes its long drawn out rebuild it will house as many people as the civilian part of the town in the new accommodation which will have finally replaced the last of the permanent barracks and office blocks, some of which have survived almost since the Crimean War.

By the mid eighteen-fifties Aldershot was a boom town, vying with the other small local towns to provide for the requirements of the troops and the army of construction workers in the camp who, at their peak, exceeded 3,000 men. Their wants were basic. Aldershot, especially, became a collection of drinking shops, cheap saloons, dance halls and brothels, given up almost entirely to separating the soldiers and workmen from their pay through the medium of drink and prostitution. These twin evils were certainly not new to the Army nor indeed to the construction camps where workmen could earn three or four times a soldier's pay, but their appearance in rural Hampshire on such a scale and at such a tumultuous pace must have seemed like a vision of the apocalypse to many of the original inhabitants. John Walters in his book *Aldershot Review* quotes from a description by Mrs Ewing, an eyewitness of the devastation caused by the building of the camp:

> Take a highwayman's heath. Destroy every vestige of life with fire and axes, from the pine which has longest been a landmark, to the smallest beetle smothered in smoking moss. Burn acres of purple and pink heather, pare away the young bracken that springs verdant from its ashes. Let flame consume the perfumed gorse in all its glory and not spare the broom, whose more exquisite yellow atones for its lack of fragrance . . . by some such recipe the ground was prepared for the Camp of Construction.

And all this before the real evil had properly taken root! Mrs Ewing's outcry was, at that early stage in the camp's history, only concerned with the physical destruction of the wild heathland. The social and moral effects were still to come and are also fully described in John Walter's book:

> By day the workers toiled, while the troops marched and drilled. By night the ramshackle quarters of the traders, of the drink and vice vendors, became illuminated by oil lamps and flares. The thousands of soldiers and workers flocked towards these for their off-duty fun and recreation.
>
> Many of the drink shops, put roughly together with canvas, wood or sheets of zinc, had a large area behind the bar separated by a curtain. Here there were rows of chairs and a platform where variety artists appeared. Comedians cracked dirty jokes and bawled dirty songs. Women and girls, often billed as 'songstresses' or 'chanteuses', shrieked popular songs and, in dancing, saucily flipped up their skirts to reveal their long lacy drawers. There were clog dancers, acrobats, conjurors, usually cavorting to the background music of a few brass instruments. The area was to the crude labourer and soldier a sexual paradise, but too often leading to a sexual hell . . . Nearby were 'love tents' to which the prostitutes led the men who had been successfully solicited . . .[2]

Walters goes on to detail the real price paid for the debauchery and sordid commerce in terms of rampant venereal disease, bastardy and the break-up of family and village life. In Victorian England drink, dance halls and prostitution were to be found in every port and in all large towns and, rightly or wrongly, soldiers and sailors were the natural scapegoats for the consequences. The hypocrisy and commercialism of the age allowed these evils to continue, and the underworld of vice penetrated every social class. The common practice of introducing prostitutes into the officers' quarters in Aldershot, and elsewhere, is well documented right up to the outbreak of the First World War. In the end the toll taken by disease caused such concern that the 'Contagious Diseases Prevention Act' of 1864 extended the jurisdiction of the Army

Medical Department, for the control of venereal diseases, from the garrisons to the principal towns frequented by troops — Aldershot, Chatham, Colchester, Cork, The Curragh, Plymouth, Queenstown and Woolwich. The Act provided for the compulsory treatment and hospitalisation of known prostitutes provided they refused to undergo treatment voluntarily after being found 'diseased' at an examination at a 'Certified Hospital' to which they could be directed. Double standards were applied in a situation in which the men involved were merely seen as conforming to the stereotype of the 'brutal and licentious soldier' whilst the unfortunate women were regarded as a menace to the security of the nation through their undermining of the fighting strength of the armed forces.[3]

The sordid and rabelaisian night life of Aldershot did not deter the Prince Consort from his interest in what was in reality his creation, and the Queen herself quickly developed a liking for military spectacle. She frequently attended reviews with Albert and observed the exercises and field days from her carriage. Albert's friend, Sir William Knollys, by now a Lieutenant General was appointed as the first Commander of the camp and together they planned the construction of a pavilion where the Queen could sleep when she came to visit her army at Aldershot. At the time the completed pavilion was described in *The Illustrated London News* as 'bald, cold and ugly to the extreme', but when the landscaping was completed it came to be accepted as one of the landmarks of the camp and survived until it was dismantled in the nineteen-fifties to make room for the QARANC Depot and Training Centre. The Royal Pavilion was completed and ready for use by the end of April 1856 and on the 26th of that month the Queen and Prince Albert dined and spent their first night there. Gradually the Pavilion was filled up with *objets* and bric-à-brac from Windsor and the Royal couple began to feel very much at home in what had started off as a convenient rest station when visiting the camp.

Prince Albert's early and concerned interest in the camp at Aldershot was shown in a number of ways but perhaps most typical of him was his gift in 1859 to the officers of the camp of a collection of a thousand books and the provision of a suitable library in which to house them. An article in *Torch*, the journal of The Royal Army Educational Corps, for Winter 1981, gives an account of the setting up of the Prince Consort's Library:

> One of the first brick buildings erected in the camp was the Prince Consort's Library . . . In discussing the site for the Library he stated his desire to see the building surrounded by grass, trees and shrubs since the camp area suffered under clouds of dust rising from the Long Valley and Laffans Plain.
>
> The Library was designed by Captain Francis Fowke, Royal Engineers, and was built between September 1859 and September 1860. Captain Fowke was subsequently to become famous as the designer of the Edinburgh Museum of Science and Art, the Dublin National Gallery and the Royal Albert Hall. The total cost of the building, furnishings, landscaping and additional books was £4,183 8s. 4d. Until 1935 the Privy Purse bore the cost of maintenance of the Library whilst the Aldershot Military Society provided money for more books. Since that date the Library has been under the charge of the Director of Army Education.[4]

Development of the camp and the town kept pace with each other. Camp amenities

The Prince Consort's Library, opened in 1859, has changed little since that date.

soon included three churches, the Victoria Soldiers' Library (in addition to the Prince Consort's Library), an officers' club, riding schools, a musical society and a theatre. In the town, apart from the dubious amenities which we have already described, private builders bought up plots of land for the building of shops and houses and High Street, Wellington Street, Victoria Street and Union Street were all well under way by the end of the Crimean War. The returning regiments with their accumulated pay added to the growth and prosperity of the town and already there was a movement of the more respectable or more prosperous middle classes away from the town centre towards the quieter, more salubrious small towns and villages outside the immediate camp area.

Because of its sheer size as a military garrison, and the innovation of a military town built virtually 'from scratch', Aldershot was inevitably caught up in the military reform movement which gained support from the end of the Crimean War. But even before the military reformers came to grips with the Army it was taken to task by the 'Peace Society' whose aim was to show up military misdemeanours like the vice and debauchery associated with the camp at Aldershot. The Peace Society believed that the only way to save society from these evils was to disband the Army completely. The Society's reaction to Aldershot was reported in the *Morning Star* of 25 August 1859:

> The sum of the contrast is, everyone of the 4,000 people in Aldershot Town is at work, and in earnest, while Aldershot Camp is an organisation of idleness 20,000 strong.

This was an example of double standards at their worst and the Peace Society could make very little headway with these sentiments in places like Aldershot where the 'earnest work' of the townspeople depended for its profit on the appetites of the soldiery. Army reform was another matter and whilst many soldiers, although not all, and a considerable number of officers were in favour of the abolition of flogging, the rationalisation of uniforms, better pay and more humane living conditions, reform was seen as divisive at best and subversive in its methods. When General Sir William Napier was approached by the Army Reform Association he summed up the reaction of most senior officers by saying:

> If the persons composing the Society are military their proceeding is an act of grave insubordination; if they are civilians, they are incompetent persons, perniciously meddling with what they do not understand.[5]

It is true, and could hardly be otherwise, that most senior officers were paternalistic in their attitude towards their men. Field Marshal Sir Evelyn Wood, VC, perhaps unwittingly, gives an example of how paternalism can be made to look caring and humane beside the somewhat cynical and world weary attitude that he himself betrays at times in his autobiography. At least Evelyn Wood tells the story against himself. In 1869 Wood became Deputy Assistant Adjutant General in the South Camp Headquarters of General Sir James Yorke Scarlett. Sir James had led the Heavy Brigade charge at Balaclava which routed a much larger force of Russian Cavalry which was advancing down a hillside towards them. This action would probably have become the most acclaimed feat of arms of the whole Crimean War if the British habit of regarding every great disaster as a glorious victory had not intervened. Thus the brave but incredibly bungled charge of the Light Brigade is remembered above all else. Both Sir James and Lady Yorke Scarlett had considerable private fortunes and since they were both Christians in the real sense of the word, they indulged in many acts of unobtrusive charity. Evelyn Wood recalls:

> When I had been under his Command for some time I thought it my duty to point out the result of one of his many charities . . . Sir James used to pay for a cab for every woman leaving the maternity hospital, and I told him the moment the cab put the woman down at her hut on the eighth day after her baby was born, she took up her basket and walked into the town to make good the week's marketing. Said he, 'What a capital thing to save her one journey'.

Wood tells another story of General Scarlett and incidentally, describes the 'military games' indulged in during the exercises in the new training area.

> Sir James was as usual leading a line of skirmishers of one force against another, many yards in front, as he had led the Heavy Brigade at Balaclava . . . Sir James was leading an attack up the Fox Hills, near Mitchet Lake, and with cocked hat in hand was cheering on the troops. Three times I respectfully pointed out that he was very far forward, to be rebuffed only with a curt expression beginning with an oath. On the third occasion he turned round and said, 'Young man have I not ordered you twice to hold your tongue? If I like to lead my skirmishers what the . . . is that to you?' Said I most respectfully, 'Ten thousand pardons, sir, but it is the enemy's line in retreat you have been leading for the last ten minutes'. He was short sighted, and did not wear glasses, so was unable to see

the distinguishing mark, a sprig of heather worn in the shakos of the troops he was attacking.[6]

Sir Evelyn Wood himself went on to become a very distinguished GOC at Aldershot by which time he had no doubt learned to be rather less interfering. In the eighteen-eighties he was responsible for the reconstruction which replaced most of the remaining huts with stone and brick-built barrack blocks each designed to accommodate a complete company. He also swept away many unnecessary duties, especially at sentry posts which he gleefully discovered often served a purpose long since forgotten. Being one of Sir Garnett Wolseley's 'bright young men', and thus marked for a brilliant career, Wood was concerned to improve the efficiency of the army whilst also improving the living conditions, food and general welfare of the troops stationed at Aldershot. Unlike many of his contemporaries he actively sought the views and practical help of his service advisers. In his autobiography he tells of teaching shocked cavalry officers how to judge the quality of oats with the assistance of officers from the 'not quite top drawer' Army Service Corps. His ideas on training, especially his insistence upon night exercises and on large scale manoeuvres over unknown country were distinctly innovative. Although they were encouraged by Wolseley who was by now Adjutant General they brought him into direct conflict with the Commander-in-Chief, The Duke of Cambridge. Lord Hardinge, who had followed Wellington as Commander-in-Chief, suffered a stroke whilst accompanying the Queen on an inspection of returned Crimean veterans at Aldershot in July 1856, and died the following year. Cambridge, a cousin of the Queen, although not a senior general, had been given command of the 1st Division, made up of Guards and Highland Regiments, for the Crimean campaign.

Cambridge led his division bravely if not brilliantly but spoiled a good impression by returning to England in January 1855, after the Battle of the Alma but well before the war was over. He was said to have suffered a nervous and physical breakdown but he recovered within a few weeks of his return. Unfortunately he dallied in England instead of returning to his post in the Crimea. For a while he was out of favour with the Queen. However, when Lord Hardinge had to retire because of his ill-health the Duke of Cambridge emerged from a list of equally unsuitable candidates as the front runner for the post of Commander-in-Chief. The Prince Consort pointed out the dangers but many senior army officers wanted a Royal Commander-in-Chief. The Queen forwarded Hardinge's letter of resignation to Palmerston, the Prime Minister, saying at the same time that in her opinion George (The Duke of Cambridge) 'was almost without a competitor'. This no doubt clinched the matter. But Cambridge was only appointed 'General, Commanding-in-Chief', not Commander-in-Chief since he was not at the top of the Army List. He had to wait, with increasing impatience, for the full honour for another thirty-one years until 1887 and the Queen's Golden Jubilee, by which time he had completed fifty years of army service. By the eighteen-eighties the Duke of Cambridge had assumed the full mantle of his illustrious predecessor, the Iron Duke. He gained the same reputation as Wellington in his later years for opposition to every change and for his insistence on being consulted on even the smallest matter concerning the Army. Like Wellington he remained popular with the senior officers and old soldiers, many of whom had fought with him in the Crimea thirty years earlier. His advocacy of outdated cavalry tactics and his obdurate dislike, often outspokenly expressed, of 'staff college graduates' and indeed all 'educated' officers, nevertheless tended to make him a laughing stock amongst the young and an easy target for cartoonists and anti-army journalists.[7]

Unlike Wellington, however, the Duke of Cambridge had never opposed the setting up of the field training area at Aldershot. Wellington, in true eighteenth-century style, had opposed the bringing together of large bodies of troops for training because he was convinced that the public, even in the middle of the nineteenth-century were violently anti-army, and the sight of large bodies of troops would lead to calls for their reduction or complete abolition. Sadly, he did not live to see his opinion refuted first at Chobham and later at Aldershot where the public almost immediately displayed that great interest in military spectacles, parades, exercises, reviews and sham battles that led to the inauguration of the biggest military entertainment of all, the tattoo. The Duke of Cambridge very much enjoyed the reviews and field days at Aldershot and he continued to attend them up to and even after his retirement in 1895 by which time he was probably one of the best known and certainly most easily recognised visitor to the town and camp. He had opposed the appointment of Wood as GOC at Aldershot because of his reputation as an ardent reformer but he was overruled by the Secretary of State. Despite Wood's interest in the soldiers' welfare and his membership of the so-called 'Garnett Ring', Wolseley's band of 'Young Turks', he combined in himself an odd mixture of the forward-looking military innovator and the brave but reactionary country squire who like so many officers who won the Peninsular War for Wellington were equally happy following the Duke's fox hounds between battles.

Horses and hunting were an obsession with Wood and his pursuit of these two passions was only restricted by his comparatively limited income. His pleasure in being posted to Aldershot, the most important Major General's command in the Army, was very much enhanced, he says in his autobiography, first by the number of Royal visits he received there and secondly by the opportunities to ride and to hunt which the locality provided. He was firmly convinced that to ride across country was one of the best forms of officer training and he would never accept that there would be no place in future battles for the mounted soldier. When he retired in 1904 he was probably the last of his line. Like his contemporary and fellow protégé of Wolseley, Redvers Buller, he really did regard the Army more as a very congenial way of life than as a serious vocation. Like Buller he had been selected and 'brought on' by Wolseley who admired their intelligence and charisma. They had both done well in the minor wars in which they had been involved but they were essentially men of the nineteenth century as indeed was Wolseley although with perhaps more dedication to his profession. Evelyn Wood did not have to face the challenge of modern war against a European enemy but Buller was not so lucky. When he took over from Wood as GOC at Aldershot he was probably the most popular soldier in the Army and in the country. His reputation was based on his dashing performance in the Ashanti and Zulu Wars but also on his genuine concern for the well-being of his men. Unfortunately his reputation as a strategist, planner and military thinker had become somewhat inflated over the years and only reluctantly did he agree to take over the command in South Africa in 1899. By then he was very much overweight and given to eating and drinking in a manner that might have suited the bucolic Devonshire squire that he eventually became. At sixty he was probably aware of his own limitations but he could not escape from his responsibilities nor from the false reputation which he had inadvertently earned. In South Africa, after a series of costly defeats and equally costly victories he was superseded by Lord Roberts who was made Commander-in-Chief with Kitchener as his Chief-of-Staff. On his return to England Buller took up his appointment again at Aldershot whilst Roberts returned to become Commander-in-Chief of the British Army. Buller could not understand or accept what had happened to him in South Africa and after a series of acrimonious confrontations with the Press and eventually with the Minister for War he was retired on half pay. An appeal to the King was rejected and the banishment confirmed. Despite his sorry performance Buller had been welcomed back to England as a hero by the people of his native West Country and even more enthusiastically by the garrison and the ordinary people of Aldershot town. As John Walters says, 'Aldershot townsfolk crowded towards Government House, trying to show their affectionate sympathy to Sir Redvers and Lady Audrey. Letters reached Buller by the sack load. These, it was reported, came mostly from working folk and many relatives of soldiers'. Protests and petitions against his dismissal were organised in many towns and when he left Aldershot for his Devonshire home he was still one of the most popular soldiers in Britain. It had been left to a largely uninformed British public to sense that Buller had been given a task which he had only reluctantly accepted but also a task which in the immediate circumstances of 1899 was almost impossible.

After Evelyn Wood and Redvers Buller Aldershot became more and more caught up in the reforms and reorganisation introduced by Lord Haldane as Minister for War in the Liberal Government that swept to power in 1906. French, Smith-Dorrien and Haig all commanded at Aldershot in the period between the Boer War and the First World War and all left their particular mark on the camp. General Sir John French who followed Buller was, like so many of his predecessors, a cavalry officer and had gained his experience of war and his reputation as commander of the Cavalry Division in Natal. By the time he left Aldershot in 1907 to become Inspector General of the Forces he had seen the arrival for military use of the motor car and the aeroplane although it is likely that he disapproved of both pieces of equipment. The reforming spirit of Campbell-Bannerman's Government was seen in many areas but none more obviously than in military matters. Haldane says in his autobiography, of his first interview with the Generals of the Army Council, 'After a short talk the leader said to me that they all felt they would like to have some general idea of the reforms which I thought of proposing to Parliament. My reply was that I was a young and blushing virgin just united to a bronzed warrior, and that it was not expected by the public that any result of the union should appear until at least nine months had passed'.[8] Nevertheless he threw himself into the work and reforms came thick and fast, many of them correcting faults which emerged in the Boer War and some even tackling for a second time deficiencies and lack of organisation which had become apparent during the Crimean War. Some of these defects, dating back fifty years and more, had been tackled but not completely remedied by Cardwell's equally famous reforms in the eighteen seventies.

Aldershot, being what it was and where it was, saw much of these changes and no doubt it heard much about them too since there were still many officers reluctant to leave the well-trodden parade grounds and exercise fields of the nineteenth century. These reforms saw the end of the old volunteer and militia forces and the setting up of the new Territorial Forces and the planning and construction of the Expeditionary Force. The first two divisions of the force were based on Aldershot and were the first to go to France in August 1914. But it was the will to accept new ideas and at least to give them a fair trial that brought a somewhat supercilious General French his first staff car. It was the acceptance of change, however reluctantly, which also encouraged him to find room on Laffans Plain for the experimental kite and aeroplane flights of the somewhat eccentric 'Colonel' Samuel F. Cody. The Royal Engineers Balloon Unit moved from Chatham to Aldershot in 1899 and was there in time to assist Monsieur Caudron with the first parachute jump over the camp on August Bank Holiday 1899. Cody was attached to the War Department Balloon Factory and School at Farnborough and he and two of his sons were appointed as instructors to the Kite Section of the Royal Engineers when it was formed in 1904. Cody, although a flamboyant figure, who to the delight of the soldiery and the citizens of Aldershot rode a white horse and wore 'buckskins' in the manner of Buffalo Bill, was an inventor and an engineer of genius. He soon fitted an engine to a kite and managed a four-minute unmanned flight. After this, at the suggestion of Colonel Capper, RE, the Commandant of the Balloon School, he turned his attention to powering balloons. By 1907 Cody had fitted a French engine to a balloon produced at the Balloon School which was 122 feet long and 26 feet in diameter. He and Colonel Capper first flew the dirigible over Aldershot then later it cruised at sixteen miles an hour over Buckingham Palace to the surprised pleasure of King Edward and Queen Alexandra. In the same year Cody, who was impressed with the experimental flights being made in America by the Wright Brothers, persuaded the War Office to give him a grant of fifty pounds to build a heavier than air machine. The War Office, prudent as ever even in an era of change and innovation, did not give enough money to pay for an engine so Cody adapted the engine from his successful dirigible. At first Cody could not get his machine off the ground and was forced to endure insults in the newspapers and from those members of the military who, whilst they could see little else, were quick to realise that his machine might in the future frighten their horses right off the battlefield. Eventually, in May 1908 he managed a convincing flight and a tablet on a tree at Farnborough commemorates the event as '. . . the first successful officially recorded flight in Great Britain'. The Haldane reforms had been accepted by the House of Commons because, like military reforms before them and afterwards right up to the present day, they purported to save money. When it was found that aviation experiments had cost the nation £2,500 critics demanded an end to this senseless extravagance. Haldane himself travelled down to Aldershot to give Cody the bad news. But despite the War Office decision that there would be no place for the aeroplane over the battlefields of the future, Cody was allowed to keep his flying machine and to continue his experiments on Laffans Plain on a private basis. Cody went on with his work gaining in recognition and popularity. He took up Colonel Capper as the first passenger ever to be carried in an aeroplane in Britain, demonstrating once and for all the military usefulness of his machines. In 1912 he won a prize of £5,000 in competition with the world's best airmen and machines in the great Army Aeroplane Tests on Salisbury Plain. Tragically, Colonel Cody was killed in a flying accident in 1913 whilst preparing for a competition flight around Great Britain. One of his last passengers was General Sir Horace Smith-Dorrien who had taken over from General French as GOC, and was probably the first British General to fly in an aeroplane.

Smith-Dorrien does not tell us in his autobiography about his reaction to the flight.[9] However, John Walters in *Aldershot Review* says that the five years from 1907 to 1912, whilst Smith-Dorrien was GOC 'was probably the happiest period in the history of the Camp and Aldershot town'. Walters describes him as a happy extrovert, 'effervescing with the joy of life and with goodwill towards all men but also towards all horses'.[10] In his love of horses Smith-Dorrien harked back to that 'Golden Age' at the end of the previous century when 'Hunting Leave' was almost never refused, when daily duties finished at mid-day and wars were small, always against a coloured foe and always a long way away. For a while it seemed that the twentieth century might continue in the same way and that Edwardian England might turn out to be a less inhibited but equally 'solid' version of the Victorian 'hey day', at least as far as the Army and the citizens of Aldershot were concerned. A delightful passage from *Cider With Rosie* by Laurie Lee seems to sum up this far-off world where the picture is slightly blurred as though in an old sepia tinted photograph.

> The second encounter Mother always described as though it had never happened — in that special, morning, dream-telling voice that set it apart from all ordinary life. 'I was working at the time in a big red house at a place called Farnhamsurrey. On my Sundays off I used to go into Aldershot to visit my friend Amy Frost — Amy Hawkins that was, from Churchtown you know, before she got married, that is. Well, this particular Sunday I'd dressed up as usual, and I do think I looked a picture. I'd my smart lace-up boots, striped blouse and choker, a new bonnet, and crochet-work gloves. I got into Aldershot far too early so I just walked about for a bit. We'd had rain in the night and the streets were shining, and I was standing quite alone on the pavement. When suddenly round the corner, without any warning, marched a full-dress regiment of soldiers. I stood transfixed; all those men and just me; I didn't know where to look. The officer in front — he had beautiful whiskers — raised his sword and cried out 'Eyes right!' Then, would you believe, the drums started rolling, and the bagpipes started to play, and all those wonderful lads as they went swinging by snapped to attention and looked straight in my eyes. I stood all alone in my Sunday dress, it quite took my breath away. All those drums and pipes and that salute just for me — I just cried it was so exciting . . .'[11]

The scene remembered by Laurie's mother from before the First World War could no doubt be recalled by other Aldershot folk with a greater or lesser degree of accuracy. The great parades, and especially the Sunday Church Parades, which had to be held at different times for the different churches so that the onlookers could see at least two parades on the same morning, were a great attraction for the whole area, as they were in every garrison in Britain. Although the worst or perhaps the most obvious signs of vice and debauchery had, by this time, been removed from the town centre to certain notorious little areas, like the one in Ash Vale, drunken violence was still a problem especially late at night. Traditionally this had been dealt with by frequent, strong-arm, military piquets patrolling the streets of Aldershot, removing the trouble makers but only at the expense of much noise, disturbance and occasionally near riot. Smith-Dorrien was genuinely concerned, like Evelyn Wood, with the welfare of his soldiers but also about the peace and tranquility of the Aldershot streets. Against all the advice of town and barracks he removed the night patrols and put the soldiers on their honour, in a system worthy of Baden-Powell at his best, to restrain themselves and their comrades in the interests of the town and the fair name of the Army and their regiments. Against all the odds, and with only minor breaches his plan worked and the townsfolk slept quietly in their beds. When he left Aldershot Smith-Dorrien was give a letter from the Municipal Council thanking him for the marked improvement in the behaviour of the men in the streets and adding that since the abolition of the piquets, unseemly disturbances had become a thing of the past.[12] Smith-Dorrien was in all reality a very modest man, as Generals go, and many of his small reforms and improvements in the Camp went unnoticed until they were swallowed up in the gradually accelerating preparations for the Great War. However, one innovation that he prided himself on, and which became obvious to the inhabitants of the town, concerned the tattoos which had become a popular annual entertainment since their early beginnings in the Victorian parades, reviews and 'gallops past'. In 1907 the tattoos began to incorporate tableaux, spectacle and mock set-piece battles, some illuminated by torchlight. Before he left Aldershot Smith-Dorrien included the use of searchlights on a large scale in the displays thus, in his own words, 'greatly increasing their beauty'. When the entertainment was resumed after the war it was known as the 'Aldershot Searchlight Tattoo'.[13]

Douglas Haig took up the succession as GOC at Aldershot and the contrast with his predecessor was immediately apparent. Haig was introverted and withdrawn, an excellent staff officer who had worked well with Haldane at the War Office but who seemed to find difficulty in making personal contacts or in displaying warmth or human feelings. After his spell at the War Office he had gone to India as Chief-of-Staff and when he returned as GOC to Aldershot he brought with him, with some lack of sensitivity, a number of his Indian staff officers. Of course his staff officers were white but this influx from foreign parts was known amongst the wags and the prejudiced as the 'Hindu Invasion'. But by now all the military men believed that war with Germany was inevitable and the pace of preparation had become almost frantic, matched by the growing hysteria and anti-German sentiment of the civilians. French, Smith-Dorrien and Haig each had an important part to play in the early battles of the war, but French and Smith-Dorrien did not stay the course, and they were both given appointments in the UK after the first great battles in France. Haig, who had gone to France as a Corps Commander, took over as the British Commander-in-Chief of the Expeditionary Force from French in 1915 and stayed until the end. All three Generals had played a leading part in preparing the Expeditionary Force for war during their time in Aldershot and that early training, much of it seen around the town, contributed enormously to the success, painful and expensive as it certainly was, of the few British divisions in the vital early battles of Le Cateau, Mons and Ypres.

During the First World War Aldershot played a major role in the training, first of Kitchener's Army, the volunteer force which reinforced and eventually replaced the depleted divisions of the original Expeditionary Force, and then the great conscript armies of the later years of the war. Almost every newly raised battalion passed through Aldershot during the course of the war. The camp held large numbers of trainees and the town expanded once more to provide the entertainment and other facilities required by the troops.

After the war the enormous British Army was demobilised as quickly as possible whilst Aldershot town and camp reverted to a state not unlike that of the Edwardian era. A kind of lethargy settled over most things military in the nineteen-twenties during which some of the important lessons of the war were forgotten or not followed up. One of the more obvious changes in the post-war period was the continued replacement by mechanical transport of the horse-drawn waggons and artillery limbers of the Service Corps and the Gunners. This process which started during the Great War with the introduction of lorries and omnibuses, especially in France, continued slowly and coupled with the permanent introduction of armoured fighting vehicles bore some fruit in the 'Experimental Mechanised Force' formed in 1927.

The Mobile Forces were assembled at Salamanca Barracks, Aldershot and inspected by King George V in the same year, but even so, new tactics and new weapons were slow to gain acceptance. It was only after 1934, in the face of an aggressive Nazi rearmament programme which gave Germany a large and rapidly increasing tank army, that mechanisation and the formation of integrated tank forces became the agreed policy for the British Army also. Despite the speed-up in rearming our forces the last British cavalry regiment to be mechanised, 15th/19th The King's Royal Hussars, did not finally lose its horses until 1939.

Meanwhile the town of Aldershot was slowly expanding and in 1922 it was honoured by the grant of its Royal Charter as a Borough. The importance of the army in the affairs of the town was signified by the inclusion in the Council of three members nominated by the War Office. These nominated members were usually from the medical, engineering and administrative branches of the Aldershot Headquarters and whilst representing the interests of the Army and Army families on the Borough Council they would also bring to the Council a great deal of practical and professional experience. Although this was the first time that the Army had nominated councillors, the Headquarters had been represented on the local Board of Health ever since it was set up in 1857. Following the granting of the Charter the Borough Council was invited *en masse*, at Whitsun 1923, to a reception given by King George V at the Royal Pavilion.

In retrospect the inter-war period, short as it was, appears as a space of peace and sanity between two enormous cataclysms. The quiet, almost trivial life of the town and camp now seem as far way from reality as those halcyon days before the First World War. Tennis Clubs and cricket and John Betjeman's Miss J. Hunter Dunn, 'Furnish'd and burnish'd by Aldershot sun'. Even now, I suspect many of us will forget the parades and the rifle ranges and the lecture halls but still remember his 'roads not adopted and woodlanded ways . . . and nine o'clock Camberley, heavy with bells and mushroomy, pine-woody, evergreen smells'.[14] But Aldershot, like so many other garrison towns had its rude awakening. As National tensions increased interest in the Territorial Army revived and Air Defence became an everyday topic of conversation. Even the Aldershot Tattoos assumed a more important and more directly military purpose. They were more overtly concerned with pro-forces propaganda and with the encouragement of recruiting. Two themes that were regularly illustrated in the late nineteen-thirties tattoos were first, the Entente Cordiale, which was publicised by having a senior French General to take the salute, and second, the weakness of our air defences by showing a solid wall of searchlights with a prominent gap which remained to be filled by more recruits for the Territorial Army.[15]

The coming of the Second World War saw another period of intense activity in the Camp heralded by the arrival of the first conscripted 'Militiamen' brought in under the Compulsory Training Act of May 1939. This time, however, there had been no careful preparation for mobilisation and no smooth transfer of the Expeditionary Force to France. In 1914 it took only 14 days to get 4 Infantry Divisions and a Cavalry Division to France. In 1939 it was expected to take at least 33 days to get 4 Infantry Divisions and one Armoured Division across the Channel and in the event the Armoured Division never got there at all. It had still not arrived by the time of the German breakthrough and the evacuation via Dunkirk made its retention in England one of the few bright spots in a military fiasco. By the time the disorganised but numerically largely intact BEF was back in the UK re-training and re-forming, first for home defence, and then as the fortunes of war swung in our favour for a new endeavour against the enemy overseas, the Canadian forces had begun to arrive in Aldershot. The 1st and 2nd Canadian Divisions were based around Aldershot and when they eventually went into action on the continent of Europe Canadian Army headquarters remained behind providing a permanent Canadian UK base for most of the war. The Canadian presence was commemorated in September 1945 by the granting of the Freedom of the Borough of Aldershot to the 'Canadian Army Overseas'.

The same demobilisation process occurred after the Second World War as in 1919 but this time conscription, under the name of National Service continued until 1962. Aldershot maintained its role as a major component of the army training organisation especially concerned with the technical corps. Many new corps and regiments had been formed or redesignated during the war and most of them settled permanently in or near Aldershot. The Parachute Regiment was officially formed in August 1942 and now has its home in Browning Barracks, Aldershot. The Corps of Royal Electrical and Mechanical Engineers was also formed in 1942 and has a strong presence in nearby Blackdown whilst its Headquarters is also not far away in Arborfield. The women's services, Queen Alexandra's Royal Army Nursing Corps and the Women's Royal Army Corps are also based in the camp or close by. The QARANC gives 'The Royal Pavilion' as the address of its Aldershot Headquarters and although it is a pity that the original building had to go it does seem likely that Queen Victoria would approve of the use to which the site has been put.

By the mid 1960s training and living accommodation in the camp was in a very dilapidated condition. Although most of the original huts and other buildings had long since gone, many of the late nineteenth century buildings were still in use as were most of the huts put up to cope temporarily with the expansion occasioned by the two World Wars. In 1966 a Town Plan was unveiled which has gradually trans-formed the old camp into a modern military town so that now the 'Military Town of Aldershot' is a pleasant mixture of the old and the new. New living quarters for single soldiers and families, new training facilities, offices, dining halls, messes, sports and amenity buildings mix in a pleasant blend with older buildings which have been retained because of their special significance. Amongst the surviving older buildings are the churches, the District Headquarters Building, The Prince Consort's Library, ornamental gateways from some of the original barracks and a group of the oldest surviving huts.

A small complex of the old huts has been converted into the new Aldershot Military Museum. The museum is a model of its kind and whilst it is ostensibly devoted to the history and development of Aldershot Camp it portrays much more than that. The museum presents a quite concise history of the development of the whole British Army since the Crimean War and at the same time illuminates the life of soldiers in the camp over the same period. There are also in the museum some interesting short biographical portraits of camp personalities both military and civil. Anyone interested in the camp and its history, or indeed in the town of Aldershot cannot afford to miss these fascinating and evocative displays.

Aldershot new military town, 1986.

The recent building and rebuilding of army camps has highlighted a problem which is likely to become increasingly serious over the next few decades. Unlike the old barracks, built behind a high perimeter wall which enclosed married quarters as well as barrack blocks and training facilities, the new military town is an open site presenting a surburban or garden city impression. With the growth of terrorism and its increasingly ruthless and indiscriminate nature, the open plan camp without a perimeter fence and with public roads running through it presents an ever present threat to the security of soldiers and their families alike. Aldershot Military Town was the first rebuilt military complex to suffer in this way. On 22 February 1972 IRA terrorists left a stolen car containing a large quantity of high explosives against the wall of the Parachute Brigade Officers' Mess. It exploded killing seven people and seriously injuring a further nineteen. It is a sad irony, but quite typical that only one soldier was amongst the killed and he was the Brigade Roman Catholic Padre. Although there have been many bomb outrages since then, the Aldershot explosion is the worst that has occurred so far, within the confines of a British military garrison. There have been many malicious false alarms however, and these too put a considerable strain on troops and families. The problem has not yet reached such proportions that the inhabitants of military towns would prefer to go back to living in an enclosed, defendable precinct but if, as seems likely, the threat from terrorism increases, a new approach to military architecture and military town planning may become necessary.

Wellington's statue, moved from London to Aldershot in 1884.

Perhaps it was inevitable that Aldershot more than any other garrison town should reflect the personality of its founders and famous commanders. Within a short time of the camp being built it had become the centre of the greatest concentration of British troops ever seem in these islands in peacetime. Furthermore it became the centre of military innovation and attracted to itself military scientists, engineers and experimenters, not in the narrow sense only but as enlightened staff officers, military managers and commanders. When the army stagnated, as it did after the Crimean War and between the World Wars, what little there was that was new or forward looking in the army tended to come out of Aldershot or its satellite camps. Being the most important British Military District it enjoyed a succession of able Commanders who were able to take advantage of the unique combination of training facilities in the District. Almost all of its Commanders were destined for even more important posts and many of them went right to the top of the military tree. Many of them also, and to their great credit, were reformers concerned with the conditions under which the ordinary soldier lived, and with their welfare and education as well as their military training. The Army has always been rich in personalities in all its Corps and Regiments and at all levels and no doubt the town has seen and known many more 'characters' than have been mentioned here. Early welfare work in the town attracted some very determined ladies like Louisa Daniell and her daughter Georgina. Also of course, there have been many interesting and amusing characters prominent in the Council Chambers, both before and after the town received its Charter, but lack of space prevents their proper illumination. However, before this account of the garrison town of Aldershot is closed it is necessary to return briefly to two soldiers, one of whom died before the camp came into being, and the other who produced the first plans of the camp and lived almost into the twentieth century.

Captain R. M. Laffan, RE was serving in the War Office in the early 1850s and was given the task of drawing up the plans for the first permanent barracks at Aldershot. He was posted to the camp to supervise part of the construction work and amongst his other achievements was the levelling of the plain which bears his name. Laffans Plain, which saw so much of Samuel Cody's pioneering aeronautical work, is now appropriately within the perimeter of the Royal Aircraft Establishment at Farn-borough. Laffan returned to Aldershot as Chief Royal Engineer from 1866 to 1872 after a brief spell as the Member of Parliament for St. Ives in Cornwall. His last appointment was as Governor and Commander-in-Chief of Bermuda, where he died in 1892. The Duke of Wellington, on the other hand, as we have said never saw the camp and would probably not have approved of it in any event but his presence still looms over the camp just as it looms over British military history. In one sense it is likely that if Wellington had not won his great campaigns in the Peninsula and at Waterloo, Britain would now be a different place and Aldershot Camp might not exist at all. It is entirely right therefore that the enormous equestrian statue of our greatest soldier, brought from London to Aldershot in 1884, should look out across the new Military Town of Aldershot, the Home of the British Army.

Bibliography

The Story of Aldershot, Howard N. Cole, Gale & Polden, Aldershot, 1951

Aldershot Review, John Walters, Jarrold, 1970

Bygone Aldershot, T. Childerhouse, Phillimore, 1984
(An excellent pictorial history of town and camp)

There are nine Regimental Museums in Aldershot and the immediate vicinity but the most important for the study of the Camp and its history is 'The Aldershot Military Museum', which is located in Queen's Avenue, in the Camp.

8

Bovington

REGINALD FRANCIS

BOVINGTON, the tun or farmstead of the Bovings, anciently a manor, now a farm, about two miles and a half north from Wool. In the nineteenth year of the reign of Henry III, the collectors of the aid granted on the marriage of the king's sister with the Emperor of Germany account for the expenses for three-fourths of a fee of Richard de Mucegros in 'Buvinton'. It belonged anciently to the abbey of Bindon. In 1293, the lands of the abbot here were valued at 20s. and in the thirty-first year of the reign of Henry VIII, at £10 11s. 5d. In the thirty-second year of the reign of Henry VIII, the manor and farm were granted to Sir Thomas Poynings; in the second year of the reign of Elizabeth they were granted to Thomas, Viscount Bindon. Afterwards it came from the Hoopers of Hurn-court or Boveridge. From the Reverend Mr Hooper, rector of Wimborne St Giles, it passed to his nephew, Edward Hooper of Hurn-court, who sold it in 1767 to James Frampton, esq. of Moreton.[1]

A LATER edition of Hutchins has an addendum: 'It has since continued in this family, the present possessor in 1861 being H. Frampton, esq. of Moreton'. One cannot help but wonder if Mr Frampton would be able to recognise his 'tun or farmstead of the Bovings' in the bustling, thriving modern military camp it has now become.

Bovington did, in fact, remain in the Frampton family until 1899 when, after lengthy negotiations, the War Office agreed to pay Mrs Louisa Frampton £4,300 for just over one thousand acres of the 'Heathland in the Parishes of Bovington, Turnerspuddle, Affpuddle, Wool and Elsewhere in the County of Dorset, which land shall be used as a Rifle Range or for any Military purpose or any other use or purpose of the Government or any Department thereof'.

The range was built and came into use in 1900 when over a thousand men of 1st battalion of the Royal Southern Reserves arrived for six weeks' military training and musketry practice, the first firing being carried out by 'B' (Wareham) Company, 1st Volunteer Battalion, Dorset Regiment. It was an entirely tented camp at first but eventually a low brick bungalow was built for the range warden. The existing estate keeper's cottage was let to Purchase Brothers for use as a shop for the sale of aerated drinks, groceries and other provisions for the troops and it was also used by officers while they were waiting for their mess to be built. As time went on extra rooms were added for use as a post office and canteen, and stables were erected nearby. In 1907 Purchase Brothers were listed as 'Officers' Mess Caterers, general providers and tent

Bovington village, seen here with Lulworth Ranges in the background, has hardly changed in sixty years.

kit suppliers'. In that same year the camp was enlarged: two hundred and ninety acres of Chamberlayne's Heath were bought from Colonel E. M. Mansel-Pleydell. In 1910, a further fifteen and three-quarters of an acre of the same heath were purchased from the colonel. During the first years of its existence, Bovington Camp had been used by regular units for training, mainly musketry on the ranges, but its chief use was as a summer camp for Territorials. One of the highlights of the latter was the annual meeting of the Dorset Territorial Rifle Association when, according to the *Dorset County Chronicle* of 18 June 1914, 'the sergeants' mess was placed at the disposal of any competitor who required refreshments, hospitality being dispensed ad lib'.

When the First World War began in August, 1914, the Government were surprised and unprepared for the flood of volunteers. Instead of the expected one hundred thousand, five hundred thousand men presented themselves at the recruiting offices in the first month. There was a shortage of arms and equipment and insufficient permanent camps were available; there was even an acute shortage of clothing. As regards accommodation, every existing camp — however temporary — had to be brought into use. Bovington was allocated as the initial training camp of the newly-formed 17th Infantry Division. The official *History of the Dorset Regiment* states:

> The 17th Division belonged to the north. In a happy moment the War Office turned an eye on Dorset and sent 12,000 men to invade the windy, sunlit spaces round Bovington and Wareham. It might be a distant journey but here was ideal

ground for training; wide hills, great heaths and tracts of pinewoods. So the twelve battalions drawn from between Trent and Tweed were exiled from their crowded cities, or their fields and farms, to learn the business of war where there was little temptation· or opportunity to do anything else.[2]

But there had been totally inadequate preparation for this 'invasion'. The historian of the 10th Lancashire Fusiliers records the arrival at Bovington 'where the first night was spent on the verge of the road, no tents or rations having arrived'. Similarly, the Northumberland Fusiliers found that 'Little preparation had been made, and the sky was the extra blanket for the night'. The situation became a local scandal and the *Dorset County Chronicle* came out with the headline:

'KITCHENER'S ARMY STRANDED WITH NO FOOD OR COVERING'.

Tents arrived eventually but in insufficient numbers; the weather became very wet: recruits fell sick and many had to be admitted to hospital. One young soldier died from pneumonia and was buried in the graveyard of Wool Parish Church. The winter — the first winter of the war — must have been an appalling experience for those recruits from the north-east of England. A Newcastle man wrote:

> When I arrived at the grounds, seated on top of a pile of goods on a tradesman's cart, having thus covered the three miles from Wool Station, I saw the boys at drill. None were yet in uniform . . . The footgear of the Quaysiders was much changed from the days of fancy shoes and ornamental socks. Their shoes now are – well – entirely strangers to blacking or polish, and are mostly covered in mud.[3]

Gradually, however, conditions improved: a routine of drill, musketry and physical training was established and recreation facilities developed. According to contemporary accounts, the Young Men's Christian Association did a splendid job, providing refreshments, places where the troops could write letters and buy stamps, and rooms where they could play indoor games. The enterprising vicar of East Stoke Church, the Reverend P. A. Butler, who acted as Chaplain to the camp for a number of years, formed a band which gave concerts in the YMCA, played on route marches and at church parades, which were held weekly.

The appalling conditions suffered by the troops at last prompted the Army authorities into promising that all the troops in Dorset under canvas would be accommodated in wooden huts. Huts were, indeed, built in other places but the programme at Bovington fell behind schedule. Meanwhile troops were moved into civilian billets in Wimborne, Canford, Broadstone, Ferndown and Kinson, where they expected to stay for six weeks but were obliged to stay much longer. The huts were ready at the end of March, 1915, and Bovington became an established army camp rather than the exercise area which it had been previously. Built to sleep thirty men, the huts were well constructed and lasted for many years. Some were later converted into married quarters.

With the establishment of the permanent camp, training was extended; trenches were dug and machine gun training included. Not only were troops prepared for the Western Front but local recruiting drives were held to build up reserves for the Dorsetshire Regiment which had moved in when the 17th Division departed for France. Other newcomers to Bovington Camp were the Australian Army who established a

Command Depot, the purpose of which was to receive men, who had been discharged from hospital after being wounded in France, and toughen them up in readiness for their return to France. Numbers increased rapidly after the Battle of the Somme — so much so that they had to be diverted to other camps.

The stalemate of trench warfare inspired the invention of the tank and on 2 February 1916, the completed experimental machine was put throught its trials at Hatfield before representatives of the Army Council and General Headquarters France, and six days later production was ordered. A small unit of the Machine Gun Corps, commanded by Colonel E. D. Swinton, and known as the Heavy Section, trained at Elveden in Norfolk in conditions of the utmost secrecy. After the despatch of the first detachment of thirteen tanks to France on 13 August 1916, followed by other small detachments, their potential was soon recognised, despite their disappointing initial performance over unsuitable terrain. Haig asked the War Office for a thousand tanks and, on this being agreed, the expansion of the Heavy Section necessitated a more extensive training ground than could be found in Elveden. A war diary of the time has this entry:

> The wooded country around Bovington is particularly adapted to the training of tank battalions, the rolling downs, the woods and the small streets being very similar to and as equally deserted as the battlefields of France.[4]

On 20 October 1916, Brigadier General F. Gore-Anlay, DSO, became the first Administrative Commander of the Tank Training Centre, Bovington Camp, and a week later the Elveden establishment began to move to Dorset. Thus, Bovington Camp became the home of the tank and has remained so until the present time.

As with the previous 'invasion' by the 17th Division, the transfer of the tank training set-up, lock, stock and barrel, from Elveden to Bovington, inevitably gave rise to problems. Firstly, there was the acute lack of accommodation for officers due to the fact that each tank was commanded by a subaltern; thus, a tank battalion contained far more officers than an infantry battalion. The problem was solved by allocating a barrack room to junior officers.

The most serious lack of accommodation was that required for the maintenance of the ever-increasing number of tanks arriving in the camp. 711 Company, Army Service Corps, brought with them from Elveden a Standard Mobile Workshop. An engineering officer described his arrival:

> The workshop consisted of a canvas aeroplane hangar and a few tents, with only the most primitive tools and other necessary adjuncts. After a short examination as to my capabilities in instructing on the 105 h.p. Daimler Sleeve Valve Engine, then the standard tank engine, I was placed in charge of such teaching in a canvas hut, carefully sited in the bed of a stream.[5]

Gradually the nomenclature changed: the Eastern Parade Ground was re-christened the Tank Park. It was situated at the north end of the camp, immediately to the west of the Wool to Clouds Hill road. The growing number of tanks in use and the hard wear given them by the students training over rough ground necessitated a rapid and intense increase in the maintenance facilities. Hangars appeared in increasing numbers and a permanent, galvanised iron, steel-framed building was erected at the south-east corner of the Tank Park. This building, measuring fifty feet by thirty-five feet, had a concrete and woodblock floor and an overhead five-ton travelling crane, making it possible for major repairs and maintenance to be carried out.

A mixed bag of potential tank crews arrived: trainees from Elveden; mechanically-minded and adaptable men recruited from the motor and motor-cycle industries; recruits with some experience of driving and maintaining a car; and men without any relevant experience. That training was hard and purposeful was recalled by one of them:

> The work to be got through seemed colossal and any who imagined they had come to Bovington for a 'cushy' time were quickly disillusioned.[6]

By the end of 1916, the experience gained on the Somme has been assimilated and the War Office issued 'Instructions on Training' in which a properly balanced programme was laid down, outlining the courses which make up a tank crewman's training. The first priority was the training of instructors and by January 1917, preparations were sufficiently advanced to enable the establishment of the Administrative Department of the Schools of Instruction. Individual training for each crewman was arranged in tank-driving, maintenance, gunnery, signalling, reconnaissance, bombing and the care of pigeons.

The normal course lasted three to four months. A nineteen-year-old subaltern wrote:

> My first course was Driving and Maintenance and I found it really good fun. The tanks, although very slow, had a magnificent cross-country performance and as four of the eight members of the crew were required solely to manoeuvre the vehicle, good team work was required to get the best performance. There was no tactical driving and the main object was to get the tank over the most impossible places and when stuck to get going again with the aid of pick, shovel, crow-bar and brute strength. This training was essential as each tank had to be self-supporting and recovery was in its infancy. Maintenance was very heavy, especially greasing up, as there were nearly sixty points on the outside of each tank alone which required the grease gun at the end of a day's run. The Gunnery Courses were also carried out at Bovington. These courses included indoor instruction in the huts below G Battalion lines and firing with the Lewis guns into the butts on the training ground north of the camp either from the ground or from gun sponsons removed from the driving and maintenance tanks. The six-pounder sub-calibre shooting was carried out in this area from a standing battery firing across a valley. My most vivid memory is of the so-called battle practice which took place shortly before the Battalion proceeded overseas. 18 Company marched in the early morning to Lulworth, where they found two or three store tents for the ammunition, a Standing Battery of about half-a-dozen six-pounder guns and a couple of tanks. After the whole company had fired their first live shells and a few machine gun rounds from the Battery and from a slow moving tank, they marched back to Bovington in the evening. Somewhat apprehensively after tales from my more experienced companions about the kick of the .45 revolver, I was next sent on a Revolver Course which was run by Captain Bill Watkins on a range he had built near 1 Battalion lines. The last two courses were mild ones — a Compass Course and a Pigeon Course. The

latter was necessary as each tank carried a basket of two pigeons into action. I cannot recall any incident when they proved of much use as either the tank had to be evacuated in a hurry, the pigeons were stupefied by the fumes or they were used up as an emergency ration.[7]

It is interesting to read contemporary accounts of the efforts of the instructors to simulate battle conditions: the trench system with its barbed wire used by the infantry was supplemented by shell craters and improvised objects of all kinds. The men were taken over this course again and again until familiar with the kind of problems which they would meet on the Western Front. As time went on the number of tanks available for training was steadily increased and this caused the authorities some headaches. The tank was still on the secret list so that when they arrived at Wool Station all civilian traffic was stopped and the inhabitants of Woolbridge Manor and the neighbouring farms and cottages were made to pull their blinds and keep to their back rooms. Civilian pedestrians were made to stand in a field with their back to the road. On one occasion a shepherd named Patience refused to leave his sheep so soldiers pitched hurdles around him and his sheep until the tank had passed. On another occasion, James Spicer, the owner of Bovington Farm, reported to the military authorities that, whilst he had no objection to helping them to keep the secret of the tanks, he wished they would remove the one which had broken down and had been towed into his farmyard where it had been standing for forty-eight hours!

Woolbridge Manor and the old bridge at Wool. Tess of the D'Urbevilles spent her honeymoon here according to Thomas Hardy. The road leads up to Bovington camp, two miles away.

The narrow lane from Wool Station to the camp — Cologne Road did not exist until the latter part of the First World War — made the going difficult for tanks but the worst obstacle was Wool Bridge — the sixteenth century stone bridge over the River Frome and the narrow stone bridge over the Lytchett stream. Inevitably damage was done: the Dorset County Council minute book of 12 March 1918 records that 'the parapet and retaining walls were driven into and damaged by military traffic on 24 December 1917' and that £60 of damage was done.

On 28 June 1917, the War Office agreed to change the name of the Heavy Section to the Tank Corps and expand it from nine to eighteen battalions. This, as a matter of course, led to the expansion of the training facilities at Bovington, both in the number of tanks and especially in the workshops. New buildings were provided and standard lights fitted so that repair work could be carried out at night. A new generating plant was installed, manned by Royal Engineers, to meet the increased demand. The expansion of Bovington was now in full flood: improvements, additions and extensions were put in hand in all departments. Tank training was provided for units from the United States, Canada and New Zealand. But this was not all. The War Office planned a massive expansion of the Tank Corps during 1919: six thousand tanks were to be built and the size of the Corps doubled by raising seventeen new battalions at Bovington. A complete reorganisation of buildings was planned and funds made available for new constructions without even the formality of estimates being called for. Work began in September, 1918, and progressed very quickly. One Canadian and eight new British battalions were raised, bringing the total number of officers and men trained at Bovington during the war to twenty-one thousand, fourteen thousand of whom were trained in complete units and seven thousand in individual reinforcements.

The Armistice was signed on 11 November 1918. On 12 November, the War Office cancelled the production of all tanks except the medium tank. The bubble had burst; the expansion of Bovington was at an end.

By the end of the First World War, Bovington Camp was a vast place. A soldier, visiting the camp, wrote:

> Bovington was a much larger camp than I imagined it to be. Seen under a formal constellation of electric lamps it appeared as a veritable city of wooden huts set down in a waste of barren moorland. At intervals along our road, clumps of secretive pines loomed dark and menacing in the December dusk, and as we drew nearer I saw that these were the outposts of an extensive wood which curved away to the south-west, mantling a shoulder of the ridge on which the camp was built. A long, straight road took us past hangars and corrugated iron sheds, which the driver said were workshops. Beyond them I saw the dark, toad shapes of tanks. We passed a power station, a cinema, shops, a post office, and presently stopped in front of a large barrack store.[8]

What would now become of all this? Some predicted that it would disappear almost as quickly as it came into existence. It was obviously totally dependent on the tank; and the future of the tank was by no means certain. At first the thinking was that the tank had been invented to overcome the stalemate of trench warfare and as trench warfare was unlikely in any future war the need for the tank had vanished. However, another school of thought prevailed. The tank, they considered, should have a dual role: in close support of infantry and, secondly, to carry out the role of reconnaissance and surprise attack, formerly undertaken by the cavalry.

By October 1919, the Army Council decided that the Tank Corps should be a *corps d'élite* but it was not until 1922 that the Tank Corps became a permanent, separate arm with an establishment of four battalions. During the four years previously the Corps had lost to industry many of its most valuable and skilled members. Thus, according to the Census returns of 1921, the Tank Corps Centre, which included Wareham, Swanage and Lulworth as well as Bovington, decreased in numbers from sixteen thousand to two thousand, two hundred and thirty-two. Nevertheless, demands were made on the Corps for all kinds of operational roles: the Army of Occupation on the Rhine; an expeditionary force to aid the White Russians; as armoured police to deal with trouble spots in the Middle East, Ireland, and even in the strike-stricken towns in the homeland.

The increasing demands on the Corps coupled with wastage due to demobilisation resulted in a drive to obtain recruits. A bounty scheme to encourage war-experienced men to re-enlist produced some results but the majority of recruits coming forward were young men who felt that they had missed a great and glorious adventure. An even more effective incentive was increasing unemployment and, by 1921, by which time the Depot had moved from Wareham to Bovington, as many recruits as could be handled were arriving.

The orderly build up of Battalions is reflected in this contemporary account:

> Barracks having been taken over on the 3rd, a small nucleus of officers and NCOs assembled at Bovington on the afternoon of the 5th September, feeling rather like new boys . . . Since this, three drafts have joined, and we now boast of one and a half companies, very young to anyone accustomed to war-soldiers or a pre-war foreign service battalion, but keen, smart and likely to make a name for their battalion in the future.[9]

As the battalions came up to full strength, training programmes were implemented: gunnery courses at Lulworth and driving and maintenance at Bovington. Great emphasis was laid on physical training and keen sportsmen were encouraged whether as teams or as individuals. A wide range of sports outside the conventional were catered for. Bovington, at this time, possessed one of only five Bassett hound packs in the country, and the Corps Eight practised on the Frome at Wareham before taking part in the Henley Regatta.

Competitive sport became an important factor in the life of all units, not least those of the *corps d'élite* — the Tank Corps. A non-sportsman posted to Bovington in 1920 commented:

> Sport was the only passion of Bovington's military population and the camp was — to say the least — a little better than a manufactory of athletes.[10]

Success in sport added in no small way to the prestige of a unit and in this respect the Central Schools considered itself the best of the Corps — and not only in sport. It contained the key men of the Corps — the skilled mechanics who worked long hours and, in return, received generous privileges:

> Bovington was the life centre of the Corps where mechanics ruled the roost and

where the voice of the drill sergeant was heard, if at all, only as a plaintive echo. The atmosphere of the camp was friendly and peaceful and it seemed to me the men who walked its roads were more cheerful and contented than the harassed recruits of Wareham.[11]

However, with the arrival of the Depot from Wareham early in 1921 the scene changed:

> its drill dervishes and its band caused a serious epidemic of militarism in units which, hitherto, had shown little or no interest in parade ground displays.[12]

Settling down after the immediate post-war period of uncertainty and difficulty, the Central Schools extended their range of courses to include one on which men were taught to drive a car; this was part of the Army Resettlement Scheme to help ex-soldiers to find a job. Another course was for White Russians to help them use their tanks against the Bolsheviks.

By 1920 the instruction in Central Schools had reached an advanced stage. A visitor at that time reported that he found students,

> . . . peering into models and diagrams, in section, profile, back view and sideways, while a patient but perspiring instructor explains for the umpteenth time how stuff called oil persists in poking its nose into every nook and cranny of the Ricardo engine, arriving eventually, thinner and panting, at the same old place from which it started.[13]

The report of a soldier who attended a course in the twenties brings the scene vividly to life.

> The instructor introduced us to carburetters, magnetoes, and eccentric oil pumps in a series of dramatic episodes that were described prosaically in the training manual as Carburation, Ignition and the Lubrication System. Our training at the Mechanical School was much the same as that given by a modern school of motoring. Anyone with a slight knowledge of the petrol engine would have found it elementary, for the mechanism of a tank closely resembled that of a motor car, save that it is larger, heavier and somewhat complicated by epicyclic gearing. Practical work was another story. At the Maintenance School there were fewer lectures and demonstrations by the instructors, the order being that students should 'learn by doing'. And the 'doing' of simple maintenance operations on a heavy tank is a formidable task for one unaccustomed to handling drifts, crowbars and fourteen pound sledge hammers.[14]

At the beginning of 1922 it was decided that the training of recruits should, in future, be the responsibility of units and that Central Schools should confine itself to the training of instructors. Some elementary training, however, was continued, notably that for young officers on probation.

In 1920, the Central Workshops were reorganised as the Tank Workshop Battalion. In the previous two years it had had to cope with a heavy load of work: taking on charge scores of newly-built tanks; preparing tanks in readiness for trouble during the railway strike; and receiving hundreds of derelict tanks which had been despatched from the battlefields of France. But now at last it was able to set about its main task:

'to carry out the repair and maintenance of tanks used for instructional purposes and also to keep men in suitable training for drafts overseas'. To overcome the recruiting problem boy-soldiers were recruited for technical training after a preliminary period of general education. The first batch, forty in number, arrived at Bovington on 31 January 1920. Modified from time to time, the Boys' Training Scheme continued until 1924 when the new Army Apprentices' Schools were opened. The last contingent of boys made a suitably dramatic exit. Accompanied by the band of the Royal Tank Corps, they marched to Wool Station to entrain for Gosport.

The workshop building programme, which started with such a flourish in September 1918, was half-finished by the end of the war. After that, progress was slow, due in some part to the fact that the labour force consisted mainly of prisoners-of-war with consequent reductions in size as prisoners were repatriated. The new buildings were, however, more or less completed by 1920.

No similar progress was made with living accommodation. It was not until 1920 that the War Office commenced a programme to re-decorate and renovate the huts which had been so hastily erected in 1914 and 1915 and which had suffered the wear and tear caused by the war-time soldiers who had passed through. Certain huts were selected for conversion into married quarters and this necessitated the movement of troops from one hut to another to allow the work to proceed. One man, whose troop had been moved into huts previously occupied by the Women's Army Auxiliary Corps, wrote:

> The huts were surrounded by a high fence of barbed wire, and the only entrance to this seraglio was by way of a large wooden gate, medieval in strength and design, the top of which was decorated with more barbed wire and a row of villainous-looking spikes.[15]

The provision of much-needed married quarters relieved only a few of the families of the worry of living in furnished rooms in the neighbouring villages, often paying exorbitant rents for the privilege. As more quarters became available, family life became a feature of Bovington, bringing a touch of humanity to an austerely male world. The authorities gave every encouragement, urging 'those who have a penchant for gardening to turn this dismal waste into a garden city'.

The advent of 'married families', as the Army so quaintly refers to a soldier's dependants, was a boon to the local traders, who had settled on the south side of the camp in a variety of make-shift buildings, mostly tin-shacks — hence the term 'Tintown'. At first only the needs of the soldiers were catered for but now the market was considerably enlarged and those enterprising traders who had got a foot in the camp were quick to take advantage of their opportunities. George Keen, for example, used to visit the camp on Sunday afternoons from his tobacco and sweet shop in Poole High Street, selling his wares from a suitcase; Herbert Smith cycled around the camp selling the *Daily Express*. Eventually, Keen and Smith opened adjacent stores on the corner of what is now Swinton Avenue.

Herbert Smith and his family rapidly expanded their business, opening another shop for sale of fancy goods on a site adjacent to their present store. In 1921 they erected the existing large, galvanised iron store, which, in those days, was used as a cafe and billiard saloon. In addition there were various services: barber, bootmakers, garages, taxi-service and a cinema. The YMCA continued to render yeoman service, refreshing and entertaining the garrison, as did the NAAFI and the Church of England Institute.

The question mark which had hung over the existence of Bovington Camp since the end of the First World War was finally dispersed when the War Office, after a lengthy deliberation, decided on the constitution of the new corps. A Royal Warrant, dated 7 November 1923, declared:

> Whereas we have noted with great satisfaction the splendid work that has been performed by our Tank Corps during the Great War, our will and pleasure is that this Corps shall enjoy the distinction of 'Royal' and shall henceforth be known as our 'Royal Tank Corps'.

With all doubt about its future now removed, Bovington in the twenties faced an expansion on the domestic, rather than the military, front. The increasing number of married families inevitably gave rise to the problem of children's education. At first children travelled to schools in the vicinity but, eventually, on 8th January 1923, a school was set up in a building provided by the military authorities and opened with 88 children of all ages and a staff of four with the purpose of serving 'the Camp of the Tank Corps Centre and that area in nearer proximity than any existing school'. Although entirely the responsibility of the local education authority, the school was looked on as very much a part of the camp and the staff and children were given all possible help and encouragement by the military authorities. The school was visited by HM Inspectors after it had been open only six months. They reported:

> The school was opened on 8th January, 1923. The greater proportion of the children were backward owing to interruptions in their schooling and the teachers deserve much credit for the improvement already effected. Handwriting is now generally neat and well-formed and the children show good industry and application. Homework has been started and reports are sent to parents. The Managers are showing much interest in the various activities of the school. The teachers and children are rendering the interior of the school as bright and attractive as possible by maps, charts and illustrations . . .

The change from wartime camp to garrison town was now well under way; an ambitious and imaginative painting programme was undertaken and the *Tank Corps Journal* reported that the buildings were becoming 'a maze of blues, reds, greys and greens'; drains were laid; roads and pathways constructed; street lighting installed; new Sergeants' messes organised; and the first brick-built living accommodation was erected in the form of a large Officers' mess which was to serve all the officers on the camp.

It was during this time that the camp had to be enlarged to make room for the increasing number of buildings to be erected. Land was acquired for this purpose by purchase from the estate which surrounded the camp. This was not a simple matter and in some cases lengthy and complex negotiations were required. Finally, after the War Office had paid £2,500 to the Weld Estate on 31 March 1924, for '442 acres, 3 rods and 1 perch situate in or contiguous to the Parish of Wool', the total area of the camp amounted to two thousand, one hundred and thirty-three acres.

At the Central Schools some experimentation and research was carried out. Lieutenant Colonel G. M. Lindsay, the Chief Instructor at that time, invented the Laryngaphone which enabled the tank commander to communicate with the various members of the crew in spite of the noise of the tank. In the workshops the various specialised trades were becoming more and more advanced and, as a result, at the beginning of 1925, the Workshop Training Battalion was disbanded and the work of the Central Workshops became the sole responsibility of the Royal Army Ordnance Corps. The unit was run along the lines of a civilian workshop and men who had trained there were later accepted in industry as fully qualified tradesmen.

In 1919 an Education Centre was opened and a year later Army Certificates of Education were re-introduced and the year after that they became a prerequisite for promotion. That they served a useful purpose cannot be denied: the official historian of the Royal Tank Regiment states:

> the effort put into educational training at the Depot contributed much to the progress attained in the mechanical and tactical training of units.[16]

When T. E. Lawrence joined the Tank Corps as Private T. E. Shaw in March 1923, he commented in a letter concerning his fellow recruits that they showed a complete lack of interest in technical matters or in the Army generally because every man had joined because he was down and out. On the other hand, Liddell Hart wrote, describing the Tank Corps in the mid-twenties:

> Morale and *esprit de corps* were heightened by the well-justified feeling that it was giving a lead to the military world. The exceptionally high standard of its NCOs was regarded with envious admiration by other branches of the Service. The same was true of the recruits who were coming forward to join the Corps.[17]

By 1925 the garrison was developing, growing and expanding in all directions. The Central Schools provided advanced training for officers and NCOs; the Depot received recruits from civilian life and carried out basic training before despatching them to units at home·and abroad. On the domestic front, the increasing number of married families found a wide range of goods and services provided by the NAAFI and local traders. This was not, however, to everyone's taste. A single soldier wrote:

> With the coming of wives and children the camp lost the attractive backwoods atmosphere which had tickled my imagination in the far off days of 1919. Respectability and smugness were now the order of the day. Soon we became accustomed to seeing perambulators, well-fed women and over-dressed children on roads and paths that had once been sacred to the prancings of athletes. So, Bovington ceased to be a community and became a garrison.[18]

In the first twenty-five years of its existence, Bovington Camp had become not only a garrison but also a home — in every sense of the word — for all those who went to war in armoured vehicles.

Behind the façade of genteel domesticity, the growth and development of armour was proceeding. Its chequered history shows, however, that progress was impeded and confusion caused by the way higher authority repeatedly selected for key posts in this field officers who had no previous experience of it in preference to those who had both knowledge and enthusiasm. A happy exception was Lindsay who was appointed Chief Instructor of the RTC Central Schools in 1923. But for him it was not an easy decision:

> One of the things that influenced me in deciding that I would leave my Regiment,

the Rifle Brigade, to join the Tank Corps, was that my own baby, the Machine Gun Corps, had been abolished, and I felt a burning desire to get into the most up-to-date service that I could; the Tank Corps seemed the one most suited to that purpose. Feeling that the Tank Corps was the protagonist of modern war, I thought that I could do more good for the future of the Army with it, than I could by remaining in an Infantry Regiment, even though the Regiment was the Rifle Brigade.[19]

Although situated in an isolated rural area, Bovington Camp was by no means immune to the momentous national events of the decade. The General Strike of May 1926, for example, involved the Army, and the Central Schools were called on to form a Rolls Royce Armoured Car Company. This Company went off to join a mixed force based on Chelsea Barracks with the task of maintaining order and escorting food convoys from the docks.

An interesting development of the thirties was the formation of the Royal Tank Corps Museum at Bovington. It was considered that the history of the Corps should be preserved in a tangible way in order to give recruits a picture of tank development. The project received official approval early in 1931 and the assortment of early tanks which had been lying in the open for years was cleaned, painted and completed as far as possible. Various battle relics and trophies were gradually collected. Unfortunately all this went by the board at the outbreak of war in 1939 and many priceless specimens, including 'Mother', the first tank, were reduced to scrap. The Museum was reformed in 1947 as the Royal Armoured Corps Museum and those tanks that remained were carefully preserved and formed the foundation of what has developed into one of the most comprehensive collections of armoured vehicles and memorabilia in the world. Today it is one of the major tourist attractions of south-west England.

With the Second World War, the importance of Bovington — and Lulworth — as establishments devoted to the training of instructors cannot be over-emphasised. Quite apart from the obvious commitment to the Tank Regiments, there were the tasks involved in the conversion of the Cavalry, many of whom went to war on horseback. In his autobigraphy, John Verney writes of his experiences with a Yeomanry Division and the frustration they felt: 'Though we threw ourselves into everything we did with enthusiasm, the anachronism of our equipment was disheartening. Our sabres belonged to the same era as the old gentlemen who advocated the use of pikes by the Home Guard . . . When, in the late summer of 1941, the division was at last mechanised, the speed and efficiency with which it retrained could hardly be accounted for by mere "keenness".'[20]

Additionally, there was the task of training instructors for the infantry battalions of the county regiments, hastily drawn from coastal defence in 1941 to be trained to man Churchill tanks, which were originally designed as defensive weapons. With the formation of the Guards Armoured Division even more demands were made on Bovington to provide training for regimental instructors.

Thus, during the years of the Second World War, Bovington teemed with life as courses in tank crew training abounded. Tanks in increasing numbers drove across the heath, tackled the famous obstacle course, shed tracks, and broke down. The training was nothing if not realistic. Trucks loaded with No. 19 sets, operated by operators wearing ear-phones and a strained expression, tore around from Swanage to Wimborne, filling the air-waves with the sound of voices — 'Hullo Molo, Bolo calling'.

Off-duty there was the cinema in a large tin-roofed barn, where the back two or three rows were reserved for officers. The Military Police kept a low profile but were always present; thus, if the sight of Betty Grable's legs inspired too many wolf-whistles, they would step smartly down the aisles to make their presence known.

The cinema was owned and organised by the same Mr Smith who, as previously mentioned, also owned the present store. He and his family were and still are something of a legend. When he was asked if it was true that he first arrived in Bovington with some kind of mobile shop selling polish, blanco and bootlaces, he admitted that it was, in fact, true — he did sell necessities to the troops — but not bloody bootlaces!'.

Bovington Camp established itself as the pivotal centre of the Royal Armoured Corps. It housed not only the training wings but the Depot and a number of ancillary organisations all geared towards increasing the efficiency of the troops and their equipment. Besides the training of instructors, courses were organised for a variety of purposes. For example, as D-Day drew near, a Tank Commanders' Course was designed to provide intensive training for those who would be responsible for taking their tanks into battle. It consisted of short, revision courses in tank driving and maintenance, wireless operating, and gunnery, culminating in a five-day exercise. This exercise had the innovative idea of manning the tanks with men of equal rank: thus, the Squadron Leader's tank was manned by five Majors, the second-in-command's by five Captains, and so on down the line. In this way, all members of the course had some idea of the stresses and strains which would be faced by the members of their crews in battle-conditions. In addition to the simulated conditions of order and counter-order were added the appalling weather conditions of the winter of 1943/4.

This was only one aspect of the training which was going on in Bovington throughout the war years. Many other aspects of preparing troops and equipment were in progress, not least in the technical field, where 18 Command Workshops were kept at full stretch.

After the Second World War there was a continuing demand for instructors. Units responsible for training National Servicemen and for providing refresher courses for reservists needed instructors who 'knew their stuff' and who also knew how 'to put it across'. The Bovington Schools had had years of experience in this field — the training of instructors — but there was some difficulty at this particular time. The majority of war-experienced specialists had been demobilised and it was not easy to find suitable staff to lead and organise the courses. However, increasing numbers of men, for one reason or another, decided to re-enlist and by 1947 most officers and senior NCOs were well qualified and had seen war service overseas.

Bovington was gradually returning to its pre-war establishment. With the conversion into married quarters of the huts built to accommodate troops in the First World War, the families moved in. Many lived in accommodation which had long been condemned as sub-standard but in those days when long family separations were fresh in the memory most service families were grateful that they could be together. The authorities played fair: the rent was a nominal £1 per week and there was a generous allocation of free coal. The latter was particularly welcome during the exceptionally hard winter of 1947/8. The senior officers, strongly supported by their wives, paid considerable

A new training complex at Junior Leader's Regiment, RAC.

attention to the welfare of the staff and their wives. Many of the latter were natives of foreign lands — from Hong Kong to Gibraltar — and sometimes found English customs strange and incomprehensible.

The camp school was situated in some of the larger black huts, and smaller private schools for primary-age children came into existence, notably, the one organised by Mrs Knowles, the Warden of T. E. Lawrence's cottage at Clouds Hill.

It seems incredible that two years after VE Day prisoners-of-war were still in this country; a pathetic reminder painted in huge yellow letters appeared on the pavement in the Officers' Married Quarters area — SEND US HOME.

The social scene became very active: parties, receptions, sports meetings, amateur dramatics, all contributed to the life of the Centre. The swimming-pool set in the heath was a popular venue where life-saving classes were held and galas become regular features. The 'Seven Stars' in Wool was the scene for many end-of-course parties — some of which transferred to the Swimming Pool for a midnight dip. Coming out of the 'Seven Stars', drivers tended to forget the water splash on the way back to camp with consequent dramatic effects. It is now no longer a hazard — a bridge has been built over it.

In 1952, the Boys' Squadron, RAC, was formed and stationed in Bovington. The first scheme for the training of boys in Bovington for service in the Army ended in 1924 when the Army Apprentices' Schools opened. The new unit, commanded by a major, consisted of 44 Junior Soldiers but their number soon increased to 200. They were fifteen-year-olds who were to be trained to take their place as crewmen in the Regiments of the Royal Armoured Corps. The Junior Leaders' Regiment developed gradually from the Boys' Squadron and by 1956 the steady increase in numbers required the formation of a second squadron. When the Regiment formally came into existence in January, 1957, it was commanded by a major but during 1958 the appointment was upgraded to lieutenant colonel. During that year the strength of the Regiment rose to 450, including 100 Junior Bandsmen, and a third squadron was formed.

The re-building of Bovington was now in full swing. The black huts were slowly being phased out though even as late as the mid-sixties some were still in use as married quarters. New, modern, purpose-built barrack blocks came into use and the Education Wing of the Junior Leaders' Regiment moved from its hutted accommodation in the area of the Tank Museum across the road to the top two floors of an excellently appointed tower block which it shared with the Regimental Instruction Wings. The Regiment was at last concentrated in a compact area with instructional facilities, living accommodation, messing, and staff quarters all within walking distance.

Similarly, other areas of Bovington were developed: modern, brick-built quarters appeared, a new Secondary School on the perimeter and new cinema became prominent features. During the last twenty years much has changed. It is hard to find any traces of the old 'Wild West' atmosphere which some old soldiers sentimentalise about — the busy shops, the bank, the chromium on the garish Garrison Hall, the modern, sharp-edged architecture, the smart cars, and the general air of newness have obscured it all. But not quite all — the church is still in one of those unforgettable black huts.

One thing is certain: 'the tun or farmstead of the Bovings', so picturesquely described by Hutchins in the eighteenth century is now in the 1980s a bustling, thriving modern military camp which could — very easily — pass as a military town.

Bibliography

The History and Antiquities of Dorset, John Hutchins, republished by E. P. Publishing Ltd., in collaboration with Dorset County Library, Dorchester, 1973

History of the Dorset Regiment (1914-1919), Henry Ling, Dorchester, 1932

Tinned Soldiers, A. Dixon, Jonathan Cape, 1941

The Tanks, B. H. Liddell Hart, Cassells, 1959

The RTR 50th Anniversary Souvenir Book, 1967

From Rifle Range to Garrison: An Essay on Bovington Camp (1899-1925), George E. Lanning, available for reference only at the Royal Armoured Corps Museum, Bovington Camp

BRITISH GARRISONS
OVERSEAS

9

Rheindahlen

PETER DIETZ

FROM AN aircraft above Joint Headquarters in the old Rheindahlener Wald, in the outer suburbs of Moenchengladbach, it is just possible to pick out the site of the small Roman camp discovered when the present camp was being built in the early nineteen-fifties. Seeing the evidence of the Roman camp prompts the thought that not since the Roman occupation is it probable that an army engineer has been given the task of building an 'army town' from scratch. No doubt soldiers everywhere have had to provide shelter and other facilities on a temporary basis on the lines of communication between garrison towns or when troops have been exposed with baggage, stores, sick and wounded, families and camp followers in hostile country. But on these occasions the settlement would not be permanent. Most military towns, and certainly most of the towns dealt with in this book have either grown up gradually round a military camp, like Bovington or Gibraltar, or have as an already existing town or population centre become a focus, and often the reason, for the military presence. This was the case in Edinburgh and York and more recently in Aldershot.

Five sites were examined in August 1952 when it was decided to move the main Allied Headquarters in Northern Germany to the Western side of the Rhine. The criteria used in the selection of a suitable site were of a non-military nature apart from the requirement to be 'behind' the Rhine. Of the five sites, four were in the Aachen area, at that time under Belgian control, and were without independent access to utility services or communications. Furthermore it seems the Belgians were not keen to have the new headquarters on their doorstep. The final site offered was in the Hardter Wald some seven kilometres from the medium-sized German town of Moenchengladbach. This site was in thick woodland, was sufficient in area and was within reach of the electric grid, gas, and established water supplies. The Hardter Wald and the Rheindahlener Wald immediately to the south of it, were solely owned by a local textile magnate. Single ownership made acquisition, even in the more favourable conditions of the immediate post-war decade, much easier. At the last moment the Germans changed their minds. Wishing to retain the Hardter Wald as a 'lung' for Moenchengladbach they offered the less heavily forested Rheindahlener Wald plus some adjoining woodland strips as an alternative. The planners considered the new site to be reasonable and since, as we shall see, time was running out, it was accepted and the requisition went ahead. This is why most servicemen and their families know the Headquarters Camp as 'Rheindahlen' although a real town of Rheindahlen has existed for many centuries only a few miles away to the south.

From the air the forested strip between the Rhine and the Dutch border looks flat and uninteresting; on the ground many attractive features become apparent. Over the whole area there are low hills, swampy valleys and many streams which flow west into the Schwalm, the Nette and eventually into the Maas near Roermond. The woods and swamps harbour game and many species of wild birds, and the 'wanderwegs' built through the forests and along the brooks attract large numbers of walkers, especially at the weekends and in holiday times. In the Roman Army, the soldiery complained as they do now about unnecessary tasks invented merely to keep them occupied and out of mischief. A regular chore was the making and upkeep of the causeways across these same bogs and marshland which supported the road running from Neuss on the Rhine to the confluence of the Roer and the Maas. The road ran along the southern edge of the Rheindahlen camp site. In excavating foundations for one of the camp buildings evidence of Roman fortification was found. It is thought that this was one of the 'Castells' referred to by Livy when he says in *L'Annaei Flori* that Drusus, the nephew of Caesar Augustus, erected causeways and fifty castells in the Rhineland. It is a humbling thought that, as in so many other military camps and settlements in Britain and continental Europe, the Romans were there before us. The Romans too had a period when they moved back behind the Rhine. After Herman destroyed the legions of Varus in the battle of the Teutoburger Wald in AD 9, the policy of expansion towards the east was abandoned and the Rhine replaced the Elbe as the natural frontier between the Roman Empire and the unpacified German tribes. Eventually, a new strategy divided the tribes and the Romans under Germanicus were able to advance again to the Weser.

The new British Headquarters area at Rheindahlen was not intended to be a defended locality in the sense that it was not sited with tactical considerations in mind. Its function was to be administrative, it was to have no fixed check-points and its restricted areas were established behind ornamental railings and gates rather like a great country house, or perhaps more appropriately like a nineteen-thirties model factory. It was only later with the increasing threat of terrorism and the constant pressure from political activists that the idea of the 'open camp' seemed suddenly rather naive, and after the Aldershot bombing, downright dangerous. It is argued that little can be done to protect a scattered garrison living a 'normal life' from the random and infrequent attacks which now occur. In an emergency of course the garrison does its best to protect itself and its families from the new horrors and at the same time to continue with its job. With foresight it might have been possible to make the cantonment more defensible, but at the present level of violence most of its occupants would vote for an open camp and a life as near normal as possible.

The present Headquarters area has had its share of fighting and of enemy occupation in the past. We have seen how the Romans were well established in the forests and swamps west of the Rhine and how they needed to protect their lines of communication even in the 'pacified' sections of the country. After the withdrawal of the Roman Legions the local Frankish tribes were sufficiently militant to defeat the invading Norsemen, an event commemorated in the 'Beowulf Saga', the oldest document in the Anglo-Saxon language. The British connection with the area is not only through wars. The village of Rheindahlen three miles away from the camp was raised to the status of a town by Marquess William of Juliers. He was brother-in-law to the English King Edward III who visited Cologne in AD 1340, creating his brother-in-law the first

Earl of Cambridge. Cambridge House, the Army Education Centre in the garrison is named after him. During the Reformation the Moenchengladbach area fell by hereditary succession to the Duke of Cleves. King Henry VIII chose his daughter, Anne of Cleves, to be his fourth wife and a token of his leadership of the Protestant Church.

During the War of the Spanish Succession in 1704, the year the British captured Gibraltar, Marlborough led his army through Rheindahlen on his famous march to the Danube and his victory at Blenheim. His army was also billeted in the town on their march back to the Low Countries. In the Seven Years War, celebrated by many of the oldest regiments of the British Army because of their participation in the Battle of Minden in 1759, where six regiments of British infantry advanced upon a superior French cavalry force and literally 'shot it to pieces', Moenchengladbach had the unhappy experience of being occupied by both sides. In 1814 a Cossack cavalry force passed through the Rheindahlen forest following up the retreating French Army under Napoleon. One of the Cossacks left his sabre in a hole in a tree near to a cooking fire and it was found one hundred and forty years later by a corporal of the Royal Engineers. At the Congress of Vienna which followed the Battle of Waterloo in the next year, the whole area around Rheindahlen and Moenchengladbach was allotted to the Crown of Prussia but it was stipulated that the border with Holland should not come nearer than cannon shot of the River Maas and that is where it still is.

In the Second World War some of the most bitter fighting in North West Europe took place between the Dutch border and the Rhine since it was necessary to clear the great stretch of forested, low-lying hills on the left bank before the final assault over the river could be successfully launched. Lieutenant General Sir Brian Horrocks's 30 Corps, under command of 1st Canadian Army fought a bloody battle to clear the Reichswald in late February 1945. Meanwhile it was the American 102nd Infantry Division fighting north from Aachen and then Erkelenz who cleared the German Army from the Rheindahlen and Moenchengladbach area. After taking part in the Ardennes counter-offensive, the Roer crossing and the capture of Erkelenz, the 102nd took up the advance towards Moenchengladbach on the 27 February. They were opposed by the remnants of three German divisions including about 3,500 men and a few tanks from the 130th Panzer (Lehr) Division. 405 Regimental Combat Team of the American division captured Venrath by 0830 that morning, Beckrath by mid-morning and Wickrathhahn by 1330 but then they had to dig-in in the face of fierce opposition from German units around Wickrath. The 406th Regimental Combat Team advancing on Rheindahlen and Hardt was also held up until heavy air and artillery support enabled them to advance and reach their objective by nightfall. Early the next morning 406 RCT moved out of Rheindahlen towards Hardt. The 1st Battalion of the Combat Team advanced down the left or west of the road across the area where JHQ is now located whilst the 3rd Battalion advanced along the east side of the road. There was heavy fighting in the woods of the Hardter Wald. In one action Staff Sergeant Ova I. Madsen won a posthumous Distinguished Service Cross for silencing two machine guns, and 2nd Lieutenant Earl F. Adams won the Silver Star for eliminating another machine gun with grenades. The Americans took Hardt at dusk, lost it to a counter attack after dark and finally re-took it during the night with the help of tanks which had finally caught up with them.

German resistance in Moenchengladbach and Rheydt continued until the American forces by-passed the two towns and continued their thrust north towards Krefeld. The enemy forces holding out in the area east of Hardt withdrew over the Rhine, and Moenchengladbach was finally secured for the allied forces on 1 March 1945. After Aachen, the Moenchengladbach, Rheydt urban complex was the next large town to be captured by the allies. The population of the two towns together had been over 200,000 in 1940, but by March 1945 the combined population had shrunk to less than 70,000, and in Moenchengladbach over half the living accommodation had been destroyed whilst in Rheydt only ten per cent remained habitable. Much of the devastation had been caused by allied bombing but in Rheydt in particular, fierce resistance to the American advance, by German troops dug in on the western edge of the town, caused much of the damage there. The rubble from the ruins of Rheydt was heaped up into a substantial hill on the outskirts of the town, and there it remains as a memorial to the follies of war, alongside the Venlo–Aachen autobahn. Rheydt was the home-town of Dr Goebbels, Hitler's notorious propaganda chief, and it is said that the strong resistance of the town was ordered in fear of his reaction if the town fell to the allies. He certainly did react strongly and threatened that Mayor Vogelsang, newly appointed by the Americans, would be 'finished off' in a few days. The new Mayor of Aachen was in fact murdered by so-called 'Werewolves' on Palm Sunday 1945 but happily this was the only incident of its kind in the aftermath of the war. By 13 January 1946, exactly thirteen years after Hitler seized power, Moenchengladbach was able to hold its first City Council election as its first step back towards a free and democratic society.

In May 1945, after the unconditional surrender of Nazi Germany, the main task of the allied forces in Germany was to organise the zones of occupation which had been confirmed at the Yalta Conference. In the early days, after the Wehrmacht had been disarmed and disbanded, the problems were administrative in that the large population, swollen by refugees from the east, had to be fed, housed and in many cases re-educated for a democratic society. Industry and agriculture had to be revived and a civil government improvised. The British set up their Headquarters roughly in the centre of their zone in the Westphalian Spa towns of Bad Oeynhausen for the army and Bad Eilsen for the Royal Air Force. British Naval Headquarters was in Minden from where, at some little distance from any erstwhile German naval base, the process of German naval disarmament was directed. These towns were well placed for the British zone, were comparatively undamaged and being Spa towns, had plenty of good living and administrative accommodation. They were well suited for the priorities of the immediate post-war years. However, by the early nineteen-fifties the international picture had changed. The Cold War, and as a consequence NATO, had arrived. Strategic considerations again began to cast shadows over the allied planning conferences.

Already by 1950 thought had been given to the establishment of a peacetime Headquarters for the British forces west of the Rhine. The project was hurried on by the forthcoming ratification of the Bonn Convention which would restore full sovereignty to the new Federal Republic of West Germany. After the ratification the full cost of occupying requisitioned properties would fall on the British taxpayer and not on the German Occupation Budget. It was therefore essential to get out of the requisitioned buildings in the Spa towns and elsewhere as quickly as possible. Even more important was the necessity to get a new Headquarters complex constructed in the right location whilst there was still time to set off the full costs of the project against the German Occupation Budget. It was obviously going to be a race against time. In 1952 preliminary plans for the new Headquarters were prepared at HQ BAOR and put to the Treasury for approval in principle. Provisional agreement was given but only on certain conditions. It would have to be a Joint Service Headquarters. Office and living accommodation would be based on 'Barrack Synopsis, 1948 Scales' (less twenty per cent), and these scales were to be applied to all three services. All costs were to be borne by the Occupation Budget and not a penny would be required from the Treasury. This was exactly the kind of 'heads we win, tails you lose' agreement that the Treasury can never resist, and all now hinged on the speed with which the building project could be pushed through.

In military history the appearance of the right man at the right time and place has accounted for many famous victories. Whilst it would be cynical to disregard the powerful processes of career planning or discount the careful selection procedures which should match the man to the task in hand, in wartime at least it has to be admitted, plain good luck can play a crucial role. The need for 'luck' in war could almost be elevated to the level of one of the great principles of war. The availability and appointment of Colonel Harry Grattan, Royal Engineers, to be Chief Engineer (Works) with responsibility for the Combined JHQ project, appears to demonstrate the importance of luck in military affairs in peacetime, no less than in war. Grattan was born in 1903 and went to the Royal Military Academy, Woolwich in 1921. From 1923 to 1925 he was at the Royal School of Military Engineering, Chatham where he received almost all of his formal engineering training. After Chatham he was posted to India where he stayed until the Second World War. In India he was involved in the rebuilding of Quetta after the earthquake of 1935. No doubt this last experience helped him to accept philosophically some of the admittedly less cataclysmic, but none the less serious, natural disasters that occurred during the Rheindahlen build. The rainfall on the site in November 1952 was 207 per cent of normal and the winter of 1953/54 was said to be the most severe for thirty-nine years. Along with a philosophic approach to the vagaries of the weather he may also have picked up, or at least strengthened, another gift during his service in India. Whilst he was quick to deny any kind of mystic power he did admit to some success as a water diviner in India and elsewhere, and this was to be of considerable value in the new camp as we shall see later. By the early fifties he was serving as CRE (Commander Royal Engineers) at Minden, and by the time of his involvement with the new Headquarters build most of his military career was behind him. He retired from the Army in 1955.

Colonel Grattan maintains a soldierly reticence about himself in his writings, but his ability to lead and inspire soldiers and civilians, British and German alike, is obvious from his achievements. If a memorial were required, to adapt a misquotation, it is only necessary to visit the Rheindahlener Wald. In the conclusion to his article, 'New Headquarters in Germany' printed in the *Royal Engineers Journal* in March and June 1956, he says, 'There has never been a project like this. It has never happened that one Chief Engineer and his staff have been able in the span of one military appointment to help choose the land, plan the site, and see it built, occupied and working. It is a task we have enjoyed and appreciated'.[1] The essence of what went so well in the Rheindahlen build, and what makes it unique in British military building experience, is clear in those words. Unity of control, availability and dedication of the necessary funds and the spur of a clearly understood time limit produced a singular success which contrasts interestingly with what has happened so often elsewhere.

Grattan himself refers to a somewhat similar scheme in Cyprus. The Dhekelia project involved building a complete garrison complex, although smaller than that at Rheindahlen, but including a Military Hospital and a District Headquarters. Interestingly, it too was originally scheduled to cost about £14 million. Planning commenced in 1950 and it was anticipated that the build would be phased over seven to nine years. On average it was expected to spend about £2 million every year. The project ran into the Cyprus emergency but even by 1953 many problems had emerged which were avoided in Germany. The Treasury insisted on a scaling down of the total cost from an original £14.7 millions to £10 millions. This was largely achieved by reducing provision below synopsis scales, by specifying a lower standard of 'finish' to contractors and by abandoning the concept of central boiler houses. There were also many alterations to 'Q' Briefs which gave details of the users' requirements, after they had been accepted by the users and in some cases, even after building was well on. The complaint in Cyprus that not enough planning time had been allowed must be a common one everywhere, but in Germany, where the complaint must have been equally valid, it appears to have been turned very successfully to advantage.[2] Another important difference between Cyprus and Germany emerges very clearly from the two published accounts. In Germany Grattan compliments his German workers for their workmanship and for their grim and dogged determination to stick at their jobs despite appalling weather conditions. The story from Cyprus is one of poor workmanship and less than whole-hearted involvement in the project. No doubt the very different political situation in the two countries influenced the attitudes of the workmen to the outstanding advantage of the German project. In the end the key factors favouring the Rheindahlen build were first, the glad agreement of the Treasury to the immediate spending of large sums of German money and secondly, the clearly understood time limitation on the whole project.

By the early nineteen-sixties some of the principles involved in town and community planning developed in the immediate post-war years were being applied to the planning of new and the rebuilding of old army settlements in the United Kingdom. The Tidworth rebuilding plan for example was an enlightened scheme based upon the idea of developing a 'total environment'.[3] In order to counter the perceived sterility and isolation of the garrison it was intended to include military and civilian accommodation, a town centre with shops and amenity buildings including a community centre. A novel idea was to include an estate for light industry which would provide work for Army wives. A survey had shown that some kind of paid work was essential for many of the wives, partly as an economic necessity, but also to relieve the intense boredom which many of them felt with cantonment life. The scheme failed to be accepted in its original form, the planned population being reduced from 50,000 to 25,000. The main problems at Tidworth were first, the inability of the Treasury to fund amenities on a scale sufficient to change significantly the camp environment, and second, the unwillingness of the military authorities to release training area land for even a modest amount of building. In the end even the reduced scheme was only partly implemented and development has proceeded in what seems to be a very *ad hoc* fashion. Again one becomes aware of the advantages enjoyed by the Rheindahlen planners. Even in post-war Germany however, no less than in Cyprus or Tidworth, the failure of the 'financiers' to accept the necessity for a generous provision for amenity in new or rebuilt army towns has cast a long shadow. Until recently all amenities which were not restricted entirely to the uniformed members of the community had to be seen to be strictly self-financing. Even thirty years after the building of JHQ Rheindahlen, community centres are not accepted as a normal requirement there, or in other British garrisons in Germany. Accommodation is often found for amenity purposes but on a short-term, goodwill basis and only because of the changing pattern of military occupancy which occasionally throws up spare buildings for a limited period.

The concept of the 'total environment' applied to the planning and building of military communities is admirably developed in a Defence Fellowship Study conducted by Lieutenant Colonel D. F. Densham-Booth, OBE, RE, 1968/69. The report, written over fifteen years ago is now a little dated, but the principles are still valid and surprisingly relevant.[4] The first years of the Dhekelia Project are described in articles in the *Royal Engineers Journal* for 1954 and 1955, by Lieutenant Colonel J. D. Edgar, RE.[5] Read together they throw much light on the comparative success of the Rheindahlen building and on the building of military towns since the last war.

Colonel Grattan's articles in the *Royal Engineers Journal* must provide the basis for the factual account of the building of Rheindahlen camp. Some witnesses of the build are still alive, and even after thirty years at least one of those witnesses is still working in JHQ. But memories are notoriously unreliable unless aided by notes made at the time in question, and informal talks that the author has had with early participants in the build and early occupants of the camp have been interesting but have added sadly little to the published account.

It is perhaps necessary to stress at this early stage that the new Joint Headquarters, planned and built under the sole control of HQ British Army of the Rhine, was meant to house four separate headquarters. Apart from HQ BAOR these were, HQ Northern Army Group which controlled an army made up from troops from Britain, Germany, Belgium, Holland and Denmark, HQ 2nd Tactical Air Force, again a multi-nation force, and HQ Royal Air Force Germany which had the same function for the Royal Air Force as HQ BAOR had for the Army. In this chapter whenever reference is made to JHQ or JHQ Rheindahlen or Rheindahlen Camp or the garrison, all offices, installations and living accommodation within the camp, regardless of nation or service is meant.

The overriding consideration for all concerned in the building of the new camp was the need for speed. It was thought that the ratification of the Bonn Convention might be achieved on 1 January 1953 or at the latest by June 1953. After that only one year would remain for the allocation of Deutschmarks. Twenty-five million Deutschmarks had to be spent by the start of 1953, a further seventy million by July 1953 and the bulk of the remainder, about thirty-five million Deutschmarks by January 1954. Even so it was not permitted to ignore barrack synopsis scales or to indulge in time saving extravagancies. As far as possible standard barrack construction had to be used with existing drawings and contracts to make up the bulk of the building. New planning of buildings and services had to be done on the spot. On 6 August 1952 Colonel Grattan received his brief. Site selection commenced on 8 August and even with the change of mind over the Hardter Wald, and the substitution of the Rheindahlener Wald, the Board of Officers under the Chairmanship of Air Marshal Sir Robert Foster ratified the choice of site on 10 August. Colonel Grattan says, 'The site consisted of mature timber, both deciduous and coniferous, some scrub, large nurseries of immature trees and saplings and millions of roots of forests felled in previous generations. It had forest roads of sand with no bottoming. It was three kilometres long and about one kilometre broad. The soil appeared to drain well and had good bearing properties'.[6]

By 6 September the Germans were handed the plans of the road network and the layout of the water mains. These were put out to contract immediately together with a temporary system of H.T. electrical supply so that by the spring contractors would have roads and services to hand for their work. In early October the Chief Engineer moved into an office in Moenchengladbach and within a day the first contractors' representatives arrived to show their wares. Among them was a sleek gentleman who was prepared to supply a 'maison' for the troops complete with attractive 'filles de joie'. He had to be persuaded that such facilities were not included in barrack synopses. There is a story told of an equally enterprising but rather more acceptable businessman. It is said that the North German Director of a large oil company with British connections was driving along the road from Hardt through the Rheindahlener Wald early in 1953 when he saw a lot of activity in the woods. Leaving his car, he walked into the woods and discovered the camp building going on. When he got back to his car he had an agreed site and a signed contract for the camp's service station and garage in his pocket. Such was the urgency of the situation and the delegation of authority that this story has always been accepted as more than reasonable.

To house the Royal Engineer Staff in devastated Moenchengladbach, even without the long waiting list for quarters, would have taken at least nine months so approval was obtained to build twelve officers' and twelve soldiers' houses at once on the new site. These houses were started on 4 November and occupied by the following 6 March 1953. This achievement and that of forcing the concrete roads ahead in winter is the more remarkable since it was the wettest winter for fifty years and produced conditions likened by the German workers to the Russian battle front. With this work completed and the stockpiling of some nine and a half million Deutschmarks' worth of pipes, steel, sanitary equipment, cooking equipment, kitchen equipment and boilers for the heating installations, and by paying advances on all contracts for standard barrack building, payment for over twenty million Deutschmarks was passed by 1 January 1953. By June payments of fifty-five millions had been made but by then it was clear that the 'ratification' was going to be delayed and the urgency subsided somewhat. Foundations for most of the standard buildings had started in February, and by June the whole site was seething with activity. Grattan, apologising for possible mistakes in planning, refers to the headlong rush. He says, 'It will certainly be argued in future that two or three storied barracks and messes should have been built, and would have been cheaper if more compactly sited, but in the early days the overriding consideration was to put to contract and pay running bills for every item of work for which standard designs already existed'.

Whatever is thought by the experts and the paymasters, anyone who has lived in Rheindahlen will give thanks for the overriding necessity which led to the houses and barrack blocks being well spaced out and low in profile. Even so, says Colonel Grattan in his 1956 articles, the effect is thoroughly suburban. If the camp looked suburban in the late fifties it reminds us now much more of a Garden City; it has a purpose, it has focal points and it is self-contained. It would not be fanciful to see it as a kind of 'Company Town' in the American sense. It was planned around the main industry, in this case defence, which is housed in the central 'plant' in the dominating headquarters

Early days of the building works at Rheindahlen HQ.

block. The administration is a benevolent autocracy which provides as much comfort and amenity as it can, given the kind of business that it runs and the source of its funds. All in all, for most of its inhabitants, it is a very pleasant place to work and live in. Even Harry Grattan was able to tell the writer that when he revisited Rheindahlen on the occasion of his eightieth birthday, two years ago, he wasn't too disappointed in the way the place had turned out.

Despite the alleged aesthetic disappointments, and most of us would now say these were overstated, what was achieved in the time available is truly remarkable. Apart from the staff quarters, building started in June 1953, in about twenty-three contractors' lots supervised by eighteen architects nominated by the German Ministry of Reconstruction. Many disagreements over style, fittings and facilities had arisen during the planning stage but an agreed design had been hammered out over the winter. From Colonel Grattan's terse comments one imagines that the hammering may have been loud and even painful at times. Traditional differences in house design often worked in favour of the occupants to come. Thus all the houses were able to have at least partial cellerage, although this was above the 'synopsis scale'. This was a great boon when the family packing cases had to be stored and washing hung out to dry in wet weather. Similarly, although it caused some raised eyebrows amongst the German architects who regarded open fires as incredibly old fashioned, all the officers' quarters, despite efficient central heating, had a traditional English fireplace in the drawing room. At a time when the whole camp area was littered with old and newly felled trees, and almost every house had easy access to fallen timber, this was very much appreciated, and of course helped to save fuel. There were many other examples of the marriage of different traditions, not all of them quite so successful. There were also some acknowledged mistakes. Parquet flooring, easily available in Germany at that time, used in the main rooms in the soldiers' NAAFIs, very quickly succumbed to cigarette ends and ammunition boots, and the lack of garages, even by German standards was quite obvious at the time. Despite strong representation no garages over scale were allowed for officers and none at all for soldiers, even though street parking was and still is illegal in Germany. A little money was no doubt saved but the lack of garages or even of parking space near the quarters is chronic and would now be hopelessly expensive to put right.

It was planned to have the camp ready for occupation by July 1954, but in the event a three months extension was given. The move-in started in October and, as the Commander-in-Chief had promised, all the headquarters families were settled in before Christmas. In the fifteen months of intensive building, 282 soldiers' quarters and 500 officers' quarters were completed, and in a later phase a further 244 houses were built, bringing the total to 1,126. Twenty barrack blocks for the soldiers, each accommodating seventy single men were built and eight blocks each accommodating fifty-two British service women. Further blocks were erected to house directly employed, male and female labour, the German Service Organisation, the Mixed Service Organisation and domestic, NAAFI and other personnel to a total of 2,356 bed spaces. The Headquarters Block, comprising nearly 2,000 offices and stores was occupied at the same time. Messes, a primary school, clubs, churches, a cinema, a lecture theatre and NAAFI shop were available as the occupants arrived and the amenities and general facilities in the camp were enlarged and improved over the next year or two. A secondary school to serve all Army and Royal Air Force units west of the Rhine was opened in September 1955. A second cinema, an Olympic standard swimming pool, a book shop, further churches and clubs and a three acre German shopping precinct were ready by the end of the same year. Seven and a half miles of main road, six miles of secondary and four and a half miles of minor road were open. District heating and hot water supplies, gas, electricity and sewage disposal were all in operation. There had been a host of minor snags, especially in the quarters, and a few major ones, but these were dealt with in the main as they occurred. An improvised 'flying squad' of seventy German artisans made light work of most of the difficulties.

A potentially more difficult situation could have arisen over the different perceptions and requirements of the three services to be housed at Rheindahlen camp. One complication was avoided when the Royal Navy decided that Flag Officer Germany would move his flag to Bonn in 1955. It removed only a very slight complication since the naval contingent numbered only twenty-two officers and ratings. Many thought the slight complication would have been worth while. As one WRAC driver said, 'a few sailors round the place are always good for a laugh'. The Royal Air Force component was of course much larger. In very broad terms the Army made up about five-eighths of the garrison whilst the Royal Air Force made up the remaining three-eighths. Inevitably there were some misunderstandings between the services especially since the Army had overall responsibility for the build. Most of the Royal Air Force accommodation and facilities were located to the west of the site although married quarters were happily much more intermingled. Separate sports facilities, clubs and cinema were provided and although at the time this seemed the right thing to do, there is now a certain amount of embarrassment over this evidence of service insularity. It has been said that the border between the Kreis of Erkelenz and the Stadt of Moenchengladbach, which runs through the centre of the camp and roughly divides the Army from the RAF, accounts for some slight differences of provision between the two services. However, there always have been these differences and long may they remain, but it does mean in times of contraction that a service may lose the whole of a much regarded facility such as the RAF cinema which is now closed. Similarly, the insistence on separate clubs and messes may, in the end, lead to arbitrary closures which might have been avoided. The garrison does now comprise many more non-British servicemen than was originally envisaged and perhaps the two British services find they have rather more in common than they thought. Certainly the differences so determinedly enjoyed between the Army and the RAF are greeted with some incredulity by our allies in the camp although, in recent years, they have been appreciably lessened by financial constraints.

Of course there are many shared facilities. The Garrison Theatre, originally planned and authorised as a model room, is used by the Royal Air Force and Army drama groups, both of which groups accept members from both services as well as civilians. There is also a Music Society which performs regularly in the theatre which also draws its members from all sections of the garrison. The uniquely designed swimming pool which has an off-set, fifteen feet deep, diving bay is also used by everyone living in the camp and a few highly privileged local residents. The main shopping facilities, churches and of course the one remaining cinema are happily shared by all. If a new camp were to be built now it is more than likely that it could be based on completely shared facilities but it is going to be a long time before another Colonel Grattan gets his chance. In the meanwhile the spare capacity that has emerged with the modest degree of rationalisation so far achieved means that new requirements from the operational as well as the amenity side can be accommodated without new building. An example of this is the siting within the garrison recently of the Forces Television complex.

Perhaps the most important facility, enjoyed by everyone and shared with the local population without friction is the delightful rural setting of the camp. Enhanced now by the original careful landscaping and the preservation of every tree that could be saved, the mature estate with its colourful gardens, shrubberies and thickets, merges imperceptibly into the original forests and agricultural clearings. The tree preservation, landscaping, shrub and creeper planting were supervised by a committee, not always the fastest or best way to come to a harmonious conclusion. Colonel Grattan says, 'the future will see whether the Committee did their job properly'. After thirty years the committee, wherever they are, may rest assured they can be proud of that particular piece of work. There can be very few army quarters anywhere in the world where, in winter, deer can be fed over the back fence, or where the quite rare Black Woodpecker can fly overhead as you walk to the NAAFI. Both things happen regularly in Rheindahlen thanks to the dedicated efforts of the early planners who were determined to preserve the forest wildlife.

We cannot pass over the story of the building of JHQ Rheindahlen without referring to the fascinating business of water divining. As we have said, Colonel Grattan served in India before the Second World War, and along with learning how to deal with the aftermath of earthquakes, he discovered in himself the ability to discern the presence of water under the ground by the classic method of the bending twig. The water supply in the camp area was thought to be unsatisfactory in both quality and quantity. It was anticipated that water would have to be brought from public undertakings at what was then the high price of twenty pfennigs per cubic metre. This would have cost, in 1954, £20,000 per year to keep the headquarters supplied. Colonel Grattan was not satisfied with the German reports on the local water situation and brought his own powers into play. After an extensive series of divining trials he was more than ever convinced that useful water existed under the site. He got permission for a number of trial bores to be made in areas where he had divined the presence of water. A large field of soft, faintly acid water was found at approximately twenty metres below ground. Water works were constructed within the camp area; the camp is self-sufficient and secure in its water supply and a large financial saving was made. Grattan was quick to deny any mystic powers and has always said that the ideal combination is to use divining skills to find possible water locations and then to use professional engineering techniques and resources to prove the existence of the water and to extract it.

Family and social life in JHQ Rheindahlen is very much what it would be in a UK garrison town or camp with a few significant exceptions. In Rheindahlen the atmosphere is obviously 'foreign' and slightly exotic despite the overwhelmingly British nature of the settlement. The presence of the vast German hinterland, available for shopping, holidays and local walks and excursions is an exciting challenge for many inhabitants of the camp. Families certainly, seem to make good use of their overseas location, although single male and female soldiers, and single officers tend to take their leave in Britain. The ownership of a motor car is obviously very important if full advantage is to be taken of an overseas posting, in Germany at any rate. Although it should be said, there is an excellent bus service through the camp into Moenchenglad-bach run by the Stadt, it is not fully used by the British. But with tax concessions, cheap petrol, a buyer's market for good secondhand cars and plenty of opportunities to learn the language, most people can get out of the camp and into the splendid countryside whenever they are free. It is a sad fact, however, that despite the incentives and the opportunities some soldiers and their families prefer to stay in the 'safe' and familiar environment of the camp rather than venture out into the wider world beyond. This is in part because all military towns are a little artificial in their composition. Mothers, fathers, grandparents and in-laws do not live nearby and so the Sunday ritual of the family visit is missing. There is no close family to leave the children with when the parents want to go out for the evening or away for a weekend. Rheindahlen has an additional peculiarity. Because of the nature of the Headquarters the personnel stationed in the camp tend to be more senior and more elderly than their counterparts in other British garrisons in Germany. They are less affected by the absence of close family, have fewer social and marital problems of their own, and in the case of officers and senior NCO's, need spend less time in caring for and counselling junior ranks and their wives in the role of surrogate family.

The Queen's School.

There is certainly more social life in Rheindahlen, more entertaining aided by cheap liquor, and probably more eating out even amongst quite junior ranks and their families than would be found in Britain. The availability of good but reasonably priced restaurants, and the continental cafe rather than the pub, as an evening resort for the whole family, has helped to popularise the 'evening out' amongst the families in Rheindahlen. At a rather higher level in the price range, a feature of the area is the number of converted water mills situated on the streams in the surrounding woods. Converted into excellent, although in some cases rather expensive restaurants, they provide a most enjoyable ambience, usually combined with a mercifully restrained 'gemutlichkeit' which is quite acceptable to even the most conservative British taste. Most of the rural German 'gäststatten' have excellent facilities for *al fresco* eating and often there are small animal parks and play areas for the children. Around Rheindahlen many of these cafes are situated on the network of 'wanderwegen' the carefully planned, engineered and mapped tourist walks that have been a feature of the German countryside for over a hundred years. The JHQ camp area is of course open to all. Public roads and footpaths run through the camp area and groups of German walkers descend from buses on their regular bus routes and are often seen following some real or imaginary footpath through the woods within the garrison boundaries. Even if it were possible to ban local people from a facility which has always been theirs it would be churlish, and even from the start of the build the camp has been a subject of intense interest. It is said that early building operations were actually impeded on occasions by the number of sightseers. Even now, a drive round the camp and JHQ building is advertised as a feature of coach tours of the district run from Moenchengladbach. Again, parties of old age pensioners are brought out to the camp by bus and are organised and led off through the woods singing happily in uniquely German fashion. This kind of interest in a large Allied Headquarters is not unreasonable but it does present problems in times of intense terrorist activity and even in the face of anti-nuclear, pacifist or extreme conservationist demonstrations. The inhabitants, servicemen, wives and children have learned to live with the threat and have recognised that almost their only defence is a steady but unhysterical vigilance. In the late seventies a car containing explosives was found in the NAAFI car park, left there by the IRA, and since then there have been many other alarms which have served to remind us that women and children are as much targets for the terrorists as are military installations and soldiers.

At one time it was possible to dismiss protesters as amiable eccentrics. In May 1956 a determined attempt was made by the German owners of thirty-six requisitioned buildings in the Moenchengladbach area to regain possession of their property. Many of the owners were quite elderly, and their spirited attempt to re-occupy the houses, then being used as messes, troop billets and senior officers' quarters was treated with weary but good humoured tolerance. Two old people advancing on the town in their invalid carriages collided with each other and had to be rescued from a ditch by the military police. The most extraordinary feat, however, occurred at dawn on the 6th May. An elderly lady dropped by parachute from a light aircraft on to the roof of the Garrison Officers' Mess. Unfortunately for her, her attempts to gain access through a skylight were heard in time, living-in members were alerted and she was driven off with fire extinguishers. One is tempted to say 'they don't make them like that any more', and to raise a subscription for a memorial. What would happen in a modern re-run of the incident is dreadful to contemplate.

Rheindahlen camp was saved most of the aggravation caused by the requisitioning of property in Moenchengladbach. There were only two German occupied houses on the site. Haus Helbach was lived in by the owner of the Rheindahlener Wald. He appears to have accepted the situation philosophically, leaving his home with regret but seemingly no hard feelings. Haus Heinen on the other hand was evacuated by a forester, a notoriously hard breed of men, and two days later only the walls were left standing. Roofs, windows, doors and floors all disappeared overnight. However, it would be true to say that JHQ worked hard to establish its good relations with the local civil population. From the beginning, every effort was made to persuade servicemen and their families to learn something of the German language. To learn the language of what was soon accepted as the host country was Army policy for the whole of Germany. How effective this policy has been has depended very much on the perceived priorities of successive Commanders-in-Chief. But even in the bad times, German language classes at all levels have been well attended at both the Army Education Centre and the RAF Command Language Training Centre. Two Anglo-German clubs have flourished in the camp almost from its first occupation. These clubs have encouraged joint activities and visits, hospitality between German and British families, and lasting friendships which have resulted in visits to Germany and to Britain away from a service context. There have of course been many marriages between servicemen and German girls and some between German men and British service girls, and Rheindahlen has had its share of them. This seems to have worked well and after British born girls, girls of German origin are by far the largest contingent amongst British service wives. The Anglo-German Clubs and the Anglo-German marriages have formed a bridge between the two communities which has made the acceptance of the Headquarters easier. The HQ and the British camps around Moenchengladbach employ about 6,750 local people. We were assured by the German employees we talked to that they were regarded like any other civil servants or local government workers by their fellow Germans. Interestingly, this was not always the way in which they saw themselves. For the older employees, loyalty to the British, and the adoption of some of their 'funny little ways' has become quite marked. They now occupy a kind of middle ground. They all have a good grasp of English and many of them have refused better paid jobs elsewhere because they now prefer the more easy going, informal atmosphere of the British offices. This is a phenomenon found in service employment all round the world, not least in Britain itself. Naturally, many civilian employees are ex-servicemen, but even the female employees quickly identify with the service environment and adapt the outlook and almost the way of life of the organisation they serve. This accounts to some extent for the special strengths and homogenous nature of garrison towns but is none the less remarkable in Germany, given our recent shared history.

It seems that the only continuing source of irritation amongst some otherwise well disposed local people is the admittedly startling, and sometimes shocking noise from low flying British aircraft. It is generally understood that modern very low level flying tactics require constant, intense and realistic practice, but undoubtedly the sudden build up of high pitched sound from the German as well as British planes is a matter of major local concern. The problem is not helped by the usual 'media hyperbole', where often such incidents are reported under headlines like 'Terror From The Skies'. But notwithstanding this particular discontent, the Royal Air Force is popular in the area. This was demonstrated recently on the sad occasion of the coach crash in Bavaria in which over half of the RAF Staff Band, based on Rheindahlen camp, were killed. The Stadt of Moenchengladbach was one of the first places to set up a fund to aid dependants of the dead bandsmen.

Life in JHQ Rheindahlen, especially domestic life, is lived at the slightly higher level of intensity that is typical of garrison life everywhere, and there is always the 'German Dimension'. In the early days of the camp this 'Germanness' manifested itself as a host of petty regulations about what you could, or more usually, could not do, in and around your quarter. As recently as 1981 the following paragraph could be found in the official 'Welcome to Rheindahlen' information booklet:

> If you are new to Germany it is as well to be aware of some of the more unusual customs, practices and law relating to certain activities on Sundays. For example cars may not be washed (it is in fact an offence to wash a car on the road at any time), laundry should not be hung out, bonfires which may cause offence should not be lit, windows may not be cleaned and all forms of manual labour, e.g. gardening, are frowned upon.

The handbook very sensibly goes on to say that in the interests of good Anglo-German relations the British should try to refrain from carrying out any activity which causes offence to the local population. But there is very little 'local population' nearer than two or three kilometres, and for the soldiers, there is almost nowhere to wash a car except in the street where it is perforce parked and garaged. (Probably another offence under German law.) Many soldiers in the Headquarters, for example cooks, drivers and signals personnel, work a shift system which makes the old-fashioned German Sunday very difficult indeed. Happily, the German regulations are now played down, and even when a nuisance is being perpetrated a friendly warning is the usual corrective. Many apprehensions were caused by hangovers from the excessively harsh, not to say, feudal German forest laws. Newcomers to Rheindahlen used to be told that it was dangerous to stray from the paths in the woods and that all unleashed dogs would be shot on sight whether accompanied by their owners or not. Luckily for the German Forstmeisters this regulation has not been put to the test. The seemingly boundless powers of the German Foresters, even in and around British locations, has led to the not unreasonable belief that a myth was fostered for ulterior reasons. One only needs to walk in the woods around Rheindahlen to see that the Germans are no longer terrified by the 'Forest Laws'. Dogs are usually walked unleashed although most of them are much better controlled than their British equivalents. Germans picnic and play in the woods as we do in Britain, perhaps as a result of the post-war re-education process.

The German dimension is seen more today in terms of the many colourful festivals and local activities which seem to be very much a part of life on 'the Continent'. Karneval is seen at its most spectacular in the Rhineland towns not far from the camp and the great illuminations and firework display of 'The Rhine In Flames' is a popular attraction for sightseers from Rheindahlen. Many of the villages round the camp hold a regular 'Schutzenfest' or huntsmen's festival which is colourful, musical in a tuba-ish kind of way and conducive to a monumental hangover. In the same vein the Munich 'Oktober Fest' has been incorporated into camp life and most messes in the camp hold their own Oktober Fest at which vast quantities of beer are consumed. The Royal Air Force Officers' Mess has the reputation for holding the most authentic and enjoyable 'fest' in the garrison. Special festival beer is brought up from Munich, a Bavarian brass band is hired, Bavarian delicacies and dances are indulged in and there is a competition to wear the most outrageous Bavarian style costume. Many a local

German who has never visited the famous Oktober Fest in Munich will boast of his night at the RAF Fest and proudly display his specially produced RAF Oktoberfest souvenir beer mug. Most of the local villages hold May Day celebrations and 'Kirmes' which was originally a religious festival but is now much like any other fest or fair. Tall, decorated poles are erected, rather like May Poles, and there is dancing and much wearing of regional dress.

Despite all this the atmosphere in the central camp area can be disconcertingly British on occasion. Every year a combined church fete is held on the main square which would be absolutely at home on any village green in Britain. An annual dog show is organised by the scouts and there is usually a Gymkhana. On almost every afternoon in summer cricket matches are held on the green pitches which are situated within the housing areas, again strengthening the village atmosphere. All these peculiarly British activities are of much interest to the Germans and to the many different allied servicemen and their families working and living cheek by jowl in the camp. The mobile 'fish and chip' van calls for as much explanation as the rules of cricket but both provide opportunities to socialise and to break down national barriers and prejudices.

Children swimming and canoeing in the garrison pool.

Several events in the camp calendar have been organised with the intention of bringing the different nations together. There is an Anglo-German Sports Committee and annual athletic competitions and football championships in which Germans, British and other Allied Nations represented at JHQ take part. The two British

Secondary Schools in the garrison area exchange classes with German schools, have exchange teachers and invite German children to school social functions. The three garrison churches also play their part in encouraging friendly relations with the local civil population. Open and joint services are arranged and there are joint committees to organise church activities, especially charity work. Most of the allied contingents in the camp hold a parade, or if they are too few to parade, a reception on their respective National Days. A combined Allied Forces Day parade and reception is also held at JHQ. Since the British form a large majority of the garrison the Queen's Birthday is celebrated in great style. A parade, fly past and a very large party are held in June, and all the local civic dignitaries are invited. Often a 'Beating of Retreat', that quintessential ceremony of British garrison life, is mounted during the evening Birthday party, and is regarded with nostalgic envy by our allies and German civilian friends alike.

Being the headquarters of the British Army and the Royal Air Force in Germany, Rheindahlen happily receives a large number of Royal visits. As a matter of course, local representatives of the Federal German Government, and local officials are always included in the various welcoming parties and have a place of honour at the receptions held at JHQ from where Royal Tours usually commence. Invitations to British ceremonies, and hospitality and deference at social functions are ways in which members of the Headquarters and garrison acknowledge that the British are guests in Germany and that the camp itself, in local government terms, exists only as a suburb of Stadt Moenchengladbach. The camp authorities and the Stadt and Land Departments co-operate easily and efficiently over a wide range of functions from roads, transport including the camp bus service, fire and accident prevention and policing to the overall security of the whole camp area. Even so, it must be galling occasionally for Moenchengladbach to be treated as less than the civic superior of JHQ Rheindahlen, and the Stadt must feel sometimes that it has a rather boisterous cuckoo in the nest.

It is difficult, for the British especially, in what to them is a British town set down in a rather pleasant part of 'abroad', to regard JHQ Rheindahlen as anything other than a British military town. For the soldier or the airman the camp probably has more in common with Tidworth or Halton or even Gibraltar than with the small German towns round about. But it also has more in common with all British garrison towns, camps or settlements, however they are defined, than the whole panoply of civil life in Britain or Germany. It is possible, even in the extraordinary agglomeration of offices, barracks, quarters, training facilities and general amenities which make up the structure of JHQ Rheindahlen, to see some of those features which we have identified as being typical of the British garrison.

It is perhaps fitting that we leave the last word on Rheindahlen to one of Colonel Harry Grattan's officers. Lieutenant Colonel J. Biggs, who was in charge of contracts and financial control, reminisces some twenty-five years after leaving Germany:

> The first winter 1953/4 was the coldest for fifty years and the number of workmen went down from 7,000 to 56, all night watchmen and foremen. There was a terrible storm in May, three inches of rain fell in five hours. Queen's Avenue, in front of the tennis courts was about a foot deep in grass seed, washed off the newly sown areas. There were six horses on the establishment to get around the

Beating the retreat, with the flags of Britain, the Netherlands and the Federal Republic
of Germany being lowered, 1980.

site. There was only one holly tree on the site, it was in front of Haus Hellbach. The policy was to preserve as many deciduous trees as possible. The kink in Queen's Avenue was to avoid the line of oak trees.

Enormous trouble was taken to preserve two oak trees in front of the HQ building, one was killed by lightning and after the building was occupied the other was cut down to allow a helicopter strip. Well over a million trees were planted on the site.

Three unexploded bombs were uncovered on the site, it was not known whose they were but we had to pay for the removal and loss of working hours. We converted twenty-three pairs of houses to accommodate extra large families. Four of them were Royal Engineers officers, each with eight children.

The names of the roads were decided on by a high powered committee at HQ Rhine Army. I was disappointed about this because I wanted two of the roads named after Colonel Grattan, The Chief Engineer and Major Dix the Site Supervisor. Colonel Grattan didn't think much of the idea. The telephone exchange was one of the first buildings to be started and there were at least three spies working on the job, one was British! The corridors in the HQ building are about three hundred yards long and the foreman used to ride a bicycle along the corridors shouting 'achtung, achtung'.

Finally it was my job to settle all the contracts and final accounts. This proved to be a long drawn out affair. Fortunately I had been there from the beginning, knew the site inside out, knew all about all of the jobs and so knew all the phoney excuses, etc. I shudder to think of a stranger trying to settle the account. Eventually, by the end of June 1956 I thought I had just about finished all I could do. There were thirteen outstanding accounts. Ten were bankrupts and three were under Police investigation. So I pulled down the RE flag on 30 July 1956 and retired from the Army after thirty-four years' service.[7]

Bibliography

The only published work on Rheindahlen Camp is the reprint of Colonel Harry Grattan's two articles which appeared in *The Royal Engineers Journal* in March and June 1956. His booklet *'New Headquarters in Germany'* may still be available from 34 Army Education Centre, or Garrison HQ, Rheindahlen Camp, but it is fast becoming a collectors item.

The Royal Army Education Corps Officers in HQ, BAOR, and at 34 AEC are trying to compile and maintain a record of the garrison, its history and activities. They are sadly hampered by the lack of documentary and photographic records and it is not expected that the work will be available, even for consultation, for some time.

The 'Dhekalia Project' appears in the *Royal Engineers Journal* for 1954 and 1955.

The report on 'Social Planning, Army Housing in the United Kingdom 1970s-1980s', is published as a *Defence Fellowship Study 1968/69* by Lieutenant Colonel D. F. Densham-Booth, OBE, RE and may be available from the Ministry of Defence Library, Old War Office, Whitehall.

10

Gibraltar

PETER DIETZ

THE MILITARY history of Gibraltar at its most exciting and most typical is contained in the story of its many sieges. Of course there have been quiet periods in its history especially during the nineteenth century when the 'Pax Britannica' held through much of the world. But the 'Rock' is best remembered and visualised in the popular mind as a mighty fortress besieged by countless foes who against any other fortress could not fail to triumph. The truth has sometimes been different. Between AD 711 when the Rock was first attacked and then occupied by a Moorish force from North Africa, and 1985 when the Spanish finally lifted all restrictions on access after many years of political and psychological warfare, Gibraltar has been under recognisable siege fifteen times. Some of these sieges have been of short duration whilst others have lasted for several years like the 'Great Siege' of 1779 to 1783, or indeed the last *de facto* siege, just ended, which lasted for sixteen years. The sieges have varied in intensity from short periods of bombardment and violent assault to long periods of watchful inactivity where boredom, hunger and disease presented the main challenge to the garrison and civil population. In these variations life in Gibraltar probably did not differ very much for the troops from service life anywhere else. Brief interludes of danger and excitement in between much longer periods of boredom and drudgery were, and still are, the lot of soldiers everywhere.

The one aspect of life in Gibraltar which did make the situation unique is the geographical position and geological formation of the Rock. When the Rock was garrisoned by a strong and determined maritime power it was virtually impregnable. Over the long years of military occupation the defences, through tunnelling and the reinforcement of permanent works, became more and more strong so that, even by the end of the eighteenth century, the main problems in war had become those of providing an adequate water supply, food stores and proper sanitation. Yellow fever and later cholera were more feared than any conceivable enemy. It was not until nearly the end of the nineteenth century that the much increased power and range of artillery weapons put the vulnerability of the fortress seriously in question. The advent of bombing planes and nuclear weapons has only confirmed the end of Gibraltar's role as Britain's great bastion in the Western Mediterranean.

However, in the eighteenth and early nineteenth centuries Gibraltar could not be reduced by the classic method of 'sapping and mining'. Walls could be breached and towers brought down as they repeatedly were up to the end of the Peninsula War and even later during the Indian Mutiny, but it was not possible to bring down the great

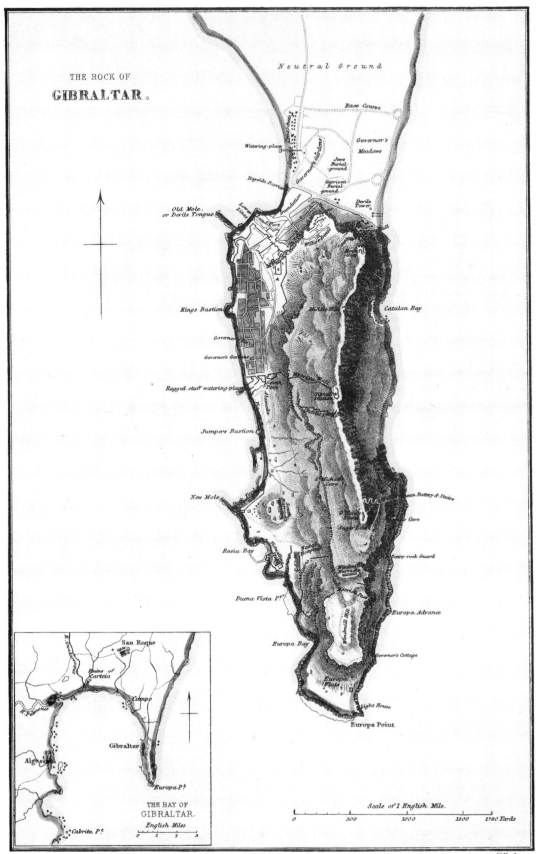

THE ROCK OF
GIBRALTAR.

Neutral Ground

Race Course

Governor's
Meadows

Watering-place

Jews
Burial-
ground

Bayside Barrier

Garrison
Burial
ground

Devils
Tower

Old Mole,
or Devils Tongue

Lower
Lines

Land Port

Inundation

Willis's Battery

Kings Bastion

Middle Hill

Catalan Bay

Governor's

Governor's Garden

Ragged staff watering-place

Signal
Station

Jumpers Bastion

St Michael's
Cave

New Mole

Ocean Battery & Stairs

Cave

Sugar Loaf

Rosia Bay

Scarp-rock Guard

Buena Vista Pt

Windmill Hill

Europa Advance

Europa Bay

Governor's Cottage

Europa
Flats

Light House

Europa Point

THE BAY OF
GIBRALTAR.

San Roque

Ruins of
Carteia

Campo

R. Guadarranque

R. Palmones

Gibraltar

Algesiras

Europa Pt

Cabrita Pt

English Miles
0   1   2   3

Scale of 1 English Mile.

0   500   1000   1500   1760 Yards

W. Hughes. sc.

An early nineteenth-century map of the peninsula.

north face of the Rock of Gibraltar. After the fifteenth century it is doubtful if any serious attempt was made to capture the Rock from the landward side. Almost always from then on attacks were made from the sea against the more vulnerable western side of the Rock, supported in spirit if not always in fact by orthodox siege tactics against the northern front. It is even less likely that a hostile power during the nineteenth century could have applied anything other than political and commercial pressures, and in the face of the overwhelming strength of the British Navy and the dominating position of Britain in world trade, these pressures need not have been taken seriously.

It is this long period of absolute invulnerability which gave Gibraltar its reputation as the pre-eminent British bastion overseas. It also gave its inhabitants and garrison a feeling of confidence and superiority which emerged again during its most recent, although happily least bloody, siege. Sixteen years of isolation and economic hardship have shown once again that external pressures and imposed privations can only strengthen the will and determination of a free and close-knit community to resist the demands and blandishments of a less happy and less stable political system.

The Rock of Gibraltar is situated in the south-west corner of Europe at the western entrance to the Mediterranean Sea. It is about three miles long from north to south and almost a mile wide at its widest point. The Rock is precipitous on its northern and eastern sides but less so to the south and west although there are sheer sea cliffs on the southern half of the west coast and at Europa Point at the extreme southern end. It is separated from, or as some would say, joined to Spain at its northern end by a flat, sandy isthmus which is completely dominated by the massive north face of the Rock which rises to a little over 1,300 feet. North Africa is nine miles away to the south across the Straits and Spain lies not only to the north but to the westward across Algeciras Bay which is about five miles wide. It is the height of the Rock, its comparative isolation and the difficulty of the landward approach which in the past gave Gibraltar its importance as the dominating fortress on the Straits.

The climate of Gibraltar is of course Mediterranean, with long, hot summers and short, cool and usually wet winters. However, being so close to the Atlantic Ocean the climate is modified so that hot summers are rarely too hot and cool winters rarely too cool. Enough rain falls in an average winter, carefully collected and stored, to meet the needs of the permanent population. A growing tourist industry requires water to be imported. In the past when water ran out it could be brought in from Spain. More recently it has been brought in by tanker from North Africa and occasionally even from Britain. The most unpleasant climatic feature of the Rock is the growth of a cloud cap on the summit when a strong easterly wind is blowing. This is known locally as the 'Levanter' and its warm, sticky presence can be very trying if it persists for more than a few days. Luckily it is usually short lived.

For most servicemen, and especially service families, Gibraltar has come to be regarded as a very good posting. When the frontier is open there is easy access to superb Mediterranean and Atlantic beaches and to the most exciting and romantic province of Spain, Andalusia. Even when the frontier has been closed Gibraltar has its own good beaches and North Africa is only two hours away by ferry through Tangier. The Rock has an incredibly varied social and sporting life and the garrison and their families are able to share the many opportunities for recreation with a civil population whose main language is now, thanks to Spanish short-sightedness, English.

Gibraltar has been a free port for over two hundred and fifty years, and although some taxes are now imposed on some imports Main Street is still a shoppers' paradise. When the land frontier is closed, fresh food, especially fruit and vegetables, must be brought expensively from Morocco or elsewhere, but there is no hindrance to the flood of consumer goods from Japan, Hong Kong, Britain and the rest of Europe outside Spain.

Frequent reference to the Straits of Gibraltar and the Rock's dominating position at the western entrance to the Mediterranean has perhaps implied that the Straits are important only for east–west traffic into and out of the great inland sea. That they effectively separated Europe from Africa has been strongly challenged by Fernand Braudel. In his famous study of The Mediterranean World at the time of Philip II[1] he points out that the Straits have always been a bridge between north and south, joining rather than separating the two continents. He insists that for many centuries Spain and North Africa were one country, joined not separated by a narrow strip of water easily and frequently crossed. This interpretation makes Gibraltar, especially in its early history, doubly important, and provides a useful point of departure for a brief examination of the history of the Rock up to its capture in July 1704 by the British and their Dutch allies.

There is fossil evidence of a Neanderthal type of people living on or frequently visiting the Rock around 40,000 BC. There is much more evidence of visits and settlements on the Rock and round the Bay of Algeciras by the Egyptians, Phoenicians, Carthaginians, Greeks and Romans. Carteia, a short excursion across the head of the bay from Gibraltar, was a Carthaginian city captured from them by the Romans about 190 BC. Julius Caesar defeated Pompey's sons Cnaeus and Sextus at the Battle of Munda within a few miles of the Rock. Roman Carteia, which included Gibraltar, became a prosperous and powerful colony after the battle in AD 45, having its own mint amongst many other privileges. The Gibraltar Museum, which is a model of its kind, displays vividly much of this early history, but Gibraltar's importance as a military base and permanently garrisoned fortress dates from AD 711.

By AD 650 the first great flood of Islam had spent itself on the borders of what is now Tunisia. But the conversion of the Berbers, who were the original inhabitants of north-west Africa, gave a renewed impetus to the spiritual and political advance. By 696 the whole of the North African coastline was in Arab hands. As Braudel has said, the short stretch of water between Africa and Spain provided an easy route for the experienced Arab sailors and in 711, after a brief reconnaissance, the Arab armies were ready to move across the Straits into Spain. A full scale invasion of Andalusia was mounted by an army of 7,000 foot soldiers and 500 horsemen under the command of a freedman, Tarik ibn Zeyed. It is not certain if Tarik actually landed at Gibraltar but it seems very likely that he made a fortified base there and installed the Arab garrison which was maintained on the Rock, with one short break, for over 750 years. What is more certain is that he gave his name to the Rock. Gibel Tarik, the 'Mountain of Tarik', eventually became the modern 'Gibraltar'. The Moors swept on into Spain and within twenty years occupied all but a narrow strip along the north coast. They remained in Spain, establishing an Emirate independent of North Africa and ruled by a succession of Arab dynasties until the fifteenth century. By then Islam had lost its fervour, the Arab world had split into a large number of rival Emirates whilst Spain, united at last under Ferdinand and Isabella, sustained by a new religious fervour of its own and financed by its newly found treasure in the Americas, was finally able to drive out the Moors and in the process regain possession of Gibraltar. Towards the end of the Moorish occupation rivalry between the Sultan of Fez and the Kingdom of Granada, the remant of the Arab empire in Spain, led to war between them over Gibraltar. This dissension led to the total defeat of the Moors in Spain and, as we have seen, to their final expulsion in 1462.

It was only towards the end of the Moorish occupation of Gibraltar that the fortifications and other buildings which remain as evidence of the Arab presence were erected. The Moorish Wall which runs down from the summit of the Rock to the south end of the town was probably completed about 1160. The wall was built to protect the southern end of the town from enemy landings in the area of the Red Sands below what is now the Alameda Gardens. The small original town was developed below the Tower on the site of Casemates Square. A mosque, which later became the Catholic Cathedral, a windmill and a water system with reservoirs were also constructed. Another interesting reminder of the Moorish settlement is the restored bath house located in the basement of the Gibraltar Museum.

After Spain repossessed the Rock the harbour was developed as a base for the growing Spanish navy and the great commercial fleet called into existence and paid for by the gold and spices of the Indies. It was also used in the frequent operations against the Corsairs operating out of the North African ports along the Barbary Coast. During the sixteenth century particularly, the Corsairs became a serious menace in the Western Mediterranean. Braudel recounts how a strong force of Barbary pirates landed on Gibraltar, made off with eighty captives, and then were sufficiently confident to sail into the harbour to arrange for ransom, buy fresh provisions and fraternise with the population. Raids on the southern Spanish coast were frequent and usually less convivial than the raid reported by Braudel. In one great raid in the early sixteenth century 4,000 prisoners were taken from the Province of Granada alone. Fifty ships were seized in the Straits in one season and twenty-eight Biscay ships were taken off Malaga in the same period. There were more than a hundred Corsair ships at large in the Mediterranean at the peak of their power dominating the Straits and controlling all coastal traffic. The Corsairs were in many cases only nominally Muslim but they operated from Arab ports owing allegiance to the Turkish Sultanate. The Turkish fleets were continuously at war with the Christian powers in the Mediterranean and so they naturally protected and co-operated with the Corsairs. It was not until after the Italian Admiral Andrea Doria and the legendary Don John of Austria, achieved their series of victories over the Turks, culminating in the battle of Lepanto in 1571 that the Corsair menace abated. With the cleaning out of the Corsair strongholds on the North African coast and the decisive shift of Spanish maritime interest to the Atlantic, Gibraltar was increasingly neglected. It was not until the Rock was visited by Philip IV in 1624 that any attempt was made to restore the defences. His visit is chiefly remembered because he managed to get his carriage stuck in the Landport Gate, and had to be reminded that it was so designed in order to keep out the enemy. But he obviously took the point. New bastions and defensive ditches were constructed on his orders. The Line Wall defences on the western side of the Rock were strengthened and gun platforms and batteries were placed to cover the harbour and the New Mole. By 1627 Gibraltar was one of the most strongly fortified bases around the Spanish coast.

During most of the seventeenth century dynastic wars were fought in Europe and elsewhere without directly involving Gibraltar. Charles I of England showed an interest in Spain and might have involved England in a war there but eventually his troubles at home overwhelmed him and Spain was forgotten. Oliver Cromwell also took a hard look at Gibraltar and saw the Rock as a possible base from which Britain's growing maritime power could expand into the Mediterranean, but the time was not ripe and British interest again declined or at least was for the moment submerged in a naval war with the Dutch. In 1662 when Catherine of Braganza married Charles II she brought Tangier to Britain as part of her dowry. As a result interest in the Straits revived for a time. A trading company was formed and Samuel Pepys visited the settlement as a member of a government management committee. Tangier was well placed as a naval base for the sea route round the Cape of Good Hope. Sadly, interest and cash ran out and Tangier was abandoned in 1684 after a brief occupation of only twenty-two years. Pepys was again involved in the winding up of affairs in the short-lived colony and there is some evidence that he arranged for his brother-in-law, a naval officer, to carry out a reconnaissance of Gibraltar at this time. Pepys was a very shrewd man and as Secretary of the Navy he would have been privy to State policy. In any event Britain began to take a more serious interest in western Mediterranean affairs and it is likely that a more informed if more discreet concern over Gibraltar dates from this time.

In 1689 Britain, in alliance with Spain, The Netherlands, Austria and Bavaria was at war with France. The British and Dutch fleets had a series of engagements with the French in which on several occasions the French had the advantage. On one such occasion in 1693 a fleet of four hundred merchantmen escorted by a naval force under Admiral Sir George Rooke were outgunned by a superior French fleet and had to disperse. Some of the ships, naval and merchantmen made their way to Gibraltar which was bombarded by the French ships and attacked in the harbour by fire ships. Improvising a defence by mounting ship's guns on the New Mole, the British sailors saved what remained of the fleet. Little had been done to improve the defences of Gibraltar in the previous seventy years but the spirited defence of the ships and the usefulness of the Rock as a defended base, particularly against the French, and after the abandonment of Tangier, was obvious. Admiral Rooke was to return to the Rock in ten years' time and this time the British were to stay.

The war with France ended with the Peace of Ryswick in 1697 but by 1700, when Charles II of Spain died, a new cause of friction had arisen. Charles had died childless. Of the two candidates for the Spanish throne one, Philip V, was a grandson of Louis XIV of France, whilst the other, Archduke Charles of Austria (Charles III), was a Hapsburg.

Britain and her allies could not accept the possibility of a union of France and Spain under a Bourbon monarchy. Britain, The Netherlands and Austria went to war in 1702 with the object of placing Charles III on the Spanish throne. There was no war with Spain as a whole but both candidates for the throne had their Spanish supporters and inevitably they were drawn into the war.

In February 1704 Charles sailed to Lisbon. Admiral Rooke was in command of the British fleet supporting him. The aim was to secure a base on the Spanish mainland from which Charles could be put on the throne. A hoped-for rising of the Catalans in Barcelona in support of Charles did not materialise and Rooke failed to find and engage the French fleet. These two disappointments weighed heavily with a Council of War held on Rooke's flagship off Ceuta. A spectacular success was necessary to retrieve the situation and to restore Charles's prestige and Rooke's reputation. Councils of War usually recommend a cautious line of action. On this occasion, knowing that the garrison was weak and the defences still not improved since Rooke's battle there with the French in 1693, it was decided to make an attempt on Gibraltar. On 1 August about 2,000 British and Dutch Marines were landed on the sandy isthmus at the north end of the Rock. Over 15,000 rounds were fired from the fleet and in six hours the defenders of the New Mole were completely overwhelmed. Captain Hicks managed to land on the Mole but his force of sailors and marines was almost completely destroyed when a magazine below the Mole blew up. A little later Captain Whittaker got ashore in Rosia Bay with two hundred men where they soon captured a small bastion overlooking the mole. The bastion was later named Jumper's Bastion after one of the officers who had managed to get on to the mole in the earlier assault. The Prince of Hesse, in command of the landward attack, advanced from the isthmus at the same time whilst calling on the Spain garrison to surrender. Fighting gradually died away during the night and the Spanish finally capitulated on the morning of 4 August.

Admiral Byng was in charge of the landing operations which, despite the disaster on the Mole, were a great success, but he was much less successful in maintaining order after the surrender. Plundering, rape and general violence were the normal consequences of failing to give up a fortress or defended town when summoned and Gibraltar did not escape. Although disorder was short lived, the town had to witness scenes that were all too familiar throughout Europe after a successful assault, until well on into the nineteenth century.

Admiral Byng's son, John, also became an Admiral and was also involved with Gibraltar but in tragic circumstances. To anticipate the story a little, Byng's son was given command of an expedition sent to relieve Minorca in 1756. He fought an inconclusive battle with the French fleet off Minorca and then returned to Gibraltar to succour his wounded, preserve his ships and, incidentally perhaps, to safeguard the fortress. He was recalled to England to face a charge of cowardice. The Court Martial found him guilty but only of a lesser charge which nevertheless carried a mandatory death sentence. On appeal George II showed no mercy and Byng was executed by firing squad. Voltaire in *Candide* commented, 'in that country they shoot an Admiral from time to time to encourage the others'.

The War of the Spanish Succession continued indecisively for several more years after the capture of the Rock and it was not until 1711 that negotiations were finally begun to end the war with Spain and France. The Treaty of Utrecht made in 1713 gave Gibraltar to Britain. Although the Rock had been occupied ostensibly in the name of a Spanish claimant to the throne, by 1713 the advantages of a permanent settlement were obvious. The Tories had returned to power in Britain in 1710 determined to wind up land operations against the French and to pursue a maritime strategy. Gibraltar was essential for this purpose and although there were discussions from time to time, and suggestions for exchanges, too much blood had been spilt to make any accommodation possible. The Treaty of Utrecht said the Rock was 'to be held and enjoyed absolutely with all manner of rights for ever', but there were unfortunately, many ambiguities. There was to be no communication with the country round about, allegedly to prevent smuggling. Moors and Jews were not to reside in Gibraltar. The sandy strip between the Rock and Spain was to remain strictly neutral. All of these conditions were ignored by both sides when it suited them. Smuggling from Gibraltar into Spain quickly became a major industry engaged in as much by the Spanish as the inhabitants, and food and wine have been imported through the frontier into Gibraltar whenever war between Spain and Britain was not being actively pursued. Finally, before the outbreak of hostilities both sides would attempt to occupy as much 'neutral ground' as possible. All these uncertainties gave the Spanish some hope that they would eventually recover the Rock but they were given no encouragement in that fond hope by the British. Queen Anne made Gibraltar a Free Port in 1712, even before the Treaty of Utrecht had formally ceded the fortress to Britain. General Bland, the then Governor, persuaded her that British influence would be much increased as a result and that the port would then rival Leghorn, the only Free Port in the Mediterranean at that time. A more practical consideration was that Morocco would not trade in food except on a reciprocal basis.

In 1726 the Spanish tried to capture the Rock again. The defences, after twenty years of peace, had been neglected. But Spanish weapons and equipment appear to have been in an even worse condition. An attempt to explode a mine under Willis's Battery at the north end of the Rock failed after nearly a whole year's work. The Spanish artillery, in what was almost entirely a gunners' war, began to wear out and, most important of all, they were unable to seal off the Rock to prevent supplies and reinforcements coming in by sea. Although hostilities ceased, peace negotiations were as usual long drawn out. It was not until November 1729 that the Treaty of Seville confirmed the agreement made in the Treaty of Utrecht. The ambiguities remained but the peace held despite war with France in 1756 and the loss of Minorca which, as we have seen, led to Admiral Byng's demise. Gibraltar enjoyed fifty years of calm until 1779 when the fourteenth siege, the 'Great Siege' commenced.

When the fighting ended in 1728 it became clear that the British were determined to stay on the Rock. What at first appeared to be a temporary garrison took on a more permanent form. Until 1728 all outsiders had been limited to thirty days residence, but from then on the ban was no longer enforced. 'Englishmen, foreigners, rich Jews and Moors flocked thither from all quarters', says a contemporary account. The Jews particularly began to build houses for themselves but the other settlers quickly followed suit, anxious to establish themselves under the protection of a permanent British garrison at one of the important crossroads of western Europe. H. W. Howes, who has made an analysis of the registers of population and trade from the year 1704, gives the following figures for the population in 1753:

Civilians:	British	351
	Genoese	597
	Jews	575
	Spaniards	185
	Portuguese	25
	Total	1,733[2]

To this total of 1,733 should be added 83 British nationals employed by the Navy and Victualling Office. This is hardly evidence of 'flocking in', but it does mean that the loss of population that occurred when the British and Dutch captured the Rock had probably been made good by the mid-eighteenth century.

The successful British resistance during the Great Siege, the courage and fortitude of the servicemen and their families and the civilians remaining on the Rock, the ingenuity and resource shown in the defence and the comparatively civilised relations that were maintained with the enemy, make up one of the most exciting and inspiring episodes in British military history.

The happy outcome of the siege, from the British point of view, depended upon the arrival in Gibraltar, before the siege commenced, of two outstanding military personalities. Colonel William Green, an engineer and competent gunner, had been wounded at the taking of Quebec and posted to Gibraltar in 1761. Although the defences of the Fortress had suffered from the usual peacetime neglect it was not until 1769 that he was allowed to go to England to persuade the government to accept his plans for their improvement. By 1772 he had replaced the civilian artificers on contract from England and the Continent with a military company of soldier artificers. The civilian artificers were described as 'indolent, drunken, disorderly and overpaid'. They could also leave the Rock at any time regardless of the local need. The new company of artificers, forerunners of the Royal Engineers, were drawn from volunteers from the regiments in garrison, of whom sixty-eight were selected. Sergeant Ince was the senior 'other rank' and the Company quickly made an impact on the sapping, mining and construction problems of the Fortress.

As Chief Engineer, and with his knowledge of artillery matters, Green's advice and energy were of inestimable value to the Fortress Commander. He and his wife Miriam, of whom more later, were typical of the many military families in Gibraltar during the siege who through their courage and high spirits sustained the life and hopes of its inhabitants.

By great good fortune a new commander was appointed to Gibraltar in 1777. It was one of those providential coincidences that produce exactly the right man at the right time and place. General George Elliott was educated at Edinburgh and Leyden Universities and spoke several languages. He was trained as a field engineer, receiving his first military education at the Royal Military Academy, Woolwich. He was wounded at both Dettingen and Fontenoy and retired in 1776. However, he was offered Gibraltar in 1777 and accepted. Originally commissioned in the Horse Grenadier Guards, (afterwards the 2nd Life Guards) he was a most experienced and enlightened officer. His qualities of leadership were the most important single factor contributing to the British victory in the Great Siege.

At the beginning of the siege the Spanish Navy was in the ascendancy around Gibraltar and was able to enforce a blockade. After waiting for three months for the Spanish to start the land attack, General Elliot decided to force the action. On the signal 'Britons strike home',[3] the first cannon shot was fired into the Spanish lines by the wife of a member of the garrison. The strength of the British batteries at the north end of the Rock, much improved by Colonel Green in the two years before the siege, made an attack on that side almost impossible. The batteries, positioned one above the other up the flank of the Rock, were continuously extended and strengthened throughout the siege. Quite early in the siege a gun was hauled up to crown the highest peak of the Rock at 1,300 feet. This became known as Rock Gun. Eventually the north front was covered with batteries and most of the enemy siege works could be enfiladed from the British positions. The story of how the last great problem was solved is recounted in Connolly's *History of the Corps of Royal Sappers and Miners*, published in 1855.

On a fine day in May 1782, the Governor, attended by the Chief Engineer and staff, made an inspection of the batteries at the North Front. Great havoc had been made in some of them by the enemy's fire; and for the present they were abandoned whilst the artificers were restoring them. Meditating over the ruins for a few moments he said aloud, 'I will give a thousand dollars to anyone who can suggest how I am to get a flanking fire upon the enemy's works'. A pause followed the exciting exclamation, when Sergeant Major Ince of the Company (Sappers and Miners) who was in attendance upon the Chief Engineer, stepped forward and suggested the idea of forming galleries in the rock to effect the desired object. The General at once saw the propriety of the scheme and directed it to be carried into execution. Work was commenced on the 25 May 1782 with Sergeant Major Ince in charge.

A footnote adds:

Whether the Sergeant Major received the thousand dollars as a douceur from the General is a question never likely to be satisfactorily answered. The probability is, that he did not receive the reward for the suggestion in this form, but some daily allowance commensurate with his skill and the importance of the duty . . . Ince contracted for the work and, such was the story current in his day, for all the excavations he received one guinea per running foot.

The Chief Engineer called for a gallery six feet wide and six feet high. Before September 1782 five heavy guns were placed in the gallery and in little more than twelve months from the commencement the gallery was pushed to the 'notch'. A battery was established there and distinguished by the name of St. George's Hall.

Two other artillery problems were tackled during the siege. Explosive shells were in use by 1779 but it was found that when they exploded on the sandy isthmus they did little damage. An infantry officer, Captain Mercier, suggested the use of a short fuse to produce an air burst and this proved to be effective. It so happens that a Lieutenant Shrapnel was serving in the garrison during the siege and it is quite likely that his 'shrapnel' was based upon Mercier's short fused shell. The other problem was caused by the difficulty of firing guns on the Rock downwards at a steep angle. Lieutenant Koehler designed a gun carriage which could be depressed so as to fire down from the rock face batteries. An excellent model of the carriage can be seen in the Gibraltar Museum. Again, it is likely that the invention influenced later recoil systems.

It became clear to the Spanish that their best hope of subduing the Rock was by siege and blockade. The Spanish naval ascendancy near Gibraltar meant that supplies were cut off from the Rock for most of the four years of the siege. Relieving fleets did get into Gibraltar in 1780, 1781 and 1782 but there were long periods when food and ammunition were desperately short, when prices rose and accusations of hoarding and profiteering were widespread. The blockade occasioned many naval skirmishes and at least two fleet actions. Because these actions took place near the Rock, everyone who was not manning the lines would seek a vantage point from which to cheer on the British ships. It was also the thing to become a 'watcher' of the Spanish lines so as to be an early bearer of good tidings. As always in these circumstances rumour abounded. Miriam Green, wife of the Chief Engineer, kept a journal in which she reports on 27 August, (about three months into the siege):

It now became quite fashionable to get all the news each one could collect; and by way of gaining all that, everybody was using spy glasses from morning to night. All those that affected great cleverness were ever ready with a pencil and paper, and it was really laughable enough to see with what a jealous eye each aide-de-camp look'd at the other fearing he should be the first to communicate his ideas of what he supposed the enemy was about! Various therefore was the Reports, and could not always agree. Those remarks I have made (such as I could not possibly make from my own observation) I think may be depended upon as they are from our own Corps, and mostly from the Gentleman that is in the Colonel's family (his ADC?), who would hardly bring me a false account.[4]

Sadly, there are no records of the observations brought to her by the 'Gentleman of the Colonel's family', but one can only admire Mrs Green's Corps loyalty.

Miriam Green tells us in her diary of the siege something of conditions on the Rock at that time. Paving stones were removed from the streets which were then ploughed up to reduce the danger from shell-splinters. Most of the houses in the town had bomb-proof shelters dug beneath them and where possible the inhabitants moved to the south end of the Rock, out of range of the enemy cannon. The Greens were lucky in not only did they have an official quarter in the town but, during their long service on the Rock, they were able to have a private house built to the south of the town. They were able to alternate between their two residences depending upon the intensity of the enemy bombardment. On finally leaving Gibraltar Colonel Green sold his house, Mount Pleasant, to the government. It is still in existence, after some alteration and additions, as The Mount, official residence of the Admiral.

In November 1781, General Elliott, never prepared to let the enemy dictate the course of events, ordered a sortie against the Spanish siege works. The sortie was something of a risk since it used one third of the garrison in the attack but it achieved complete surprise and destroyed most of the enemy's advanced works. The sortie was under the command of General Ross but Elliott was quite unable to resist taking part in the action and was in the front line whilst the fighting was going on.

The Spanish regained Minorca for the second time in 1782, and after that they were able to divert more resources to the attack on Gibraltar. The defenders numbered between 5,500 and 7,000 men but because of their solidly built fortifications they were able to hold the Rock against Spanish and French forces numbering at their peak over 40,000. But these numbers could not be adequately deployed on the land front and the fighting became mainly a duel between opposing gunners. One last attempt to capture the Rock was made in September 1782. It was the most ambitious attempt ever made. Floating batteries were prepared with overhead cover for the gunners and a water sprinking system as a safeguard against red hot shot. The attackers were able to muster 246 guns against the defender's 96. The battle started with a bombardment from the Spanish guns on the landward side at ten o'clock which went on all day. By afternoon the Spanish floating batteries, which had come close to the west side of the Rock and at first seemed invulnerable, began to burn and by nightfall the bay was lit up by the burning and exploding ships. The land bombardment made little impression on the well-protected British artillery. The attack was not renewed the next day much to the chagrin of the many Spanish spectators, including it is said, the Queen of Spain herself. The hill from which they watched the *débâcle* is now known as 'The Queen of Spain's Chair' and is gleefully pointed out to visiting tourists from the summit of the Rock. A large convoy arrived to reprovision the Fortress in October and following on so shortly after the unsuccessful attack of September it effectively marked the end of the siege although hostilities were not officially suspended until 3 February 1783.[5]

Peace returned for a short time and with the peace the inevitable problems of the eighteenth century British Army abroad. In the *Journal of the Society for Army Historical Research* there is an interesting account by a soldier, only identified by the initials G.B., of life in Gibraltar when he joined the garrison in 1797. 'G.B.' confirms that very heavy drinking was commonplace in all garrisons at that time. The men were often paid only at two-monthly intervals and with so much money to spend parades, except for the guard, were abandoned until the money ran out and the Regiment sobered up. Regiments, he says, had to be paid at intervals so that the whole garrison would not be drunk at the same time. On a more elegiac note he says he found the best time was when he was 'on guard duty on one of the elevated and retired guard stations on the very summit of the Rock, 1300 feet above the level of the sea from which the view is surely grand and where a fine opportunity is afforded for meditation. I sometimes took my bible to guard with me'. In a splendid anti-climax he adds 'but I never made use of it'.[6]

Gibraltar must have been particularly disorderly. In 1801 reports on the state of affairs there reached Britain and a very popular Governor, General O'Hara was succeeded by the Duke of Kent who had been instructed to restore discipline. O'Hara had received an income of £7,000 a year from licensing the ninety taverns within the Fortress in which the garrison regularly got drunk. But he entertained lavishly, was very well liked and enjoyed the nickname of 'The Cock of the Rock'.

By 1793 Britain was again at war, this time against Revolutionary France. British sea power preserved Gibraltar from yet another siege but there were two sea battles in the bay in both of which the British ships were triumphant. One of these sea fights was witnessed by seventeen-year-old Sarah Fyers, the daughter of another 'sapper' family. Her father, who was later Chief Engineer on the Rock, arrived with his family in 1787. He took a great interest in the welfare of the garrison and is perhaps best remembered as the founder of the Garrison Library.

Sarah recorded this eyewitness account of one of the actions:

> It was I think on the 6 July that we were sitting at breakfast in a room which commanded a view of the bay and of a great part of the straits, with the African coast and Cabrita Point in Spain, when my father, riding up, called to us. We ran out to the corridor, and he told us English men-of-war were rounding Cabrita Point close in to the Spanish coast . . . It certainly was a beautiful sight to see those magnificent ships, their white sails shining in the sun and following each other at intervals. The breakfast room was soon deserted as we hastened to an eminence near the pluviometer, whence we had a perfect view of the town of Algeciras opposite and the whole of the coast on that side of the bay.
>
> The day was beautifully clear and fine. We were presently joined by several officers of the Royal Engineers . . . Mr. Mann, Mr. Jones and others. We were not kept long in suspense as to the intention of the British squadron, for the ships began firing against the French ships-of-war at anchor and at the Spanish Forts at Algeciras. The fire of our fleet was warmly returned both from the

French ships and the Spanish defences including the little island opposite the town of Algeciras. With what interest was the scene watched from our side of the bay. Every soul in the place seemed to have congregated either on the Line Wall or on the heights, and the murmur of so many voices came to us like the sound of the sea waves.[7]

We can easily appreciate the excitement of Sarah and the other onlookers. The outcome of the battle was of very real concern to them although her colourful description belies her anxiety. Sarah married Lieutenant Cornelius Mann who watched the battle with her from 'near the pluviometer' quite soon afterwards. They were married in Engineer House and General O'Hara gave the bride away. She no doubt made an excellent army wife and Cornelius went on to become a Major General.

At the Peace of Amiens in 1802, Minorca was handed back to Spain but the 'Peace' was very much an armed truce. In May 1803 Pitt declared war on France. In May of 1805 Nelson visited Gibraltar with the British fleet. Five months later, after the Battle of Trafalgar, Nelson's damaged flag-ship the *Victory* was towed into Gibraltar. Nelson's body, after his death during the battle, was taken ashore at Rosia Bay, preserved in wine and then taken to England for burial. The wounded from the battle were also landed at Gibraltar. Many of them died of their wounds and were buried in the cemetery just outside the Southport Gate. The cemetery is now known as the Trafalgar Cemetery but it was first used in 1804 for the victims of one of the Rock's worst outbreaks of yellow fever in which 1,000 members of the garrison died as well as very many of the civilian inhabitants.

Napoleon's 'Continental System' prevented European countries from trading directly with Britain. This led to a big increase in the *entrepôt* trade through Gibraltar. After the British victory at Trafalgar, the French navy was not strong enough to prevent full use being made of the port by neutral shipping. In 1808 the Spanish rose against the French occupying their country and became the ally of Britain in the Peninsula War. French forces came as close as San Roque but did not attack the Rock. In 1811 troops were sent to Tarifa which was under siege by the French, but in the following year with Wellington's growing successes, the French withdrew from Tarifa and the whole of the area near the Rock. Gibraltar then became a supply base for the British and Spanish armies fighting in Spain. The Peninsula War made an enormous impact on the Spanish people. The Author recalls visiting Spain when stationed in Gibraltar in the middle fifties, long after the end of the Civil War, and how astonished he was to find local people referring to 'The War' and meaning, in fact, the war against the French. There is also a popular song still sung in the villages not far from Gibraltar which tells of how the Spaniards and the British came together to throw the French out of Spain.

After the Napoleonic Wars Gibraltar's problems, in a century of comparative peace, were concerned in the main with health, trade and population growth. There were outbreaks of fever in 1813 and again in 1828; in the latter outbreak there were 1,667 deaths. By then the civilian population had grown to almost 17,000. Trade continued to grow for a while after the war but eventually declined with the growth of steamship traffic which tended to carry cargoes and passengers direct over long distances. However, the opening of the Suez Canal in 1869 brought many more ships through the Mediterranean and into Gibraltar.

The Trafalgar Cemetery. Sailors from the Battle of Trafalgar are buried here, but before the battle in 1805 it was used as a burial ground for yellow fever victims in the epidemic of 1804 when over 1000 people died.

Cholera became the scourge of Gibraltar, as it was of many other European towns in the nineteenth century. A serious outbreak in 1865 in which 578 soldiers and civilians died, led as in England at an earlier date, to the setting up of Sanitary Commissioners, which was the first step towards effective local government on the Rock. By 1880 the development of long range artillery led to discussions about exchanging Gibraltar for Ceuta on the North African coast, but nothing came of this. By 1890 Germany had begun to challenge British supremacy in her naval building programme and in her growing share of world trade. As a consequence, in 1893 the South Mole, naval harbour and dockyard were put into construction and completed in less than two years. This was the great age of the 'Ironclad' and when the Home and Mediterranean fleets combined at Gibraltar for joint exercises, sailors, 'at liberty' in the town and just across the border in Spain, could number up to 30,000. This of course was very good business for the bars and taverns in Gibraltar, which together with catering for the needs of the permanent garrison, was why they were there. Vice, apart from heavy drinking, had as John Stewart says in his book *Gibraltar The Keystone*,[8] been for the most part exported with true Victorian hypocrisy, to across the border. All garrison towns had, and in many cases still have, an area given over to providing for the rest, relaxation and entertainment of the largely bachelor, lonely, bored and for short periods, rich members of the armed forces. Of course these areas were not patronised exclusively by the military. Seaports, whether military or not, have always catered for the same appetites; all large Victorian towns had similar areas which, for peculiarly Victorian reasons, were popular with all grades and classes of society. Today, these districts tend to become tourist attractions. However, as John Stewart says, Gibraltar's district of 'vice and shame' was exported across the border early in the nineteenth century and, since crime, both petty and organised, flourishes in these areas, most of the local criminal fraternity live there also. A clause of the Treaty of Utrecht hoped to prohibit smuggling across the border but, as we have seen, this was a vain hope because so many people on both sides of the border depended on smuggling for a livelihood. This was still the situation when the border closed in 1969 and will continue to be a problem in the future. Until recently the main item of contraband had always been tobacco but now the immense profits to be made from drugs has introduced a new and more vicious dimension. It may not be possible to keep serious crime out of Gibraltar and the need for co-operation to deal with it may make a much closer relationship with Spain imperative, regardless of other considerations.

The early twentieth century was for Gibraltar a period of consolidation both in its defences and in its social and political life. The old smooth bore guns with a maximum range of about 4,000 yards were only gradually replaced but the increasing Spanish fortifications around Algeciras hurried the process after the turn of the century.

Spain remained neutral during the First World War. This made the Rock a valuable base for use against German submarines, for convoy collection, contraband inspection and by the American Navy from 1917 onwards. The Rock continued to be supplied with food from Spain and Spanish workers continued to come across the border to their work in the dockyard each day. Just before the end of the war General Sir Horace Smith-Dorrien was appointed Governor. In his biography he says very modestly '. . . I believe I did no greater harm in the appointment than other Governors have done.'[9] He was in many ways an ideal choice. His experience before the war as GOC at Aldershot had prepared him for co-operating with the civilian component of a garrison town and he was able to form an elected City Council for the administration of local affairs. He also introduced an Executive Council to advise the Governor on all matters of a non-military nature concerning the Rock. The service authorities on the Rock had always jealously guarded their very restricted sports grounds and, rather against their will, he 'persuaded' the Army and the Navy to make some of their facilities available to the local people. He reports how they took immediately to football and become expert at the game. This expertise at soccer and their enthusiasm for all ball games is still very evident and there are very few games in which Gibraltarian teams cannot match local combined service teams.

He also claims to have closed down some houses of ill-fame which is a little surprising considering the view that 'that sort of thing' had been banished to La Linea many years before. There are two possible explanations. There were and still are, many bars and dance halls in Gibraltar where a rudimentary floor show is featured. It may be that at times some of these places have been used for soliciting by freelance visiting ladies. It is more likely, however, that during the First World War, with the greatly increased garrison, and highly paid American sailors in port, facilities to help relieve them of their pay were not long in re-establishing themselves on the Rock.

Although Smith-Dorrien could not be classed as an eccentric, his love of sport and his penchant for looking into some very odd corners was in the best tradition of Governors before and after him. Gerald Pawle, in an article entitled 'The General's

Last Campaign', published in *Blackwood's Magazine* in 1949, gives an amusing account of the antics and eccentricities of two twentieth century Governors. The choleric Sir Archibald Hunter, for example, lashed himself into an absolute frenzy of reforming zeal just before the First World War, and held mass meetings at which he lectured the populace. At these meetings he would condemn their poor command of the English language, their indolence and their insanitary habits. He objected to almost everything, including the uncouth behaviour of the dockyard workers, the siting of the Jews Market, the Gibraltarian habit (he said) of reading 'indecent literature', and the design of the donkey shelters. General Hunter was just getting into his stride when the incensed Gibraltarians dispatched a delegation to Whitehall and had him removed. Sir Alexander Godley appears to have been worse, at least in some respects. General Godley became very involved with the Calpe Hunt which is reputed to be founded from a pack of hounds left in Spain by the Duke of Wellington after the Peninsula War. The pack, which was kennelled in Spain and hunted the country around Gibraltar, was a joint venture with Spain and occasioned much fellow feeling and mutual hospitality, at least until the new Governor took a hand. His first mistake was to try to get rid of the joint Spanish master of the hunt. He never really recovered from the controversy that this caused on the Rock. The British members of the hunt were divided evenly between those who supported his action and those who were bitterly opposed. Unfortunately he carried on a vendetta against those who opposed him to such an extent that they were made to feel unwelcome even at the garrison church services. A wag on his staff divided the warring factions into the 'Godleys and the UnGodleys'.

General Godley was also involved in the early history of aviation on the Rock and it may be that he caused almost as much chaos in that area as he did with the Calpe Hunt. It has been said that the only reason that the Rock has an aviation history at all is because a ship sent by Oliver Cromwell, complete with wheelbarrows, shovels and possibly 'transported' Irish labourers, with the intention of cutting a ditch across the sandy isthmus of Gibraltar and thus turning it into an island, was thwarted when the Spanish captured the ship. The story is no doubt apocryphal and must have originated with the Royal Air Force, but it is a fact that only across the narrow isthmus was it possible to build an air-strip. Flying activities certainly pre-date the airstrip, however. In 1903 a Royal Engineers Balloon Section was stationed on the Rock for a trial period. A site was prepared at Bruce's Farm and volunteers for flying duties were obtained from the infantry regiments in garrison. It was hoped that manned balloons flying above the Rock, especially when a 'levanter' cloud sat on the summit ridge, would give an uninterrupted view in all directions over very long distances. The experiment does not appear to have been a success. The section left after three months, returned at the end of 1904 and left finally in 1905. They complained of the weather which seems a bit hard, but it is interesting to know that the difficulties involved in flying from the Rock were present right from the start, and even with balloons.

Surprisingly little is known about aviation at Gibraltar during the First World War.[10] A letter from a pilot who flew aircraft from the race course refers to Caudrons and BE's. (Bleriot Experimentals), which were amongst the first types to be used in operations. The problems in flying from the North Front airfield can be the same today. In his letter he says 'we only operated land aircraft for about three months because we got into trouble with Spain for dropping a BE on their side. So our experience was not a long one. The Spanish brought our activities to an end'. Some effort was made to operate flying boats but this also was not a success. 'Our seaplanes and flying boats were so elementary that we got practically nothing done at all . . . the Levanter made it almost impossible. However, apart from the occasions when a North wind is blowing it is possible to use North Front in nearly all conditions of wind'.

In the nineteen-twenties the then Governor of Gibraltar and his opposite number in Algeciras worked out a joint plan for an Anglo-Spanish airfield on the Spanish side of the border fence where it would not interfere with the race course or other amenities of mutual interest. It was not approved by London or Madrid. In 1931 a local company, Gibraltar Airways Limited, was set up and given permission to use the race course as a base for a regular service between the Rock and Tangier. Then as now, Tangier was a popular leave resort, but because of repair and maintenance difficulties it only operated for one year. One of the planes tried out in this short-lived service was an amphibian named General Godley after the Governor, but even his illustrious name could not exorcise the early aviation problems. In 1932 an instruction reached General Godley from the War Office requesting him to prepare plans for an airfield which could be made operational at short notice. This was hastened by Mussolini's brash claim to the Mediterranean as *mare nostrum* and by his unsavoury behaviour in Abyssinia. A long and confused debate took place despite the growing urgency, and much opposition had to be overcome before it was accepted that the race course would have to go. It was not until just before the outbreak of the Second World War that a start was made on a permanent runway at North Front.

Mussolini was not the only perceived threat in the thirties. Gibraltar was able to observe the Spanish Civil War at close quarters. Dorothy Ellicott describes in one of her books how, visiting the Feria in La Linea in July 1936, she and her companions were suddenly aware that troops were landing from Spanish Morocco to begin the Nationalist rising against the Spanish government.[11] Soon Gibraltar was crowded with refugees; never less than 2,000 and sometimes as many as 10,000. Although the air war, waged by proxy by Italian and German air forces, took place mainly over the larger cities, and well away from the Rock, the naval war, almost as in Sarah Fyers' day, could be seen close by. An international patrol was set up to enforce non-intervention. But since the patrol included German and Italian warships it was obvious that the Spanish Government Forces would regard the patrol as hostile. The British destroyer *Hunter* struck a mine and was towed into Gibraltar in a sinking condition and the German battleship *Deutschland* came in after being damaged. In 1938 there was a naval action to the East of the Rock between a Spanish Government destroyer and a Nationalist cruiser. The destroyer, which had been trying to get into the Mediterranean, was badly damaged but managed to get into Gibraltar harbour where she was interned for the rest of the war. These events emphasised the importance of Gibraltar as a base and, as we have seen, ensured that by 1939 an operational airfield was available on the Rock.

The Second World War began quietly in Gibraltar as it did in Britain but the period of the 'phoney war' was used to extend the tunnel system. Storage galleries, machine gun and artillery positions were improved and shelter and hospital areas were hewn from the rock. Communications tunnels were extended and most of the rubble dug

Building the airstrip, 1939.

out was used to extend the runway at North Front into the bay. After Dunkirk, however, it was decided to evacuate most of the civil population. Families were sent first to North Africa, then as relations with the Vichy French deteriorated, to England and Northern Ireland. Some of the evacuees ended up as far away as Jamaica and Canada. Ironically, those who came to the British Isles were probably in far more danger than the 4,000 or so essential workers who remained behind on the Rock. After the meeting between Franco and Hitler at Irun in October 1940, when the Spanish refused to allow German troops to move through Spain to attack Gibraltar, the tension eased. Italian aircraft attacked the Rock ineffectually on a few occasions and after the sad but necessary attack on the French fleet at Oran, French aircraft also bombed the Fortress. It is said that the French desisted only after Winston Churchill threatened to bomb Paris which had been declared an open city after the fall of France.

As in the First World War the Rock played an important part in the Battle of the Atlantic but this time it was as a base for air operations as well as a forming up place for convoys and as a protected anchorage and general repair and reprovisioning yard for the allied navies. The Malta convoys were organised and escorted through many bloody battles to the beleaguered island and it was whilst covering a convoy that the carrier *Ark Royal* was torpedoed. She struggled back to within twenty-five miles of the Rock but finally sank, almost within site of succour.

Shipping anchored off Gibraltar, even though it was protected by regular patrols dropping depth charges, was a tempting target. From September 1941 until December 1942 Italian naval underwater swimmers, divers and midget submarines made a series of attacks on vessels outside and inside the harbour. The attacks were pressed home with great courage and it was only after an attack where all the midget submarines were lost and five out of six crew members drowned that the attacks were finally abandoned.[12]

In June 1941 Germany attacked the Soviet Union and by the end of that year the United States of America had entered the war and Gibraltar became the base for the amphibious attack on the axis powers in North Africa. General Eisenhower arrived in Gibraltar in November 1942 to plan and command the invasion. The airstrip at the North end of the Rock became even more important during the invasion. Afterwards it was used as a staging post to North Africa and eventually to Sicily and Italy. Flying from the Rock had always been difficult and it is surprising that there have been so few accidents to the aircraft flying in and out. Unfortunately, one of the few serious accidents involved General Sikorski, commander of the Free Polish Forces. His Liberator aircraft crashed on take-off. The death of Sikorski came at a time crucial for Soviet-Polish relations and this, together with a history of what could have been minor acts of sabotage on the Rock, lent an air of mystery to the event which even now has not been entirely dispelled.

Although the Second World War ended in 1945, it was not, incredibly, until 1950 that the last evacuees were finally returned to the Rock. By then the City Council had become a Legislative Council with a majority of elected members. The Governor remained the executive authority with an Executive Council of four official and four elected members. Spain, meanwhile, still saddled with a fascist dictatorship, was becoming concerned at the growth of democratic self-government in an area which she hoped soon to incorporate. The visit of Her Majesty The Queen to Gibraltar in 1954 led to such patriotic pro-British fervour that the Spanish became really alarmed. The Spanish Consul was withdrawn and restrictions placed on the frontier crossing at La Linea. The history of petty restrictions, harassment and uncertainties continued for the next fifteen years until, in 1969, Spain finally closed the frontier at La Linea, refused to admit travellers coming from Gibraltar at Algeciras, severed the telephone link and placed restrictions on overflying. This opening of the fifteenth siege was the culmination of a long and fruitless campaign at the United Nations. The UN Special Committee on Decolonisation debated the issue of Gibraltar's future on several occasions and despite the appearance before it of a delegation from Gibraltar asking for the status quo to be confirmed, resolved in 1964 that Britain and Spain must negotiate. Earlier in 1964 a revised constitution had abolished the Executive Council and replaced it with a Gibraltar Council on which there was an elected majority. With the colonial status of Gibraltar almost defunct the Spanish began to take a still harder line. Britain refused to negotiate under duress and the stalemate and siege dragged on until 1980. By 1980 a new factor had emerged. In Gibraltar there was still a very large majority against closer ties with Spain but in Spain itself the death of General

General Sikorski, before his fatal air crash, with Lord Gort, the Governor of Gibraltar.

Franco, the return to democracy and the revival of a more outward looking foreign and commercial policy made membership of the European Economic Community desirable if not essential.

Under these circumstances a limited agreement to open the frontier was arrived at in 1982 but was postponed at Spain's request at the time of the Argentine invasion of the Falklands. Negotiations were resumed after the Falklands War and a partial re-opening took place at the beginning of 1983. This was not satisfactory since only long term residents of Spain and Gibraltar were allowed to cross the frontier. By the end of 1984 British support for Spanish entry to the EEC had become vital and so a full opening was finally agreed and put into operation on 5 February 1985. Thus ended the longest and, thankfully, the most peaceful siege in the history of Gibraltar.

Whilst the fifteenth siege did not involve war with Spain it did spark-off an incident quite unique in the experience of Gibraltarians. In 1967 a referendum was held in which all the people of Gibraltar were asked whether they wished to continue the link with Britain or if they would prefer a link with Spain. 12,182 valid votes were cast from an eligible electorate of 12,762. 12,138 voted to maintain the link with

Britain whilst only 44 voted in favour of Spain. Rather foolishly, but with some courage, a small group of Gibraltarians wrote to the *Gibraltar Chronicle* early in 1968 suggesting negotiations with Spain. The six signatories, who called themselves 'The Doves', said that Spain would agree to negotiate, admitting at the same time that they had already had some preliminary conversations in Madrid. The 'Doves' were then rather badly let down by their Spanish contacts who said that they were willing to negotiate but only after Spanish sovereignty over Gibraltar had been acknowledged. This was too much for many Gibraltarians who had so recently and decisively rejected the Spanish connection. A bizarre day of rioting followed. A mob of between two and three hundred Gibraltarians followed a few ring leaders and proceeded to stone and burn some of the business premises and vehicles owned by the 'Doves'. The Police were taken completely by surprise by a riot for which they had received no training. Pyschologically they were equally unprepared. The riot was for Britain and the *status quo*. The 'mob' were all known to the Police, and in many cases were related to them. Happily no one was seriously injured, although there was a nasty moment when the senior Police Officer present attempted to halt the mob advancing up Main Street by inadvisedly and certainly inexpertly igniting a tear gas canister. He, and a very small party of supporting Policemen were apparently overcome by the fumes and had to take shelter in an open doorway. The mob proceeded on its way and eventually burned to the water-line a motor launch owned by one of the 'Doves'. By late afternoon the mob had caused quite a scare, not least to themselves. At this stage the Governor put troops on standby to assist the Police if necessary. No doubt word of the Governor's action reached the mob and its leaders then wisely decided it was time to go home for a late lunch. That was the end of the day of demonstrations. The point had been made in Spain as much as in Gibraltar. The international media made much of the first riot in living memory that was for and not against Britain. Although it turned out to be a storm in a tea cup it is worth relating the story of the 'Doves disturbances' in some detail since it does illuminate some aspects of Gibraltar and the Gibraltarians which could be misunderstood. Most Gibraltarians regard their British connections as worth fighting for. Living in Britain it is possible to take for granted our democratic institutions, our enlightened and popular monarchy, Police and armed forces firmly under civil control. From the Rock it was only necessary, until recently, to look across the frontier to see the results of their absence, and to appreciate the stability, moderation and decency of their own version of British society.

Even though the 'Doves' riot happened several years ago it showed a mistrust of Spain which has certainly not been reduced by the years of virtual siege that followed it. A newly arrived Spanish democracy must earn the trust and respect of the people of Gibraltar, however long that takes, and at whatever inconvenience to Britain. The Gibraltarians make up for their lack of numbers by their literacy, their unanimity and by their easy availability to the mass media. They are accustomed to appearing on the world stage and they have learned how to use it.[13]

Politically, the immediate future for Gibraltar is hazardous. The Rock is no longer required as a British military base but it may have some attractions for NATO or to a more centralised and more sovereign EEC. But even if some mutually acceptable agreement is arrived at with Spain it is unlikely that the limited air facilities and the harbour and dockyard, overlooked from so many points of the compass, could ever be viable as a major military post again. This is not to say that as a staging-post into

Africa or elsewhere it may not have some value in circumstances that cannot yet be foreseen. However, few countries can afford to maintain an overseas base in the absence of contingency plans for its use. In the long run it seems likely that Gibraltar will find its future as a small, picturesque, Mediterranean seaport, well placed for the western Spanish, Portuguese and Moroccan resorts. It will fit into the general tourist pattern in the area, and the heavy investment in tourism in the sixties and seventies should now pay off handsomely. A modest but growing trade with the Spanish hinterland will be a bonus. The dockyard should also provide some diversification. As a traditional major employer of labour, which was trained locally in technical and managerial skills, it should continue to make a contribution to the prosperity of the Rock. Most Gibraltarians would now accept this somewhat scaled down future as realistic, but it will only work for them as long as they have complete freedom to choose where their main contacts and influences will be. In the past many Gibraltarians have managed to get the best from both worlds. Spanish and British cultures have flourished side by side and to their mutual advantage. With a democratic and friendly Spain, determined to win the confidence of Gibraltar, this situation could return. Almost as soon as the frontier was reopened cultural contacts were re-established. The thriving amateur theatre in Gibraltar, which is a particular feature of its cultural life, is already playing an important part in this process, being well placed because of its bilingual ability.

It would seem that the days of the British garrison are numbered. It is possible that we shall see out our third century on the Rock but this may be under some new and as yet unknown authority. In the meantime it is again one of the most pleasant postings in the world. Gibraltar, with its colonial buildings, moorish antiquities, semi-tropical gardens and the upper Rock to wander over, has much to offer in itself. The fortifications, batteries, tunnels and galleries are in a fine state of preservation and cannot fail to interest the military historian. The Garrison Library, like so many clubs founded under the aegis of the services in more expansive times, is a little run down and in search of a role, but it does have an exciting and unique collection of books and documents on Gibraltar and the surrounding area. It must represent a treasure just waiting to be discovered and used by writers and students. The shops in Main Street continue to provide a limitless range of goods from every manufacturing country in the world and with easy access from Spain this is bound to continue. Of course there is an immediate problem in the relationship between Gibraltar's almost completely 'freeport' status and Spain's policy of economic protectionism. However, under the EEC, both systems must move closer together and, as we have said, coping with drug smuggling is likely to make real co-operation essential in the near future.

Gibraltar is the last town to be described in this collection and it is particularly appropriate to end with this archetypal military town. Gibraltar developed as a town because of the need to garrison the Rock. The first civilians came to provide goods and services for the soldiers and sailors stationed there, but they stayed to make it their home, and now they have inherited the Rock. The population, made up in part from 'stay behind' British, sometimes with their families but more often after marrying local girls, mixed increasingly with people of Spanish, Portuguese, Italian and Jewish origins, has absorbed many of those qualities that we associate with garrison towns everywhere. The inhabitants have a very well-developed sense of humour, often displayed in satire and caricature. A particularly cynical attitude towards authority,

The ceremony of the 'keys' outside the Governor's residence always attracts a large crowd of tourists.

and especially previous Spanish authority and Spanish petty officials, is typical. They have great courage, and over what they regard as fundamental issues a dour determination not to give way. Above all they value the British connection. They display this regard in a noisy, exuberant patriotism which can embarrass the more phlegmatic, less demonstrative native British. In Gibraltar as in many other garrison towns, in the United Kingdom no less than abroad, there is a healthy scepticism about the doings of the military. In reverse it would be foolish to suggest that all soldiers and sailors are able to adjust easily to a population which is mainly of a different religion, speaks Spanish not English at home, has basically a different way of life but even so, has been quick to insist upon and to incorporate a full measure of British justice, democracy and toleration. It is perhaps these last characteristics which give a homogeneity and strength to the town as a whole. The ties between Gibraltar and Britain are strong. Most Gibraltarians have British friends and many have British relatives. Very many British servicemen and their families develop friendships with local people which survive despite the transient nature of service life. It is finally perhaps, one of the great bonuses of garrison life, that it does encourage the development of close bonds between those who have suffered siege and bombardment together, or perhaps have only stood together at a quiet moment, and pitied the poor benighted foreigner on the wrong side of the wall.

Bibliography

Gibraltar, The Island Series, P. W. C. Dennis, David & Charles, Newton Abbot, 1977

Gibraltar The Keystone, John Stewart, John Murray, London, 1967

History of the Corps of Royal Sappers and Miners, T. W. T. Connolly, published by Longman, Brown, Green and Longman and Roberts, 2nd Edition in 2 vols., London 1855

The Mediterranean and the Mediterranean World in the Age of Philip II. Fernand Braudel. Collins, 1973

Sea Devils, Valerio J. Borghese, translated by Jane Cleugh, Melrose, 1952

Historical Notes on Gibraltar, The Gibraltar Tourist Office, 1985

Dorothy Ellicott has written many short books on Gibraltar and its relations with Spain but they are only available in Gibraltar.

Epilogue

FOR CONVENIENCE we have divided this study of British military towns into four types. These types can be described first, as the historical garrisons established for geo-political reasons and dating from the earliest written history of these islands. Second, the port garrisons which arose to protect our maritime bases at the time when sea power was our most important national asset. Next, the great training camps, called into being in a later age of mass armies, large formations and the need to exercise the new weapons of mechanised destruction. Finally we have looked at two of our overseas garrisons in Europe and found perhaps that they could be fitted into one of the previous categories; Gibraltar amongst the sea power garrisons, and Rheindahlen as an interesting example of the current tendency to build military towns the shape of which is dictated largely by the latest military technology. Control, in one form or another, has always been the purpose of the garrison town, whether the control of strategic routes or significant populations or of the seas or of the training and communication between great armies. The typology is only important because it allows us to compare our garrisons and draw conclusions about similarities and common underlying principles.

The first common fact about garrisons, leaving aside the business of control, although what follows is another aspect of it, is that garrisons are set up for a purpose more urgent than the social or economic or self-defensive reasons which led to the founding of the civilian settlement. Some asset, geographical, strategic or economic is to be defended for the nation or the community or the monarch, not as personal property but in trust. It is here that the notion of honour arises with all its fearful potency. The garrison defends its position and maintains its task to the death, or at least until it is no longer effective. To betray the trust, to open the gates or to treat with the enemy is traitorous behaviour of the worst kind, not only for the military but for the civilian component also who, whether they like it or not, partake of this trust and honour. This is why we are excited and exalted by a Waterloo or an El Alamein but we are moved to tears by a Lucknow or a Ladysmith or a Tobruk or a Kohima Box and to tears of shame by a Singapore, however undefendable it may have been in 1942. Honour and the sacred task explains the heroic nature of the defence of so many vital locations even though inspired leadership, fear of exemplary punishments and occasionally a knowing dread of the result of capitulation, may also play a part. Heroic defence calls for especially courageous and self-sacrificing attack and to 'die in the breach' has always been regarded as the acme of honour for the military profession. The ferocious nature of siege warfare also explains, without excusing, the inevitable fate of a town taken by storm, even up to the present day. Badajos, given over to three days of rape and pillage, despite all the efforts of Wellington and his officers to protect the unwilling Spanish hosts of a French garrison from battle-crazed

British Peninsula veterans is different only in degree from the Russian sack of Berlin, defended for too long in 1945.

To the notion of honour and trust we can add that sense of common purpose which is typical of most military towns. Where the main industry and employer in an area is the military, it may not be surprising that the civilian workforce and their families identify with and to an extent emulate their uniformed colleagues. The extreme examples of this tendency amongst our chosen towns are Bovington and Rheindahlen which latter resembles, as we have said, a company town on the American model. Catterick and Aldershot, both of which owe their existence, or at least their present size and shape, to military necessity also fall into this category. Of course all military towns follow this pattern to some degree since all are involved in the provision of goods, services and amenities to their respective garrisons, but in some it is the overriding business of the town. We have seen also that in the older military settlements local marriages, births and retirements have forged another link. What was a matter of policy in Roman Britain has continued to the present time, through necessity and convenience, strengthening the bonds between soldier and civilian and at the same time reinforcing the common outlook. One can find now, public houses in York or Edinburgh and in many naval bases, which are not only named after a famous ship or regiment and which naturally became a rendezvous for off duty sailors or soldiers but which also serve whole families, over several generations and all connected directly or through marriage with the armed services. In Plymouth, and in Devonport especially, there can hardly be a bar without a lovingly preserved ship's name plate which in one sense at least is the focus of honour and respect for every serviceman and civilian who wishes to drink there. This is an obvious way in which the spirit and ethos of the armed forces makes itself felt throughout the garrison.

Another strand in this tapestry of garrisons, and perhaps a less happy one, is the conservative, backward looking nature of the military town. Its object is to hold or maintain all that is there. Everything about the garrison combines to support this philosophy. The buildings, the military purpose and in many cases the history of the town encourages the psychological tendency to caution, to conservation and limitation rather than towards expansion and change. Coupled with this innate conservatism, which incidentally is present to a surprising degree in all armies everywhere, is an enhanced patriotism and almost chauvinistic ethno-centrism. It is only necessary to observe the thriving British Legion Clubs, active Old Comrades Associations, the frequent ex-service parades, religious services and 'Acts of Commemoration', often complete with banners, to feel the strength of a still living force. A new feature of this characteristic veneration of the past is the rapidly growing interest in the preservation of military architecture. Organisations for Military archaeology are flourishing in Chatham where, as we have seen, Fort Amherst is being restored and preserved, and in Gibraltar, Plymouth and Edinburgh and many more, quite outside the existing groups traditionally interested in the preservation of the local historical heritage. An important feature of these new activities is their concern with comparatively modern aspects of military buildings and artefacts. So that, for example, the Aldershot Military Museum, new as it is, is already encouraging an interest in the founding of the camp in the eighteen-fifties and its history up to the very recent military past.

For the military future there would appear to be two options. We have seen how the development of the modern military town presents many hazards to its inhabitants.

Aldershot and Rheindahlen have been the subject of terrorist attack and who can doubt that British military cantonments will become increasingly the target for similar outrages. The trend in military town planning is to ignore this threat and to continue the concentration of military facilities, troops and families within boundaries which are at least recognisable. At the moment the latest military towns, new and rebuilt, follow the 'open town' plan. Defence and security requirements are hardly considered. As we have said, it is unlikely that this situation can continue for much longer. Terrorism appears to be an important and still growing military option and sooner or later if military communities are to remain concentrated in certain areas they will have to be more seriously protected. It is likely that this protection will take the form of increasingly sophisticated electronic surveillance and barrier systems rather than a reversion to barrack walls, barbed wire and guard houses. However, the end result will be the same and garrison, troops and families alike, will feel the added enclosure and the increased isolation almost as though they were living in a moated and walled eighteenth-century fortress town. This artificial reversion to an earlier, and it was to be hoped outmoded, form of military settlement might well heighten the 'garrison syndrome' and some of the virtues that we have discerned in the military town could then become a liability. In an age of increasing freedom of information and communication, of openness in government and civic responsibility, the advent of new closed areas and protected communities would be viewed with more and more suspicion and the very strengths and virtues of the garrison would be seen as anachronistic and counter-productive.

There is another way. It has often been suggested that the various military communities should be broken up and dispersed amongst the civilian population. Military town planners, often despite their masters, have favoured the idea of having a much more even mix between military and civilian families. The Tidworth planners wanted to achieve something like this but they were thwarted by resistance from both sides. It seems that the military would not make enough land available for non-military purposes and the civilian authorities were unrealistic about the level of amenity that the services would have to provide. Even so, in every area which has a military presence, regardless of whether quarters are provided, many service families live, and increasingly choose to live, deep in the civilian community. This may be the pattern for the future. There has been a debate for some time about the expense to the exchequer and the 'hostage to fortune' aspect of providing accommodation and facilities for military families abroad. The debate has been extended to question the wisdom of providing quarters, furniture, welfare and other services, sometimes in parallel with similar local provision, in the United Kingdom itself. It has been said that it would be more efficient, cheaper and often more acceptable to give a money allowance instead.

A policy of dispersal amongst the civilian population is a much more attractive option now than in the past. Encouraging the soldier to buy his own home has been a policy attracting only lukewarm support from the authorities but for the future it may be the only sensible course of action. Even abroad there have always been some officers, NCOs and soldiers living with their families in private accommodation or in blocks of accommodation on local estates, hired from a foreign government or local authority or private landlord. There is no reason to believe that a system of almost total dispersal could not be achieved and made attractive to the military family. This policy would probably speed up the existing trend whereby the soldier's family stays put in their house, once they have started to buy one, whilst the soldier is temporarily accommodated at his place of duty, whether at home or overseas. With the general increase in home ownership it is reasonable to suppose that most military families will want to remain in one place and even where the family live in rented accommodation the pressures to stay put are sure to grow. A policy of dispersal, especially within a sympathetic, caring and alert community, would reduce the threat from terrorism but it could also have additional advantages. In the end we may only be giving a little, more necessary, impetus to an existing situation. In historical and emotional terms the dispersal and end of the military town would be a sad loss but there is no reason why the garrison virtues could not be carried a little more into the civil community. A properly managed and monitored dispersal might be one way in which some of the very real qualities, nurtured in military garrisons over hundreds of years, could be put to use in the wider world outside.

Notes
and References

Chapter 1 Colchester

1. The town continued to be called Camulodunum (The Latinised form of the Celtic name) under the Romans. It is not clear when it became Colchester but for convenience this name is used from here on.
2. It is reputed that the grounds of St. John's Abbey were used for a mass grave for victims of the plague and that a mound in the grounds, which are now the gardens of the Garrison Officers' Club, marks the spot where the grave was located.
3. Colchester was used as a stop on the routes from London to the ports of Harwich, Ipswich and Yarmouth. The journey by coach from Colchester to London could be done in seven or eight hours and there were regular daily services.
4. The Contagious Diseases Act was passed in 1864 and extended to most garrison towns in Britain and Ireland in 1866. The Act was a focus of discontent for army reformers and early feminists alike in the latter part of the nineteenth century.
5. It is a testament to the durability of these Nissen huts that they still survive, having been in continuous use since they were erected. However, their days are numbered. The first phase of a new purpose-built accommodation for the MCTC has recently been completed and the remainder of the re-build should be finished in two to three years' time.
6. The new barracks were opened by Christopher Soames, the then Secretary of State for War, and his remarks at the time are indicative of authority's changed attitude to the regular soldier. As he observed, in addressing the men of the Duke of Wellington's and the Queen's Royal Surrey regiments who were in occupation of the barracks, 'You have been in these barracks a while and I hope you find they provide a high standard of comfort and amenity for all ranks. They were designed that the minimum of time need be devoted to those chores and fatigues which demanded so much effort from a unit living in the old type Victorian barracks. We are determined that the soldier, be he married or single, will be provided with the high standard of accommodation which he rightly expects and which is surely his due.'

Chapter 2 York

1. Frere, Professor Sheppard. *A History of Roman Britain*, Routledge & Kegan Paul, 1967.
2. *Egil's Saga* is one of the major Icelandic Sagas. It is the story of the medieval Viking poet Egil Skallagrunsson.
3. Wenham, P. *The Great and Close Siege of York 1644*, Roundwood, 1970.
4. The *Articles of Surrender* show how generous were the conditions imposed on the City of York. This no doubt reflects the importance of the city and the necessity to keep on good terms with its inhabitants. Colchester, which came under siege some years later was much more harshly treated on its surrender. See Chapter 1.
5. *Sir John Reresby's Diary* can be consulted at York City Library.
6. Ibid.
7. A facsimile of early copies of the *Yorkshire Gazette* is held at the York City Library as is a collection of early photographs from the paper.

Chapter 3 Edinburgh

1. Fergusson, R. *The Poetical Works of Robert Fergusson, With his Life*, Alnwick, Davison, Edinburgh, 1814.

2. Borrow, G. *Lavengro*, John Murray, London, 1851.
3. Maclean, Fitzroy *A Concise History of Scotland*, Thames & Hudson, London 1970.
4. Scott, Sir Walter *The Heart of Midlothian*, The Waverley Novels, Border Edition, John C. Nimmo, London 1893.
5. Carlyle, Dr Alexander, Nicknamed Jupiter. A Minister and leader of the Scottish 'Broad Church' Party. *Autobiography* published Edinburgh, 1860.
6. Scott, Sir Walter, op. cit.
7. Fergusson, R. op. cit.
8. *Edinburgh Castle, Troops in Garrison.* A list, not yet completed, but compiled with considerable ingenuity as the evidence becomes available by the staff of The Scottish United Services Museum. It starts from 1660.
9. Evans, Hilary and Mary, *John Kay of Edinburgh*. 2nd revised edition, P. Harris, Edinburgh, April 1980.
10. Fergusson, R. op. cit.
11. Innes, Major (Retd) C. B. *The History of Craigiehall.* An unpublished manuscript. Copies are held by H.Q. Scotland, Craigiehall, Edinburgh.
12. Oliver, John W. Sadly the poet is now dead and his work cannot be traced but his complete poem is reproduced in Innes's *Craigiehall.*
13. The Military Tattoo. Although the 'tattoo' can be traced back to the Roman Military Games popular throughout the Roman Empire including Britain its revival in nineteenth century Britain stems from the military reviews and parades which suddenly became very popular in Victoria's reign and especially once the growth of Empire, overseas trade and 'the whiteman's burden' caught the general imagination. In the present century tattoos have become increasingly elaborate and theatrical and have been adopted first by the Royal Navy with their 'Navy Days' and then by the Royal Air Force with 'Empire Air Days' in the twenties and thirties and Air Days since the Second World War. Today, the Military Tattoo is in evidence everywhere the British forces are stationed at home and overseas. Although, as in the case of Edinburgh, the ostensible purpose is to raise money for service charities, they also perform an important public relations and propaganda function. See also the Chapters on Colchester, Chatham and Aldershot.
14. Robertson, J. and Logie, M. A. *Poems of Allan Ramsey*, Walter Scott, London, 1887.

Chapter 4 Chatham

1. Pepys, Samuel *Diary*, New Edition. Ed. Latham & Mathews. Bell & Hyman, London, 1970
2. Dickens, Charles. Refers frequently to the army and army officers, usually as figures of fun. *The Pickwick Papers* and *Great Expectations* use Chatham and the surrounding area as the scene of incidents in the novels.
3. Coxwell, Henry *My Life and Balloon Experiences*, W. H. Allan, London 1889.
4. Harry, Wesley *Brochure of The Royal Arsenal Woolwich*. Printed for the Ministry of Defence, Public Relations Department, March, 1984.
5. The Contagious Disease Acts. See Colchester, note 4 and Aldershot note 3.

Chapter 5 Plymouth

1. Walling, R. A. J. *The Story of Plymouth*, Westaway Books, 1950.
2. Boynton, Lindsay *The Elizabethan Militia 1558-1638*, David & Charles, Newton Abbot, 1971.
3. Worth, R. N. *History of Plymouth*, William Brendon, 1980.
4. Walling, R. A. J. op. cit.
5. Ibid
6. *Western Morning News*, 14 January 1967.
7. Hadfield, A. M. *Time to Finish the Game*, Phoenix House, 1964.
8. Gill, Crispin *Plymouth: A New History*, David & Charles, Newton Abbot (Vol. 11), 1979.
9. Ibid.
10. Walling, R. A. J. op. cit.
11. Bracken, C. W. *A History of Plymouth*, Underhill, 1931.
12. Hogg, Ian V. *Coast Defence of England and Wales 1856-1956*, David & Charles, Newton Abbot, 1974.
13. Ibid.
14. Collier, B. *The Defence of the United Kingdom*, HMSO, 1957.
15. Goodman, Stanley. A letter to the author, November 1985.
16. Rose, Colonel Markham *The Story of the Royal Marines*, Lectures for Recruits, 1935.
17. Goodman, Stanley op.cit.

18. Ibid.
19. Ibid.
20. Price, Alfred *Blitz on Britain*, Ian Allen, 1977.
21. Goodman, Stanley op. cit.
22. Joslen, Lieutenant Colonel, H. F. *Orders of Battle, (Vol. 11)* HMSO.
23. *General Return of the Strength of the British Army, January 1941, July 1941, July 1942*, Imperial War Museum.
24. Twyford, H. P. *It Came to Our Door*, Underhill, Plymouth, 1945.
25. Baynham, Henry *From the Lower Deck – The Old Navy 1780-1840*, Hutchinson.

Chapter 6 Woolwich

1. Vincent, *Records of the Woolwich District (Vol. 1)*, Woodlands Local History Library, London Borough of Greenwich.
2. Harry, Wesley, op. cit.
3. Jefferson, E. F. E. *The Woolwich Story*, R.A. Printing Press, Woolwich, 1970.
4. Hogg, O. F. G. Brigadier, in a lecture on 'The RMA in the Eighteenth Century', before the Society of Antiquaries of London at Burlington House, 20 Oct. 1953
5. Wagstaff, Major General C. M., CB, DSO. Commandant of the RMA 1930-1934. In a statement to the Marley Committee 1931. Found in the RMAS archives.
6. A Letter of the Lieutenant Governor, RMA. Now in Records of the RMA 2/2/78 at Woodlands Local History Library, London Borough of Greenwich.
7. Jefferson, E. F. E. op. cit.
8. Graham, Brigadier C. A. L., DSO *The Story of the Royal Regiment of Artillery* (6th Edition), R. A. Institute, Woolwich, 1962.
9. The lines by Mary Cull were published in a local paper, *Jones Woolwich Journal*, 30 October 1848.
10. Jefferson, E. F. E. op. cit.
11. Hime, Lieutenant Colonel H. W. L. *History of the Royal Regiment of Artillery 1815-1853*, Longmans, 1908.
12. Ferguson, Ruby *Children of the Shop*, Hodder & Stoughton, London, 1930.

Chapter 7 Aldershot

1. An amusing account of Cardigan's career is given in *The Reason Why*, by Cecil Woodham-Smith, Constable, 1953.
2. Walters, John *Aldershot Review*, Jarrold, 1970.
3. The Contagious Diseases Act. See Colchester, note 4 and Chatham, note 5.
4. *Torch*, Journal of the Royal Army Educational Corps, Winter, 1981.
5. *Life of General Sir William Napier* (Author of the *History of the Peninsula War*). Writings edited by H. A. Bruce, M.P., John Murray, London, 1864.
6. Wood, Field Marshal Sir Evelyn, VC. *Midshipman to Field Marshal*, an autobiography, Methuen, London, 1906.
7. St. Aubyn, Giles *The Royal George, 1819-1904*, Constable, London, 1963.
8. *Haldane, Viscount Richard, Burdon, An Autobiography*. Hodder & Stoughton, London, 1929.
9. Smith-Dorrien, Sir Horace *Memories of Forty Eight Years Service*. Murray, London, 1925.
10. Walters, John, op. cit.
11. Lee, Laurie *Cider With Rosie*, Hogarth Press, 1959.
12. Smith-Dorrien, Sir Horace, op. cit.
13. The Aldershot Tattoo. See also chapters on Colchester, Chatham and Edinburgh.
14. Betjeman, John *A Subaltern's Love Song, from Collected Poems (Enlarged edition)*. Compiled by the Earl of Birkenhead, John Murray, 1958. (6th Im. 1977)
15. Tattoos, See note 13 above.

Chapter 8 Bovington

1. Hutchins, John *The History and Antiquities of Dorset*, J. B. Nichols & Sons, Westminster, 1861. Republished by E. P. Publishing Ltd. in collaboration with Dorset County Library, Dorchester, 1973.
2. *History of the Dorset Regiment (1914-1919)*, Ling, Dorchester, 1932.
3. *The Historical Records of the 9th Battalion Northumberland Fusiliers* (Appendix 1), Newcastle, 1928.

4. A War Diary of the time reproduced in 'The History of "E" (5th) Battalion' *The Tank Corps Journal Vol. 2, No. 14*, June, 1920.
5. Stack, Brigadier W. A. 'The Travails of a Tank Engineer, 1916-1918', *The RTR 50th Anniversary Souvenir Book*, 1967.
6. Ibid.
7. Brooks, Colonel G. H. 'Bovington Camp', Winter 1916-17, *The RTR 50th Anniversary Souvenir Book*, 1967.
8. Dixon, A. *Tinned Soldiers*, Jonathan Cape, 1941.
9. *The Tank Corps Journal, Vol. 1, No. 7*, November 1919.
10. Dixon, A. op. cit.
11. Ibid.
12. Ibid.
13. *The Tank Corps Journal, Vol. 1, No. 10*, February 1920.
14. Dixon, A. op. cit.
15. Ibid.
16. Liddell Hart, B. H. *The Tanks*, Cassells, 1959.
17. Ibid.
18. Dixon, A. op. cit.
19. Liddell Hart, B. H. op. cit.
20. Verney, John *Going to the Wars*, a new edition published by A. Mott, London 1983 in the War Library Edition.

Chapter 9 Rheindahlen

1. Gratton, Colonel Harry, 'New Headquarters in Germany'. Two Articles published in the *Royal Engineers Journal*, March and June 1956. Printed together in a brochure by HQ, BAOR, 1957.
2. Edgar, Colonel J. D. 'The Dhekalia Project'. Two articles published in the *Royal Engineers Journal*, 1954 and 1955.
3. Densham-Booth, Lieutenant Colonel D. F. *Social Planning, Army Housing in the United Kingdom 1970-1980*. Published as a Defence Fellowship Study by the Ministry of Defence, 1968/9.
4. Ibid.
5. Edgar, Colonel J. D. op. cit.
6. Grattan, Colonel Harry, op. cit.
7. In a letter from Lieutenant Colonel J. Biggs to HQ, BAOR in 1978.

Chapter 10 Gibraltar

1. Braudel, Fernand *The Mediterranean and the Mediterranean World in the Age of Philip II*, Collins, 1973.
2. Howes, H. W. *The Gibraltarian — The Origin and Development of the Population of Gibraltar from 1704*, Colombo, 1951. A second edition with an additional analysis of the 1777 population made by Manuel Cavilla, OBE, was published by Mediterranean Sun, Gibraltar, 1980. In the Gibraltar Garrison Library.
3. *Britons, Strike Home!* Written for Bonduca by Henry Purcell in 1695. Lewis Winstock in *Songs and Music of the Redcoats 1642-1902*, Leo Cooper, London 1970, says 'although it appears dramatic by modern standards, the soldiers liked it'. No doubt it was used as a suitable opening flourish to the bombardment.
4. The diary, Miriam Green's Journal was reproduced in part from the *Royal Engineers Journal* under the title 'A Lady's Experience in the Great Siege of Gibraltar (1779-83)'. A printed copy is held in the Gibraltar Garrison Library but it is not known from which RE Journal it was taken.
5. *History of the Corps of Royal Sappers and Miners*, Connolly, 1855, gives excellent details of the Great Seige and of the early history of 'Sappers' on the Rock.
6. G.B.'s account is reproduced in the Gibraltar Garrison Library and is taken from an unidentified copy of *The Journal of Army Historical Research*.
7. There is a bound, typescript copy of *Sarah Fyers' Journal* in the Gibraltar Garrison Library. The Library also contains a copy of a book, *The Fyers Family* by Colonel Robert H. Vetch, CB, late RE. This seems to be taken, at least in part, from the *Royal Engineers Journal* but like the typescript the journal gives no indication of when or where it was printed.
8. Stewart, John D. *Gibraltar The Keystone*, John Murray, London, 1967. An interesting although somewhat partial history of the development of the Colony.
9. Smith-Dorrien, Sir Horace. op cit. in Chapter 7, Aldershot.

10. There is a manuscript history of aviation on the Rock in the Gibraltar Garrison Library but it tends to raise more questions than it answers. It does include some photographs.
11. Dorothy Ellicott has written many interesting short books and monographs on the history of Gibraltar and about relations with Spain over the whole period of the Rock's separate existence. The books are published and are still available in Gibraltar but do not appear to be available in the United Kingdom.
12. Borghese, Valerio J. *Sea Devils*, translated by Jane Cleugh, Melrose, 1952.
13. The Gibraltar Tourist Office has produced a pamphlet *Historical Notes on Gibraltar* (1985) which gives an outline of the dispute with Spain and also traces the early history of the Rock.

Key to back cover

Woolwich

Bovington

Colchester

Edinburgh

Rheindahlen